Contents

The AgriChain Centre – Growers/ Importers/ Exporters/ Retailers – What makes convergence possible – Convergence – The plate – Strategy – The bugger index – Convergence at price level – We used to…

Introduction

This is no ordinary book - and that, I guess, is a statement made or view held by many an author.

What makes this book truly unique though is the way its structure has been derived. This book has been years in the making. I have been 'writing' it in the grey space between my ears for at least the last decade, in fact - ever since I stopped being a fresh produce retailer.

The reason it has taken until now to get my thoughts onto paper is quite simple. I had lacked an appropriate structure.

This might sound like an odd statement to make. Thousands of books are published every year and most follow a very simple structure. They have a beginning, a middle and an end.

Well, this type of structure has never worked for me - probably, because my mind does not operate along linear principles.

The structure around which this book has come together is the CON-Factor Construct. This is an analytical tool I developed to foster critical thinking and problem solving skills based on the learnings from our business consultancy work at The AgriChain Centre. As is the case so often, it took me several years to realise that the CON-Factor Construct would serve as an ideal structure for this book.

So here they are both - book and Construct.

The book consists of several segments: two introductory pieces which aim to define produce versus horticulture and introduce the concept of the value braid; the chapters following the CON-Factor outline; a group of thought pieces which address different situations within the fresh produce industry and a selection of opinions previously published in journals and newsletters. The final chapter, entitled 'Convergence' aims to pull the learnings from those three segments together and suggest a way forward.

My focus has been shaped by both hands-on involvement at growing and retail levels, as well as the intellectual pursuit of thinking about how the industry operates and how it could do better.

I started my produce industry career as an apprentice nurseryman in a fruit tree nursery in Germany in the 1970s. In the early 1980s I was growing perennial and vegetable plants commercially in New Zealand. By 1989 I was managing the fresh produce business for Progressive Enterprises, which then owned the North Island based Foodtown and 3 Guys supermarket chains. Later Countdown was added to the equation and I was able to extend my learning nationally.

I have over the years metamorphosed into an agribusiness consultant, company director, publisher and educator. At some stage in my life, I have also worked as a landscape gardener, journalist, Labour Department employment officer and university lecturer.

The point I am trying to make by sharing some of my background with you is to emphasise that the views I communicate in this book have evolved over many years and originate from more than just one perspective.

I would like to thank my business partners Anne-Marie Arts and Keith Budd for their tolerance with my urge to put pen to paper over the years. A big thank you also to Kathryn Foulkes-Baker who acted as editorial assistant and Lisa Ritchie who in her usual calm and professional style managed to turn my various outputs into something resembling a book!

Last but not least, my profound thanks to my publisher, Gordon Prestoungrange, Baron of Lochnaw, for his guidance during the last decade.

This book will appeal to anyone, in New Zealand and elsewhere, keen to understand better how fruit and vegetables get onto retail shelves and what goes on behind the scenes in order to satisfy the consumer, a challenging task in anyone's business.

For starters

Where the scene is set

Produce or horticulture?

What comes first, the chicken or the egg? The chicken, of course. No need to debate this; everyone knows that chickens lay eggs. So where does the chicken come from then? From the chicken farm, of course; .... where it probably hatched from an egg!

We all know that old argument, don't we?

So let's bring the argument into our industry then. Are we the horticulture industry or are we the produce industry? Or are we both? Can we be both? What defines us if we are different? If we are different that is...

I have thought about this long and hard over the years as my career took shape and I moved through various components of the value chain, long before it was called that. I have resolved in my mind that produce and horticulture are not the same, are not interchangeable terms and have to be treated as unique and defined elements of the same value chain. Here is where I am at with this. The focus of horticulture is production. The focus of produce is the consumer.

I am not on my own with this view. Wikipedia suggests that "*horticulture* is the industry and science of plant cultivation including the process of preparing soil for the planting of seeds, tubers, or cuttings", whereas "*produce* is a generalised term for a group of farm-produced goods, not limited to fruit and vegetables. More specifically, the term "produce" often implies that the products are fresh and generally in the same state as when they were harvested. In supermarkets the term is also used to refer to the section where fruit and vegetables are kept. Produce is the main product sold by greengrocers, farmers' markets and fruit markets."

New Zealand as a country is focused on agricultural production and Wikipedia is dead right - *produce* can mean all sorts of things, but we also fit the next part of the definition.

Our supermarkets have *produce* departments not *horticulture* departments and *produce* is exactly what is sold by the other consumer distribution channels such as greengrocers and farmers' markets.

In the US and Canada the attribute *fresh* is added and the individual in charge of fruit and vegetables in the supermarket environment is known as the *fresh produce* manager.

On that basis then, all growers are part of the horticulture industry whilst merchants, wholesalers and retailers are participants in the produce industry. And as the produce industry's purpose in life is the movement of horticultural product from the farm gate to the dinner plate, the horticultural industry is actually a part of the wider produce industry as well.

Indeed there are some industry participants who are permanently wearing two different hats at the same time, like the apple grower, for example, who is managing his own export programme!

The other issue we have is that when Government decides to engage with the horticultural industry through its industry body Horticulture New Zealand, for example, the consumer driven side of the equation otherwise known as the produce industry does not necessarily consider itself addressed - or even worse, does not know at times what is going on around it.

Before we selectively get precious though about which industry we belong to and which one we would rather not be a part of, we might just as well remember that we are lucky enough in New Zealand to have a truly pan-industry body - United Fresh. United Fresh members come from the entire spectrum of the combined horticulture and produce industries and United Fresh Executive Committee and general meetings are the only events where the entire fresh produce value chain is sitting at the same table and every member is there by right as opposed to being an invited guest.

We now need to get into the habit of using our pan-industry organisation, United Fresh, to address pan-industry issues.

For further information: *www.5aday.co.nz*

Forget supply chains
- value needs to be the name of the game

There are numerous articles available to researchers and practitioners alike which describe supply chain management in general and within the fresh produce industry in particular. I have also contributed to this collection of written expression on the topic through peer reviewed articles, pieces written for HortSource, the produce press in general and, of course, through my Sauerkraut column on the HortSource website.

Why add another one then? Why indeed.

The reason is very simple: time does not stand still. Over time, action takes place, successes are achieved, mistakes are made and lessons are learned. Or in the words of Reg Revans, the father of Action Learning, L=P+Q, where L stands for learning, P for programmed knowledge and Q for insightful questions.

Over time then, I have been: a practitioner, i.e. a supermarket executive with responsibility for fresh produce purchasing functions; a formal learner by way of completing an action research based doctoral thesis focused on the fresh produce supply chain and ways to improve it; and a consultant to industry on strategic supply chain matters. And without having set a formal investigation framework at the outset, I have in recent months reached the conclusion that a pure supply chain focus is not only insufficient to achieve sustainable value as produce moves through the supply chain, but also downright counterproductive.

To be very clear - of course supply chains do exist; and naturally, there is an absolute need for the different organisations that form the chain to cooperate in order to ensure that value is created and sustained. As we learn more about the behavior of chains we also need to be prepared to look at them in a new light.

A chain that wants to be successful in a sustained fashion does need to work on three aspects. These are firstly its own internal processes (1), secondly the cooperation with the respective up- and downstream elements of one's chain (2) and thirdly the way value is created and shared (3).

It has been my experience that most energy appears to be going into (2), some effort into the creation aspect and very little into the sharing aspect of (3) whilst internal processes (1) are taken in the main as given and if work is undertaken to optimise them, then it is typically done in isolation.

Yet without internal processes within an organisation being correctly optimised, it is literally impossible to create sustainable value for one's own organisation, let alone the chain as a whole. Value creation within one's own organisation is the starting point for future participation in a successful value chain.

I will therefore focus here on the issues within an organisation that represents one's own link in any chain which will lead to the introduction of a new concept - the **Value Braid**.

The Value Braid

Link construction

Whenever value chains are discussed in the literature, the focus is placed on chain performance and the need for participating links to work hard at ensuring that as product gets passed from one link to the next, effectiveness and efficiency are maintained without loss of momentum.

The reality is that this concept relies on the links themselves being organically _pecializ. A supply chain that works well can be compared to a well oiled machine that benefits from regular maintenance to ensure the engine runs smoothly, gets a regular oil check and is tuned as required. If this concept is accepted for the overall chain performance, it follows that a similar approach is advisable to ensure the robustness of individual chain links. Dealing with an individual link is by default more _pecialized than dealing with the chain at large because if individual links are ineffective, the chain as a whole will not work properly either. It is therefore critical that the composition of individual links is better understood than is currently the case.

My action learning approach in my professional and academic activities over the last ten years have now lead me to the following assertions:

- A successful supply chain link resembles a yeast braid, which is constructed from individual strands.
- If the dough used to bake a yeast braid is not kneaded enough, it will not rise properly.
- Dough that does not rise properly will not turn into a well baked yeast braid.
- A well baked yeast braid consists of five strands, expertly woven together by the baker's hands.
- If the five strands are not woven together well, the yeast braid might taste OK, but will present as messy, crooked and out of alignment.

The five strands that form the link an individual business represents in the supply chain are:

a. Customer focus
b. Quality status & management
c. Information capability
d. Communication skills
e. Physical product movement

Each strand will be briefly discussed to assist in explaining the nature of a value chain link - or **Value Braid**.

<u>Customer focus</u>

The purpose of a value chain is to satisfy customer needs. Each link in the chain needs to focus on four categories of customers. These are its suppliers, its direct customers; i.e., the next link in the chain, the ultimate consumer and the internal customers (such as team members) within the link itself. Each group of customers has its own needs, its own pressure points and its own set of rose tinted glasses. Unless their needs and aspirations are understood and aligned, value creation is next to impossible.

<u>Quality status & management</u>

Quality is a concept discussed ad nauseam, written about extensively and not well understood. Some years ago I introduced the concept of interactional fusion quality. This was based on the realisation that produce of good quality had the potential to be of average or poor quality by the time it has passed through the supply chain, if the journey either took too long or if the handling processes along the chain were questionable.

Similarly, produce of questionable origin entering the supply chain would not improve through travelling along a well designed, managed and skilled supply chain. The law of perishability does not allow for such eventualities. Quality management is not a destination or a point in time, but a never-ending journey and must be treated as such.

Information capability

The paperless world has yet to arrive but we are increasingly becoming dependent on electronic communication for just about all aspects of produce moving from grower to consumer. Living in a market economy means that not every IT system in use is the same. Many 'off the shelf' systems pronounce 'connectivity' as one of their virtues, referring to their supposed ability to connect with other proprietary systems up and down the value chain.

How much data do we want to share though? How much data do we need to share? At what point in the process should data be shared? In which format should shared data be presented? How can we protect our data from abuse - and to what extent does the shared data need to be 'translated' in order to meet the needs of our customers?

These are just a few questions for starters. The point being that technical capability alone is no longer enough. How we manage data is getting just as important as whether we can cope with the technical aspects of data transmission.

Communication skills

The ability to communicate well has always been one of the mainstays of building and maintaining good business relationships. Competence in the areas of accuracy, timeliness, relevance and sufficiency from both content and process perspectives are paramount in ensuring value is added rather than reduced as produce moves through the value chain.

What constitutes 'sufficient' information though? How much reliance should we place on automated data collection as opposed to the good old fashioned human approach? Can identical communication models be applied to all fruit and vegetable sectors?

And if these questions were not enough - do we need to consider the role of social media solutions such as Twitter to reach our customers?

Physical product movement

This aspect always appears to work well in any business. After all, I must be doing something right if I can get my tomatoes to my wholesaler every day in one piece?

Indeed, but what improvements could be made? To what extent is physical product movement impacted by the information needs of my customers? Could I save money by sending the truck earlier? Or later? Or getting my neighbor to deliver on my behalf?

Does it make a difference whether I am sending my produce to a wholesaler, to a retail distribution centre or direct to a consumer via an e-Bay or Trade Me listing?

How do I keep my product moving and how do I integrate this strand of my value braid with the other four?

And last but not least - the yeast.

Think of the yeast as the magic ingredient, your unique selling proposition, the critical core competence that differentiates your product or offer from that of your competitor. It does not matter how well a braid has been assembled, if the yeast is missing, the dough will not rise and the braid will not achieve its potential, regardless of how long it is kept in the oven! The same applies to your business. What is your 'yeast'?

Your 'yeast' ultimately underpins the success of your business, as evidenced by the degree to which you are able to have the five strands of the braid working in harmony as the business connects with the respective up- and downstream elements of your value chain.

A paradigm shift is needed in the way we think about our business. Before we can successfully participate in supply chains or value chains, we need to ensure the link our business represents is optimised - and that link is called the **Value Braid**.

CON-Factor analysis

Where readers get to meet me

Consumer

The purpose of achieving operational excellence within the fresh produce environment is to satisfy the consumer. Period. It is irrelevant how many levels separate an organisation and its ultimate customer. Organisational excellence is unattainable unless a consumer focus is adopted and consumer needs are better understood.

No one should be surprised about the fact that consumers get discussed early on in the piece. Anyone who works at any point within the fresh produce supply chain knows that without the consumer deciding to initiate a purchase at the farmers' market, green grocer or supermarket all the effort to get quality produce onto the shelves would ultimately be wasted.

The term 'fresh' and how it presents as a critical constraint to the entire produce supply chain will get discussed in more detail further on. What needs to be mentioned at this point is the perception the consumer has in relation to 'fresh'.

The Compact Oxford English dictionary defines 'fresh' as "(of food) recently made or obtained; not preserved....." It is a safe bet that 99% of consumers have developed their perception about 'fresh' without ever having been near a dictionary.

In fact, most consumers give very little thought to where their fruit and vegetables come from. Sure, some consumers would prefer to purchase organic produce and the concept of food miles is raising its head periodically; but by and large consumers expect their produce to be 'there' when they choose to do their shopping and regardless of where they choose to shop.

Freshness is therefore a concept in the eyes of the beholder. A consumer who turns up at the local farmers' market would expect the lettuces on sale to be have been harvested the day before at the earliest. Preferably, even the same morning at dawn.

'Fresh' lettuce and other green vegetables are characterised by their green and crispy leaves. 'Fresh' tomatoes better not just be red but also ripe. Bananas generally do not come with a 'fresh' tag in the consumers' mind. The colour stage at which they are presented sends a message about the degree of ripeness. Apples these days are anything but fresh - apart from the glorious first few weeks after harvest in late summer and early autumn.

Consumers instinctively know that eating produce is good for them. There are a whole range of additional perceptions related to the concept of eating fresh fruit and vegetables. Older consumers can relate back to the days when tomatoes were something Dad grew in the vegetable garden over summer. Lack of flavour is a common complaint raised when the quality of fresh fruit and vegetables is up for discussions.

"The fruit simply does not taste as good as it used to", is an opinion often voiced in consumer surveys and no produce grower, wholesaler or retailer is keen to hear such a statement.

One of the underlying issues the produce industry as a whole struggles with is the fact that consumers do not value produce in monetary terms. Consumers perceive that growing fruit and vegetables is a low cost affair and therefore the harvest of the nation's fruit growers and market gardeners only deserves low returns in terms of the retail price consumers are prepared to pay.

Where does this view come from and how can it be addressed?

The answer to the first part of the question is relatively simple.

Agriculture and horticulture are alive and well in all first world countries. Farmers and growers may believe otherwise and grizzle periodically, but consumers know that farming is really very simple.

A farmer grows what he feels like, looks after it whilst it grows and then sets about harvesting. The government will subsidise whatever the farmer achieves in prices and the cycle begins again.

Yes, this is a very oversimplified and cynical way of looking at things but it sums it up rather nicely - and it is more or less true, apart from in New Zealand where farmers do not get any subsidies at all. Elsewhere, subsidies are still the norm. Farmers and growers in the developed world operate with a fairly extensive safety net.

Consumers have therefore intuitively developed the notion that as they are taxpayers already paying to keep the growers in business, any monies demanded for the actual goods during the selling process should consequently be of nominal value only.

Coupled with this misguided slant on economics is the romanticised belief that growing fruit and vegetables is a lot of fun. It must be, because isn't that what Mum or Dad did for a hobby when I was young?

Put bluntly, the average consumer has no idea about the effort it takes to produce fruit and vegetables nor do they understand what is required in order to ensure fresh produce is available on the shelves when she does her shopping.

Should the consumer care? On one hand, the answer is, 'yes, of course'. After all, we are talking about part of our daily sustenance here, and surely we ought to be interested in that. On the other hand, the sad truth is that as a society we are so used to having placed what we need to survive right in front of our nose to ensure an effortless uptake, that the term 'consumer society' and all the negative connotations associated are well deserved.

If we do show an interest, it is typically related to a high impact issue of perceived negative value, such as the marginal availability of organics or the amount of chemicals being used during production or the fact that bananas have to travel long distances to reach their market and shouldn't we therefore stop eating them?

Changes in my time

I arrived in New Zealand in 1981. At that time rural parts of the country still operated their telephones via party lines, no one had a home computer, the fax machine had already been invented but had not made it to New Zealand yet, mobile telephones only existed in movies, the Internet was the domain of Californian researchers and the US Strategic Rocket Command and e-mail and blogging did not even exist in peoples' imagination.

Shops and supermarkets opened Monday to Thursday, typically 9am - 5pm. On Fridays, shopping hours extended to 9pm. The country was shut on Saturday and Sunday.

Milk was brought by the milkman and was not available in supermarkets. When supermarkets were open, they stocked the basics. This did not include beer or wine, which had to be purchased at the off-license.

The cheese range available consisted of Cheddar variations such as Mild, Tasty and Colby. Camembert was an expensive import from France, pasteurised to death with the consistency of chewy wallpaper glue. Bananas, oranges and grapes were subject to retail price controls by the government appointed import monopolist.

As consumers, we were a lot less demanding and accepted most products and services dished up to us with good grace.

Things are a little different now.

Shops are open seven days a week, new malls are springing from the ground at the rate of two a year in Auckland and it is not difficult to find supermarkets that are open around the clock in the metropolitan areas. Milk is no longer just milk. The product range has exploded into full cream, trim, calcium enriched and latte suitable. Milkmen no longer exist and liquor is now the largest supermarket category.

Bananas are at times selling at under $1 per kilo and anyone can be a fruit importer.

As consumers, we are intimately familiar with and aware of our rights and do not hesitate to insist upon them, justified or otherwise.

Society as a whole has become more tuned into concepts such as 'the consequences of one's actions', 'cause and effect' and 'quality'. We worry about the nutritional value of the food we eat, we worry about the environmental impact food production has generically, we worry about chemical residues and we worry about the quality of the goods we are buying.

Retailers worry about the stuff we worry about to the extent that they have set up approved supplier programmes which go beyond the minimum national standards. In addition, most supermarket chains organise regular chemical screening programmes and laboratory tests, dabble in organics and generally aim to convince their adoring public that they are going about their business in an environmentally friendly fashion at all times.

New Zealand was an extreme case in terms of the regulation consumers were subjected to right until the mid 1980s. The country has since gone the other way, just about everything is deregulated, whilst some of the larger world economies such as Germany still ensure that shopping does not take place on Sundays.

Perception

Perception is nine tenths of reality. We believe what we see. This is actually one of the problems with the internet. Someone hangs some info onto a website and we take it as gospel. It must be true - I can see it there in black and white, right? Well, not necessarily. Logic and rationality do not come into it, though.

The same goes for what we see in the retail environment. If the banana display does not present itself as fully stocked with plump yellow hands of fruit that invite me to pick them up and put them in my trolley, I am likely to walk through the produce department without purchasing anything else because I use bananas subconsciously as indicator merchandise for overall range quality.

Similarly, if I see cauliflower being sold for more than $2.99 per head, I draw the conclusion that the entire range is overpriced and I would be better off shopping somewhere else or restricting my purchases to the absolute minimum.

I am aided in my belief that my intuition is a robust decision making tool in this instance by my knowledge that produce quality and pricing are moveable feasts and that variations do exist as a result of fruit and vegetables being produced by mother nature as opposed to being manufactured by man.

Where do I get my knowledge from? My knowledge is partially gained from education going back to early childhood that associates soil, dirt and mud with growing plants and partially media driven.

All it takes is a little rain and suddenly the daily press runs an article on vegetable prices fluctuating widely. I am reading it in the paper - so it must be right.

It is also fair to say that as the next generation of consumers grows up, some of the knowledge created along the way is likely to get challenged. Five year olds have been known to insist that the supermarket was the source of milk, rather than cows. They must be right, because they are seeing the milk on the shelf in their plastic bottles, right? How one of these bottles can possibly come out of a cow's udder is simply too difficult to comprehend for some shoppers-in-training.

What do consumers care about?

Another way of initially asking this question is, 'how do consumers shop?' The answer is that they are certainly not shopping for all produce in a preplanned fashion. Potatoes, apples and bananas often find themselves onto shopping lists. At times, one can also spot onions, lettuce and tomatoes. More often than not though, the shopping lists include summary items such as fruit, greens or salad veggies. How do I know? Well, I made a point of picking up discarded or accidentally dropped customer shopping lists whenever I went into a store and they always made interesting reading. Even if potatoes or tomatoes were listed, I only very rarely saw 'a bag of washed potatoes' spelled out, as opposed to loose brushed potatoes or a 10kg bag. The tomato item was never defined as loose or prepacked, vine ripened or Roma, cocktail size or gourmet. And as far as bananas are concerned, all the fancy branding on the fruit label is a total waste. Bananas are not shopped for by brand at all.

This means a substantial part, if not most, produce purchases are based on impulse decisions made during the shopping trip. Appearances therefore count and so do quality, price, intended purpose and experience.

Consumers actually do not see apples, potatoes, lettuce or bananas on display. Well, they see them on a superficial level, but what they really see is the apple crumble, the mashed potatoes, the salad and the snack. Consumers buy meal ingredients, meal components or meals in their own right.

The produce manager, on the other hand, sees 424 odd SKUs, the wholesaler that range of the SKUs he supplies and the grower just sees his crop.

Everyone in the supply chain therefore sees something different which makes working towards achieving the same objectives such a difficult task. Whose perspective is the most important one, whose view matters the most? Ultimately all partial views along the supply chain need to be consumer focused but each perspective counts and is relevant as long as it is focused upon reaching the common goal of achieving consumer satisfaction.

What is that then, consumer satisfaction? For starters, it is the driver for repeat purchases. A dissatisfied consumer will seek alternative products or shopping destinations. Satisfied customers will be back to buy more. Whilst the old saying 'it is difficult to keep all customers happy all the time' has application here as well and sets limits, successful retailers generally and genuinely try to keep all customers happy because they intuitively understand that their future success in business depends upon it.

Here are some practical examples.

Consumer satisfaction is being able to buy tomatoes that taste like tomatoes. The standard hot house tomatoes are often referred to as 'water bombs', as they are often grown hydroponically, have little flavour and have a high liquid content. Consumer satisfaction is being able to buy the first peaches of the summer in the knowledge that they will be sweet and juicy rather than unripe and sour in taste. A common mistake made is that of the race to get the first of a season's fruit - of any type - off the tree and onto the shelf long before the fruit is ready. Consumer satisfaction is buying lettuces that are not limp and covered in slugs, but clean and crispy.

Consumer satisfaction also extends into the intangible areas, such as nutrient content, chemical residue levels and shelf life expectations.

Consumers also care about having produce bags available right next to the produce they want to buy. They would like to clearly identify the price of the produce they are buying and, ideally, they would like to avoid slipping on the wet produce department floor or tripping over the broom and breaking a leg. The bin to dispose the outer lettuce leaves into had better be close to the lettuces as well as emptied regularly and all produce ought to look fresh, crisp and inviting to eat. And whatever it is that I want and whenever it is that I want it - it had better be there.

Meeting these requirements is a tall task in anyone's book, but consumers have a choice these days; and plenty of it. Did I mention that the aisles need to be clean, product descriptions up to date and all shelves and bins fully stocked? The produce department needs to smell clean and inviting, but not sanitised, thank you very much, and there certainly must not be any rotten fruit about. Mrs. Consumer likes her produce department well organised and like product grouped together, such as salad greens for example. At the same time, she does not want to be afraid of having a whole apple display collapse on top her, just because she wishes to pick the third apple from the left in the second row. There also need to be plenty of ½ cauliflower and cabbages available in case she is only doing a small shop and, Mrs. Consumer would like the choice between loose apples and prepacked ones of a smaller size at all times; and no, she does not understand why a bag of prepacked fruit weighing 1 kg should be more expensive than 1kg of loose fruit. It goes without saying that the produce department needs to be easy to navigate at all times without other customers' trolleys crashing into hers or her own trolley getting snagged on a built out carton display of bourbon and coke mixer which should not be sitting in the produce department in the first place.

To put all the above into perspective: supermarket operators are out to set the scene for the overall shopping experience in the store by way of the state of the produce department. If produce looks good and is shopped the store itself will do well. If produce is largely ignored in favour of another supermarket or a nearby greengrocer, problems for the store are typically just around the corner.

Consumers are a funny bunch. They actually do not care about how the produce they want got onto the supermarket shelves. 'I want it, so it had better be there'.

Today's consumer differs somewhat from her mother and grandmother. Grandmother could already shop in the early supermarkets of the 1950s and 60s, but Granddad was in all likelihood still tending his plot of tomatoes and potatoes on his ¼ acre section. Mum and Dad no longer had a veggie garden on their section and if they had, they subdivided the section in the 1980s and made a killing on selling the front garden to a developer. They did, however, still know what a tomato used to taste like and understood the difference between Rua and Red King potatoes.

Today's city consumer not only no longer has any connection with the land but possesses only a limited concept of seasonality. 'Why should I stop eating strawberries just because no New Zealand grower is harvesting any at present? What about Australia or California? Surely someone must grow some there. Why can't they send some over?'

Merchandising

How a consumer reacts in a store is in most cases a matter of how the produce department is laid out and merchandised. Time poor and impatient customers do not wish to race from one end of the department to the other in order to get an overview of the apple category. Apples should therefore be displayed with apples, lemons in the vicinity of oranges and so on. Our minds work through association. This means we expect peaches somewhere close to nectarines, because we know instinctively that these products are related. Similarly, potatoes, onion, kumara or sweet potatoes, shallots and garlic all fall into the same group. Produce retailers group all these products because they know them as root vegetables. It is the production orientation that is responsible for the display decision. Luckily, in this instance this works for the consumer as well, only customers know these products as roasting vegetables.

Growers and retailers are production oriented. The consumer is meal oriented. Retailers need to come to terms with this.

Consumers have in the main been done a disservice in the fresh produce departments over the last decade or so.

There have been massive changes in fresh produce retailing since around 1990. As these changes, however, were very much incremental, consumers and industry participants alike could be forgiven their assumption that it has been business as usual.

In the early 1980s supermarkets were open Monday to Friday with extended opening hours on Thursday or Friday nights. Milk was something the milkman delivered and liquor was bought at the liquor store or off-license.

By the end of the decade, Saturday shopping had arrived, milk and liquor were starting to wheedle their way into the stores and technology was slowly changing the way the fresh produce department was going about its business.

And just how was this business being conducted?

Here are a couple of snapshots - then and now.

Then - say 1985

The Produce Manager and his early morning crew would arrive between 6am-6.30am and prepare for the arrival of the first owner/ driver delivery fresh from the city markets. Whilst waiting, the team reworked the vegetables that had come off the mirrorback the night before prior to closing and cleaned the empty mirrorback, prior to restocking it for this day's sales. Gaps were left in the display for any produce that had sold out the day before, in anticipation of new stock arriving from the markets prior to opening.

All perishable fruit that had been taken off the tables the night before, were taken out of the cooler and regraded before going back on display.

By the time the shop opened at 9am, all displays were refilled and ready for the day's trade. Rubbish bins had been emptied, produce bags had been restocked and the weigh stations labels had been refilled to ensure a smooth day's trading.

The female produce department assistants, typically mothers with children or women returning to the workforce, arrived between 9am-10am. Their primary job was to man the weigh stations within the produce department, to weigh every customer's purchases, to print out the price label and to attach the label to the weighed produce bag.

In between serving customers these weigh station assistants 'preened' the department. Tables and mirrorback sections were constantly graded with any soft or otherwise unsaleable produce being removed from display. The high demand areas such as bananas or seasonal fruit were restocked several times during the day - and sooner rather than later, as the weigh station assistants had a pretty good handle on what needed doing.

The, typically younger, male produce assistants were largely engaged with bringing cartons, crates or sacks of produce out from the rear storage area and delivering it to the female produce assistants for restocking the retail area. Their other key task was rear store related - bunching silverbeet, trimming lettuces and cauliflowers and reconditioning any limp greens by way of soaking them in the produce department bath tub.

By 3pm weigh station assistants and the male produce staff were being replaced by school boys and girls who kept the department going until closing time at 5.30 or 6.00pm.

At that stage all vegetables were taken off the mirrorback and placed into the rearstore cooler overnight, as was all perishable fruit. The potato displays were covered with heavy cloths to avoid unnecessary exposure to fluorescent light whilst the cleaning and nightfill crews were busy going about their business.

By midnight, it was usually 'lights out' - until the arrival of the produce manager early the next morning to prepare for the first market delivery that signaled the beginning of a new day.

Now

Twenty-five years later some things have certainly changed. Stores are open seven days and store closing times are anything from 8pm to midnight. Some stores do not close at all.

Many supermarket mirrorbacks have been replaced by refrigerated multideck cabinets, capable of running at different temperature zones per section. Produce no longer gets removed to the cooler each night - and when the store does eventually close, the last produce assistant who leaves the department pulls the thermal curtains down on the multideck to encourage the temperature within the now closed environment to drop a bit further. The produce manager is no longer running the department during most of its trading hours. Often, there are no produce staff members visible after 6pm and any display maintenance tasks are taken up by the skeleton grocery crew which runs the store. And that can be a hit and miss affair to put it politely.

Weigh stations are a thing of the past. All produce is now weighed at checkouts during the "swapping goods for payment" process. The knowledgeable mature ladies with the amazing multi-tasking ability of grading, preening, weighing & labeling as well as keeping an intelligent conversation with a customer going have disappeared from the produce departments.

So, when we look at why the independent greengrocer market segment is enjoying such a sustained revival - could this be because the consumer perceives that greengrocers take better care of their wares as they are less reliant upon sophisticated technology?

The meaning of 'Fresh'

This question is probably as difficult to answer as "what is the meaning of life?" Not surprising therefore, that these two fundamental questions are actually directly related. The concept of 'fresh' in relation to harvested fruit and vegetable is an oxymoron. The process of harvesting - plucking an apple from its tree, cutting a lettuce in the field or digging potatoes from the ground - signals the products' progression from a living organism into compost.

Luckily we, the horticultural and produce industries, have developed effective mechanisms to convince consumers that produce is safe to eat for a period of time after harvest. The length of the period may vary. Scientific advances mean that these consumption periods have recently been drastically extended in the case of some products. None of this, however, changes the fact that 'fresh' is a perception issue in the fresh produce business rather than a concrete reality.

In the absence of such concrete realities, perceptions take over as drivers and determinants. The value equation retailers, as the part of the supply network tasked with getting consumers to exchange fruit and vegetables for money prior to consumption, are faced with on a daily basis is this:

Strong product knowledge (SPK) , buying & negotiating expertise (BNE), logistics capability (LC), merchandising skills (MS) and realistic price structure (RPS) equals growing market share (GMS), good margins (GM) and good return on investment (GRI).

When expressed as a formula, we have

SPK+BNE+LC +MS +RPS = GMS+GM+GRI

The mathematical symbol for sum is

Therefore,
(SPK, BNE, LC, MS, RPS) = (GMS, GM, GRI)

SPK, BNE, MS, LC & RPS are all determinants of Fresh (F) and can also be summed up as **C**ore **R**etail **A**ppropriate **P**ractice **S**teps (CRAPS)
Therefore,
F = CRAPS

But as CRAPS are the inputs that determine F, we need to reverse this formula into
CRAPS = F

Let's call the outcome of combining **g**rowing market share, **g**ood margins and **g**ood return on investment **3G**.
In mathematical terms 3G could be described as a product. The mathematical symbol for product is
The successful fresh produce retailer model is therefore built on these formulae.
CRAPS = F and F = 3G
Therefore
CRAPS = 3G

So what was the purpose of this short excursion into mathematics? Nothing other than to demonstrate that the horticultural / produce industry is not rocket science and that there is absolutely no reason why a produce retailer cannot succeed in business as long as he/she sticks to the fundamentals. These being the need to understand how to manage the consumer fascination with 'fresh' and that consistency in this area will lead to equally consistent performance across the three key performance indicators of market share, margin and return on investment. Simple isn't it?

If only! Retail might not be rocket science - but retail is detail!

The secret to success is to understand how to juggle the CRAPS components - SPK, BNE, MS, LC & RPS - and keep them in a constant equilibrium and harmony with each other; from day to day, week to week, season to season.

SPK - Strong Product Knowledge

Retail produce staff will never have the detailed product knowledge about oranges that a citrus grower has. Nor will they be able to discuss the relative merits of the various apple rootstocks as they relate to fruit size and yield. Nor will they indeed be an expert in any crop - and, of course, it is not expected of them either. Produce managers and their team members do need to have strong product knowledge right across the fruit and vegetable spectrum, particularly as it relates to the keeping, handling and merchandise requirements of the vast product range ordered and stocked virtually every day. A little knowledge on how to use the produce on display would not go amiss either. The sales people who know their product generally tend to be the successful ones.

BNE - Buying & Negotiating Expertise

Produce does not just turn up by magic in the retail area - someone has to buy it. In some cases it is the produce manager himself, more often a head office produce buyer, or even a team of buyers, taking care of ordering the daily requirements of fruit and vegetables from suppliers.

How many companies produce is being bought from, who does the buying and whether wholesalers are involved in any transaction or not is not the major issue some people think it is. Marketplace realities will take care of these determinants.

The critical issue is that someone on the retailer's staff had better be trained as a produce buyer, because the perishability of the product and the sometimes daily fluctuating supply situation calls for well trained professionals with cool heads to ensure the business flourishes.

LC - Logistics Capability

Having purchased the produce, time is of the essence. How will the produce get into the stores? Via the market floor, directly from grower to supermarket or should it be shipped via a centralised distribution centre? Do all stores need a daily delivery? Should some stores be serviced more than once daily? Does every product have to be included in every delivery? When does the produce have to arrive in the distribution centre in order to reach the stores by 8am? Does it make sense to deliver to all stores in the morning? Should delivery vehicle be refrigerated? Do we use owner/drivers, the company fleet or an independent contractor? How much should this cost and what is affordable?

These are just some of the questions retailers have to answer in order to build an appropriate level of logistics capacity, suitable to their particular situation. One thing is for sure. Nothing happens on its own!

MS - Merchandising Skills

The produce has arrived in store. Now what? Well, somehow bananas, apples, cauliflower, mangoes, aubergines and the other 250 odd lines will have to be displayed in the retail area, in a way that is both enticing to the consumer and encouraging her to buy, as well as complementary and beneficial to the produce. In other words - merchandising skills are called for.

Merchandising at the most basic level is putting the goods in front of the customer, but there is so much more to it. Should all the apples be displayed together or should they be interspersed with pears? Lemons and avocados look good next to each other, they make good colour breaks - but should I use colour breaks or not? It might be better for the strawberries to be in the refrigerated cabinet - but if customers do not shop the whole department, I probably will not sell too many strawberries from that location. Where should I put them instead?

Every store is different, with a different layout, different size, different fixtures, different customer demographics, different geographic location and different staff. The end result has to be the same though.

A decent offer, attractively laid out, well presented, logically organised and skillfully maintained will sell fruit and vegetables. Nothing less will do.

Ah yes -and a ticket describing the merchandise with a clearly readable price is also a requirement.

RPS - Realistic Price Structure

Which brings us to the next and by no means the last point - the price. What should the retailer charge? What can the retailer charge?

Or should the questions be: what is the produce worth? What will the consumer consider to be value for money?

This is where things can get quite confusing. Consumers invariably list 'price' as relatively unimportant in their purchasing decision when asked about this by research companies. On the other hand 'value for money' tends to pop up typically as a major decision influencer.

The retail price, therefore, cannot be set in isolation but relative to the other factors in the equation. A retailer's realistic and acknowledged underlying objectives in setting the retail price are:

- cost recovery
- sales targets
- profit objectives
- customer satisfaction
- avoidance of cherry picking
- being the main produce shop destination
- repeat sales
- growing market share

How well the produce retailer will do in the business is thus entirely dependent upon how well the produce retailer understands his or her business.

Supermarkets - trick or treat?

There was a time when supermarkets were viewed by consumers as benign structures which were providing a community service by aggregating all the food and other household requirements families needed in one place. Things have changed somewhat. Many consumers view supermarkets today as monolithic structures with behaviours similar to that displayed by the medieval robber barons that harassed travellers along the great continental trade routes - or as outright highwaymen like Dick Turpin.

This negative attitude towards supermarkets is not helped by the media which take great delight in reporting supermarket activities in minute detail, from supposed price wars and resource consent objections to changing supplier relationships as a result of regional rationalisation. And on a day when the local media gives the topic a break, a business writer takes up the cudgel and develops the theme further.

I picked up a book recently with the intriguing title "The Undercover Economist" with the objective to broaden my learning on matters economical. To my surprise, the book's second chapter is called "What Supermarkets Don't Want You to Know".

Here is a little sample.

"Have you noticed that supermarkets often charge ten times as much for fresh chilli peppers in a package as for loose fresh chillies? That's because the typical customer buys such small quantities that he does not think to check whether they cost 4p or 40p. Randomly tripling the price of vegetables

is a favourite trick: customers who notice the markup just buy a different vegetable that week; customers who don't have self-targeted a whopping price rise."

Don't get me wrong. Consumers have a right to be informed, but this persistent supermarket bashing is beginning to grate on my nerves. Having worked in the supermarket business, I am fully aware of how things work in that environment and I get a little upset when supermarket operators regardless of which side of the fence they sit are portrayed as money grabbing price gougers who aim to trip consumers up at every opportunity. The law of averages suggests that there is the odd rat bag or three in the supermarket industry - as there are in any industry sector.

This supermarket bashing needs to be brought under control though as it is getting out of hand. As an industry, we offer a lot to consumers - convenience, range, innovation, and yes, value.

Are we telling consumers? Well, we are on a chain by chain basis. Many supermarkets publish catalogues of various shapes, design and frequency. The odd one has given up advertising on a product price basis and gets its messages across by different means. Others again only advertise in their local community publications.

But what are we doing as an industry to promote supermarkets generally as a shopping destination? Not much from where I sit. Should we? Not up to me to decide, but supermarkets used to be pretty good places to buy fruit and veggies. Maybe we need a bit more than just product price messages on a weekly basis. By the way, 'The Undercover Economist' is a worthwhile read. I can thoroughly recommend it.

Shit happens

More politely expressed - change is inevitable. The basics might remain the same, but everything on the periphery is likely to change. We might as well accept it, because we will have to cope with it anyway.

In order to survive, we need to eat. No change. If we want to eat, we need to procure food. No change. How do we go about procuring food? Big change!

We stopped hunting a while ago and adopted the 'let's pay someone else to find the food' principle. Open markets evolved into closed stalls, which turned into grocery shops. These gave way to self-service stores, with the 21st century incarnation being known as supermarkets which are now being challenged by farmers' markets and internet shopping.

We are unlikely to go back to hunting our food down ourselves any time soon, but we are happy to experiment with the 'how' we trade for food.

What is the matter with us? Perennially dissatisfied or can we simply not help ourselves; constantly needing to tinker?

I am sure there are elements of all these traits that contribute to our lives, but the real answer is that we are all riding a merry-go-around called 'life'. Life means nothing stays the same and everything is constantly in motion and therefore changing. We just don't recognise it half the time.

It wasn't all that long ago in the 1980s that when one wished to eat a salad and did not grow any lettuces of one's own, one resorted to buying a head of lettuce and all the other ingredients like tomatoes, spring onions, etc., in a shop or supermarket. This was simple to achieve. Lettuce, tomatoes and spring onions were always available and the good folk down at the local supermarket even made sure that all salad ingredients were conveniently grouped together on the mirrorback.

Today, the options available to someone fancying a salad have increased exponentially.

For starters, our consumer has to make a fundamental decision. Do I assemble my own salad or do I buy a ready to eat salad in a bag, gas flushed and complete with vinaigrette?

If I fancy the ready made version, I have an array of choices in terms of size, brand, type of container, flavour and - use by date. In fact, there is little difference between picking a bag of salad from the produce shelf and a can of baked beans from the grocery aisle. My preparation effort will be minimal. I just need to make sure that I heat the baked beans through well enough and pick a salad bag which still contains fresh lettuce leaves rather than wilted or slimy ones.

Should I opt for the self-assembly option, I again have some decisions to make. Do I take a field grown lettuce or a hydroponically grown one? Iceberg or Buttercrunch? What's this? Where are the tomatoes? No longer next to the lettuce - why not? Well, once the mirrorbacks were replaced by refrigerated multidecks, tomatoes could no longer be displayed next to the lettuce, as tomatoes do not tolerate refrigeration.

Ah, where are the tomatoes then? The tomato category is likely to have its own display table - halfway down the aisle and certainly not anywhere near the lettuces. But what to buy? Loose hothouse tomatoes or cocktail tomatoes? Vine tomatoes or grape tomatoes? Cherry tomatoes or yellow pear shaped tomatoes? A six pack of tomatoes or beefsteak tomatoes?

Help, all I want is something red to put into my salad.

What used to be a simple and straight forward decision has suddenly turned into a mind bender.

Time & knowledge

I have less time today than I had twenty years ago. I have more choice than I had twenty years ago. I have more to worry about than twenty years ago. And those guys who run supermarkets have become less helpful.

What do I worry about? Food safety for starters. Biosecurity. Ecoterrorism. Slipping in front of the carrot display on a water puddle.

I know there must be some staff around, because the produce does not jump upon the display tables on its own, but where is everyone when I want to ask them a question? Where did this produce come from? How do you know it is fresh? What does 'certified organics' mean? How do I cook celeriac? Have you got any bananas out in the rear store that are perhaps a bit riper?

Chances are a customer has to wait a long time before she can find someone in a supermarket produce department who is willing or able to answer all her questions. Many customers do not care. Convenience of being able to get all their groceries including produce on the one trip outweighs the fact that information is typically not forthcoming.

But it matters to other customers. It matters to the extent that if the need for information is greater than the lure of convenience, the supermarket is shunned in favour of the greengrocer or Saturday's farmers' market.

Consumer information needs are quite diverse and complex. At the most basic level the question often is, "how do I cook this vegetable?"

It is a sad reflection on our society that meal preparation skills can no longer be taken for granted. Microwaves, desktop grills and boil in the bag options have a lot to answer for. The next level up is, "how safe is this to eat?" Not a question typically associated with fresh produce - although food poisoning and worse have been linked with otherwise harmless produce such as beansprouts and cantaloupes.

The time factor has two aspects to it. Firstly, as a busy consumer who really considers shopping to be chore, I would like to move through a store as smoothly as a dolphin cuts through the ocean. This means I would like to scoop up pre-packed capsicum as I move through the produce department without the need to stop, as time is of the essence. I will do this as long as I can have confidence that the pre-pack I pick up is of acceptable quality and that I am paying a competitive price.

Secondly, I am not sure how long it will be before I use those capsicum in a meal. I am therefore looking for some assurance that the capsicum pre-pack I intend to buy will last in my fridge for at least a couple of days without shriveling up in front of my eyes.

If I have had too many poor experiences with shopping this way and if I am at the same time becoming totally dissatisfied with being constantly on the rush and not doing the things that really matter well enough and if I include meal preparation in that category - I may well end up changing my entire attitude towards shopping as well.

The slow food movement now has over 80,000 members across over 100 countries. Its goal is to "protect the pleasures of the table from the homogenisation of modern fast food and life." It promotes gastronomic culture, develops taste education, conserves agricultural biodiversity and protects traditional foods at the risk of extinction.

Consumers who adopt the values of the slow food movement will inevitably also change their shopping behaviour. Greengrocers and farmers' markets are 'in', supermarkets become the place to buy the shelf stable centre aisle goods no household can be without: cleaning fluids, bottled water, canned food, dry pasta and rice.

I do not have time as a busy consumer to pay detailed attention to how the produce ends up on the shelf of my supermarket, but I do expect it there when I do want some. At the same time, I have picked up on the wider theme that supermarkets are corporates whose sole objective is shareholder profit. I know they must be doing something right, otherwise they would not survive and prosper, but I am increasingly getting concerned about this mismatch between my value system and what seems to be important to supermarkets.

It seems the right thing to do to support the greengrocer and my neighbourhood butcher and since I am able to buy my bread from the baker in the same complex, this fresh retail cluster seems to have become a destination for me in its own right. The strawberries do seem to look fresher, more consistently red and less squashed. Maybe I need to come here more often and look, there is the lemon grass I have not been able to find at my local supermarket.

Consumers do not wander through the stores articulating their views to all and sundry. They keep their own council. When the scatter noise and dissatisfaction barometer reach a certain level though, consumers start voting with their feet.

This is less of a problem for the produce industry and more of an issue for individual channels. Industry though needs to insure that consumer dissatisfaction with one of the fresh channels, for example the supermarkets, does not turn consumers off the fresh spectrum altogether. That would be unfortunate.

It is therefore vital that the produce industry at large understands consumer needs and trends so that it can ensure consumer access to quality fresh fruit and vegetable at all times - and through the channels consumers favour.

References/Recommended Reading

Harford, Tim *The Undercover Economist* Little, Brown 2005 ISBN 0-19-518977-9/ ISBN 0345494016

Constraint

Food businesses operate under constraints. Constraints vary, but may include distance to market, seasonality, capacity, crop compatibility, financial scope and others. The key is the ability to identify the constraints relevant to one's particular business and the degree of 'stretch' the constraints are able to tolerate before quality is compromised.

The nature of the product

The most fundamental constraint relating to fresh produce is that the minute produce is harvested, the decay process gets under way. We have learned to work around that though.

Postharvest handling of crops ready for sale has become an intricate science and consumers benefit from our ability to manipulate respiration and decay rates without really appreciating it.

Whilst green leafy vegetables typically make the journey from paddock to plate with a minimum of delay, apples on the other hand can just about take a year these days; that is how efficient and effective controlled atmosphere storage and chemical compound based ethylene scrubbing mechanisms have become.

How product is treated postharvest, in other words, how much money is being spent on maintaining appearance, quality and eating quality is organised around three factors.

- What is the minimum that has to be done in order to get a decent price?
- Is the product destined for local market or export?
- Do I have a customer for the product I have planted - at least at the time of harvest? There are no generic answers to these questions. The answers

depend upon the type of crop, the time of year and where the crop has been grown. Another factor that does come into the equation is the state of the infrastructure between harvest location and retail destination. Let's look at one example. Cherries harvested in Central Otago on New Zealand's South Island typically have two potential volume destinations - Asia, preferably Japan, and the domestic markets of Auckland. Growers prefer Asia. Asian consumers seem to be prepared to pay more for fruit than their Auckland counterparts. In order to get to Asia though, cherries have to pass strict phytosanitary conditions, have to be packed in acceptable material and, of course, need to be faultless, i.e., no rots or splits, without blemishes or chemical residues. As Central Otago is in the middle of nowhere, where fox and rabbit would say good night to each other apart from the fact that there are no foxes in New Zealand and rabbits are considered a noxious pest, cherries leave by truck in the first instance, regardless of whether they are Tokyo or Auckland bound. By the time cherries are loaded onto the trucks at the Central Otago packhouses they are divided into two categories.

The first category consists of fruit that is definitely headed for the various domestic markets and has therefore been packaged accordingly. The second category is those cherries that, it is hoped, will be able to wing their way to foreign shores within twenty-four hours of leaving their birthplace. Whether they will or not, has yet to be determined.

Cherries sent to Auckland typically travel via the Cook Straight ferry which connects the country's South Island with its more populated Northern counterpart. From an export perspective, a highly perishable crop such as cherries, needs to travel as airfreight.

So if all is well, the export destined cherries leave New Zealand via Christchurch airport. If, on the other hand, the exporter has some concerns about the shipment's ability to either reach its destination in sound condition or if there are problems with the way the shipment presents itself from a packaging perspective, then the decision might be taken to divert the fruit onto the local market instead.

Such a decision immediately creates several dilemmas. Firstly, the local market may well be saturated at that point in time. Placing a large export shipment into the local market in addition to the local market volumes already circulating is likely to collapse the price.

Secondly, the now rejected export shipment would have had a certain amount of value applied to it, over and above what is required for local fruit, such as a phytosanitary inspection by a Ministry of Agriculture officer or specialised packaging. As the local market does not require such fineries, the local market price offered will not take these expenses into account.

And to top it all off, the grower possibly will not even know that his product has been rejected for export and will get a hell of a fright when he gets to see the financial details a few weeks later.

The way things used to be

Yes, there is always that old paradigm to fall back on. *The way things used to be.* I am a great fan at looking at the way things used to be. Not because I have a hankering for the past and cannot cope with the present, but because I care about the future and want to understand how some of the constraints we are experiencing today, in the present, have come about. The future does not exist in isolation. If we want to develop robust systems in just about any business discipline for the future we need to build upon past and present. A sense for history and process evolution is therefore an essential starting point.

Mankind needs to eat to survive. Our meals may have become more sophisticated, but the principle has not changed. No food, no energy and eventually no life. As we started to evolve as a society we split into two very basic population segments. Some of us add value to society by performing essential and desirable tasks that do not produce food, whilst others produce food in order to feed the rest of us. This system has evolved wherever society reached a certain degree of sophistication. It is not a new principle and can be found as far back as the ancient Egyptians and beyond.

In modern terms we refer to these two groups as town or city dwellers and country folk. Wherever towns established themselves, the country folk were not too far away, as the town dwellers needed to be fed.

One classic reminder of how things used to be that survives into our age is the open air markets in the old cities along the Rhine in Germany. All a traveller has to do is to head for the city centre in places like Mainz, Bonn or Cologne and on at least three days a week one comes across the spectacle of fruit and vegetable growers having pitched their stalls in the shadow of the town hall or cathedral, offering the wares grown in the surrounding country side.

New Zealand or the United States do not have the same historic depth as Europe, but the principle remains the same. As soon as people establish settlements whose primary function is not food production, people a little further afield arrive with fruit, vegetables and meat to feed the settlers. In the

US these were the early Indians before the white settlers decimated them. In the case of New Zealand, Waikato Maori became very innovative in the middle of the 19th century when it came to feeding the newly established and rapidly growing city of Auckland.

Prior to the arrival of motorised transport and the accompanying road network then, the following principle existed right around the globe:

Wherever towns and cities spring up, the surrounding countryside is called upon to feed the city dwellers.

Having grasped this principle, it is therefore easy to understand why every town used to have its own dairy factory, abattoir and market garden area. No food, no city. It was as simple as that.

City dwellers and country folk did not necessarily know each other or even like each other. For one, an educational gulf emerged between the two population segments that grew from generation to generation.

Nevertheless, both groups realised their mutual interdependence. City dwellers no longer had the wherewithal to feed themselves and country folk needed the guilders, talers, marks and dollars city dwellers used to pay for their food in order to buy the balance of life's necessities, cloth, salt, stock etc.

Supply and demand

Supply and demand were finely balanced. Country folk soon knew what the town they were servicing could consume and city dwellers intuitively understood that their reliance on the food supply meant that there were limits to the extent to which they could afford to drive a hard bargain if they wanted to eat well next season as well.

Both parties had no alternative but to get on. Shipping fruit and vegetables in from other parts of the country was not an alternative because of the product's high perishability factor. The same applied to shipping it out. By and large, an equilibrium existed.

From time to time, the equilibrium got disturbed. In most cases there was very little warning. The plague, for example, was something neither city dwellers nor country folk could plan for, particularly as both parties' hygiene standards, or rather the lack thereof, were a major contributing factor of the disease breaking out in the first place. Similarly, war was a frequent visitor and the country folk usually took a heavy hammering as food was in hot demand and nobody wanted to pay.

I should point out at this point that I am not aiming to produce a historically accurate account of the agricultural economies of the Middle Ages here. My objective is to paint a broad brush stroke picture about relationships and their constraints as they relate to fruit and vegetable supply.

When life was normal though, the growers 'kind of' knew how much to grow and the town folk had a good idea what represented a fair price. And if that sounds oversimplified - it is fully intentional. Over time exotic spices, vegetables and fruit were introduced from far distant lands. Some of these, potatoes and tomatoes for example, soon became a mainstay of the European diet and started causing problems of their own. A number of books have been written about the potato famine, so there is no need to take that topic much further here.

The moment the motorcar was invented the relative balance between supply and demand became disrupted. Hardly enough to be noticed in the first instance, but over time the pace of change increased.

Whilst New Zealand does not have a centuries old history of hamlets turning into villages and towns like Europe, the principles apply here as well. Farmers and growers settled on the land, villages and towns established themselves and on the edge of each town, the market gardens grew.

As towns and cities grew, market garden areas shifted further out

- always remaining at the edge of the cities. Around 1900, for example, Auckland's market garden area was around 7km from the city centre, on fields occupied today by the Auckland Racing Club.

By the end of 1945, the Mangere area in South Auckland had become the predominant market garden area. There is still some produce grown in Mangere, but the main economic activity taking place there revolves around the International Airport, 21km from the city centre.

Mangere has been replaced by Pukekohe as the area critical to Auckland's vegetable supply. Pukekohe is about 50km from the Central Auckland Post Office and there is some serious debate going on about how long Pukekohe can withstand the pressure generated by rising land values and environmental concerns before vegetable production has to shift further south again.

Supermarkets and greengrocers

Or should that be greengrocers and supermarkets? Greengrocers certainly were around long before the supermarket concept was invented. They were not always called greengrocers either. Fruit shop, fruiterer, barrow boys were also commonly applied descriptions. The Worshipful Company of Fruiterers was one of the omnipotent craft guilds of medieval London and had its counterparts all across the continent. A specialist trader selling highly perishable food products that he is intimately familiar with has been an accepted societal concept for centuries, no surprises there.

Supermarkets evolved in the US in the late 1920s and early 1930s and eventually made it to New Zealand in 1958. A Harvard Business Review article of 1938 defines a supermarket like this. "A supermarket is a large departmentised store in which the departmentised food sections are the only, or at least among the most important, sections operated."

The same article quotes US industry magazine Progressive Grocer as stating that Los Angeles had 25 supermarkets in 1929 with a combined turnover of US$3.3 million. This number had grown to 193 and just under US$36 million annual turnover in 1935.

The demands of one crop category versus the needs of many

This is truly one of the major issues within the fresh produce industry. An apple grower is passionate about his apples, a cabbage grower cares about his crop and the potato grower has at all times the best interest of his crop at heart. It goes without saying therefore, that all the equipment used on the apple orchard, in the cabbage patch and in the potato paddocks will be entirely suited for its use; it will be fit for purpose. The same goes for post-harvest facilities, equipment and transport. Growers are sensible people and they care about produce. It is their livelihood, after all.

At the other end of the spectrum sits the consumer. She cares about the produce, too. It is just that she does not think about fruit and vegetables as farm outputs, but as food or meal ingredients. Her interest therefore does not lie in economies of scale, margins and effective farm or shop labour management but in taste, value for money, quality, hygiene and the wider food safety aspects - without necessarily being able to eloquently articulate the latter.

The retailer sits fair and squarely in the middle between producer and consumer. At the moment the produce is placed on display within the retail environment, the perceptual transformation occurs from farm output to meal solution. A head of Cos lettuce turns into the basis for a Caesar's Salad. Washed potatoes are being selected for tonight's roast dinner and the rosy apples on display ensure that mom's apple pie is the crowning highlight of the family meal.

As the customer's focus is on consumption rather than on long-term maintenance of the products' current state, there is very little need to educate the consumer on that score beyond a few basic points such as,

-do not place tomatoes or bananas in the fridge;

-potatoes should be kept in a dark place;

-the fruitbowl is also a good place for capsicums.

The retailer on the other hand ought to have a few more in-depth skills. There is one problem with this: retailers are only interested in moving the produce as fast as possible from their shelves into their customers' trolleys. Whilst this is an honorable attitude and totally in-line with the commonly accepted shopkeepers' creed and motivation, it is not conducive to getting the retailer's full attention when it comes to the care requirements of individual crops.

Retailers view produce, and everything else in their stores for that matter, as product categories and merchandise departments. Getting a retailer to focus on the needs of bananas between being received at the store delivery dock and being purchased by a consumer is just about possible, given that bananas typically account for between 8-10% of produce department sales. Everything else is hit and miss. The trick for a supplier therefore consists of getting the produce into the supermarket supply chain and into the shoppers' trolley without either giving the produce assistants a chance to damage the produce or without having to rely upon them to add any significant value to the produce through their actions and behaviour.

Rather than dwell on the negative aspects of this, growers need to think positive. How can retailers be motivated to look after the produce that comes into the store? One of the reasons pre-packing has taken off in the produce industry is the attraction of being able to keep the produce out of the hands of clumsy produce staff. This theory is somewhat flawed, to the extent that even bags of pre-packed apples do require manual handling of sorts.

Packaging

How does one get produce from the paddock to the consumer?

It does not matter how fresh fruit and vegetables are when they are still in the ground or on the tree. It is of little relevance how small or large a head of lettuce or a crop of apples is. Crop quality and process care account for nothing - unless the producer is able to get his harvest to the consumer in an efficient and cost effective way that takes into account the product's perishability and delicate nature. This is by no means a new revelation, but has always been understood instinctively by the people involved in the trade: growers, wholesalers and retailers.

The New Zealand fresh produce industry was for most of the 20th Century dominated by one company, Turners & Growers Limited (T&G). This situation continued right until 1989, when the banana import business was deregulated. Post World War II wooden containers became prevalent as the preferred method of transporting fruit and vegetables from orchards and market gardens via the city markets to retailers. Through practical application and common sense three key wooden packaging types emerged for vegetables:

- Large grower bins, which when full could only be lifted and moved by forklift;
- Vegiepacks, which held, for example, six heads of lettuces or 8 cabbages, depending on product dimensions;
- Allpacks, a smaller box suitable for spring onions, radishes, tomatoes, other non-bulk vegetables and locally grown fruit.

Potatoes continued to be sent to market in jute or Hessian sacks and eventually migrated to paper sacks and plastic bags. Fruit had been traveling to market in lightweight, covered, shallow and well ventilated wooden containers for some time by the time Vegiepacks and Allpacks were introduced.

Industry did not think in supply chain terms in the 1940s or 50s, although the logistical challenges industry participants faced were in some ways more complex. Whilst fruit was grown in a variety of places, centers of gravity emerged early on, e.g., Hawke's Bay and Nelson for apples, Kerikeri and Gisborne for citrus, Central Otago and Hawke's Bay for peaches, plums and eventually nectarines. The distance of these growing areas from their key markets of Auckland, Wellington and Christchurch meant that most wooden containers used for fruit were a 'one-way' solution.

Vegetables, on the other hand, were usually grown in close proximity to settlements. Unlike fruit, most vegetable varieties do not require very specific climatic growing conditions or soil type. This meant that returning empty packing cases to a collection point for re-use was a feasible option. Green vegetables, in particular, were also far more perishable than potatoes or fruit. The latter could survive a three-day rail journey if handled correctly, the former needing consuming as close to harvest as possible.

These natural preconditions combined with an underdeveloped road transport network and laws limiting road transport opportunities in favour of rail, led to the development of a thriving returnable wood based packaging system for vegetables, whilst fruit was largely transported in one-way boxes made from a lighter type of wood.

By the time New Zealand introduced decimal currency in 1967, T&G had reached its zenith as the dominant force in the fresh produce industry. It would remain in this position for a further two decades without any substantial erosion of market share or change of business practices. When it eventually came, change was swift and brutal. Right now, though, the company was enjoying its hard earned success. This success was partially built on T&G's ability to provide growers with a packaging solution for their produce - 'one way' fruit boxes and returnable Vegiepacks and Allpacks. T&G had gone into the manufacturing and box hire business, conducting that business through its wholly owned subsidiary, the Fruit Case Company Ltd (FCC). FCC depots were conveniently attached to city markets and growers picked up a load of empty boxes after they had unloaded the produce for the next day's auction on the market floor. T&G and its associated companies were wholesaling produce in virtually all New Zealand cities and towns. The FCC concept was strongest in Auckland.

In the lower North Island, Chinese growers, who constituted the majority of the vegetable producers, operated their own container company, the Green Leaf Crate Company. Its containers were identical in size and shape to the FCC ones, but as movement of market ready vegetables between production centers was not prevalent, the Green Leaf Crate mainly circulated in the lower North Island. The returnable produce crate system was not as strong in the South Island, where right up to the mid-90s large field bins, Hessian sacks and plastic bags counted as mainstream packaging solutions for green vegetables.

From the early 1980s major produce industry changes began to occur, which also affected the returnable produce crate business. At the T&G board meeting in August 1981 Chairman Jack Turner reported that Foodtown Supermarkets Ltd, a subsidiary of Progressive Enterprises Ltd was establishing its own large distribution centre in Mangere and had asked T&G to supply it directly rather than through auctions (Stead, 1997). The Board's direction to that request deserves to be recorded verbatim, as it is a manifestation of how supermarket buying was misunderstood as recently as 25 years ago.

"The executive directors of the company have been living with this matter for a long time and it is constantly under consideration. It is our considered opinion that the auction system is the fairest and the best for all concerned and that, as leaders of the industry, Turners & Growers Ltd should not be prepared to give a lead in any action which would destroy the auction system which was officially supported by the growers' association and by the New Zealand Retail Fruiterers' Federation."

By February 1983 another sign of things to come could be found in the monthly T&G Board Report.

"The supermarkets have secured such a large proportion of the trade we must continually endeavour to retain their goodwill and as much of their business as possible."

At that point in time, 1983, the supermarkets were buying their produce from auction, from T&G by private treaty and from a small emerging number of produce brokers who were not associated with the auction business at all, but moved produce directly between grower and retailer. The concept of supermarkets buying directly from growers was very much in its infancy.

In 1984 the incoming Lange Labour government announced that it would lift the monopoly for imported fruit that had existed since it was introduced by the Savage Labour government in 1936. Between 1936 and 1952 the Internal Affairs Department had been responsible for managing the fruit import business. In 1952 the Government set up a company called Fruit Distributors Ltd to manage that business on its behalf. Shares were allocated to every produce auction company throughout New Zealand. As T&G expanded its reach and purchased its competitors, it became the majority shareholder of this monopoly company by default.

Any resolve by Government to deregulate the importation of bananas, oranges, grapes and other niche fruit would lead to substantial challenges for T&G. In the end Government gave five years notice in the case of banana and orange imports. The trade of all other imported fruit was deregulated in late 1984. Bananas and oranges would be deregulated in December 1989.

In 1987 T&G acknowledged and identified six serious competitors who had entered the wholesale produce business in Auckland: Primor Produce, Kiwi Harvest, Alex Donald, Allan Lowe, Market Gardeners and Sunrise Coast (Stead, 1999). Of these three are still in business. One of the founding directors of a fourth one (Kiwi Harvest) continues to play a pivotal role in the industry today.

By 1988 T&G was facing serious challenges:

- The stock-market crash of 1987 affected the entire economy and T&G was no exception.
- The Government that had been so keen to deregulate the fruit import business could not see fit to deregulate the apple export business, i.e., the NZ Apple & Pear Marketing Board monopoly remained in place.
- The deregulated Kiwifruit export business that had generated substantial revenue for the company (and some of its competitors) collapsed and Government created a Kiwifruit monopoly modeled on the Apple & Pear Marketing Board, effectively shutting T&G out from participation in this multi-million dollar revenue opportunity.
- Banana deregulation and thus further potential revenue shrink was only a year away.
- The supermarkets had shifted substantial volumes of business from the T&G auction to other wholesalers.

Not content with that, one supermarket chain, Foodtown, had started buying some local produce direct from growers, bypassing the wholesale channel altogether.

The produce crate dilemma

This last issue, the changes in supermarket buying behaviour, created more than just one dilemma for T&G. Not only was its market share under constant threat and dropping at an alarming rate, the company was actually facilitating its competitors' growth through its approach to the returnable produce crate business. T&G's wholesale competitors and those growers who had started selling small quantities of produce direct to supermarkets were using FCC equipment, i.e., returnable produce crates ultimately owned by T&G, to move the produce from the production areas to the stores.

Until mid 1988, T&G was taking the attitude that it could tolerate this behaviour, as the bulk of the produce was still being channelled through the markets. The reality was that the company was not in a position to stop this leakage, even if it had tried. Growers who picked up truck loads of empty equipment did not have to provide any details regarding the ultimate destination of the crates, once filled with produce. T&G was very conscious of the fact that these growers were also supplying the auction floor and the last thing the company wanted to do was to get offside with growers.

The financial structure of hiring wooden crates from FCC did not help matters either. A grower's account was debited $5 per crate at the time of pick-up. The T&G Vegiepack system worked on the basis that grower and purchaser should jointly fund the hire cost. When the produce was sold at auction, the grower's account was credited with $4.50 per crate, representing the deposit return less a $0.50 user fee. Similarly, the retailer's account was debited with $5 per crate of which $4.50 was refunded when the empty crates were returned.

FCC was not designed to operate as a 'stand-alone' company in the conventional sense. Its purpose in life was to facilitate the movement of produce from growers to Turners' auctions. When other distribution channels emerged, the FCC specific system of 'checks and balances' was of little use to a T&G management team that was increasingly getting concerned about the changing industry. As long as growers turned up to hire crates and retailers returned the crates eventually, FCC could do nothing other than issue crates - unless the 'rules' were changed.

I joined Foodtown Supermarkets in 1987 and became head of the company's fresh produce business in 1989. Some of the changes I wanted to make to the way produce was bought were hampered by a lack of an alternative to the FCC supplied Vegiepacks and Allpacks.

Foodtown's new produce distribution centre started operating in May 1989 and the company's produce buyers withdrew from participating in auction sales at about that time. Direct purchases from growers increased and whilst these continued to be received in FCC supplied containers even if T&G was not involved in the purchase, the buyers began to notice a hardening attitude at T&G with regards to growers supplying produce directly in FCC equipment.

The withdrawal from the auction system also provided the opportunity to 'normalise' the packaging cost structure from a retail perspective. Having to account for cost of goods and cost of packaging separately was an administrative nightmare. I felt that if it was possible to buy a carton of baked beans for a fixed price without having to pay extra for the carton, the same should be possible within the produce sector. Suppliers were therefore advised that the company was no longer prepared to accept packaging surcharges. It would in future negotiate a price for produce supplied. Suppliers needed to ensure they covered their entire packaging related costs when they negotiated supply.

The Achilles heel of Foodtown's future produce business strategy was the distinct lack of an independent returnable packaging system whose owner was unable to use the system as a strategy tool related to securing supply. The decision was therefore taken to invite Graeme Weck, a Pukekohe based manufacturer of bulk bins for the onion and kiwifruit trade to enter the business. Weck was to manufacture a sufficient quantity of reusable wooden boxes that were identical to Vegiepacks and Allpacks and offer them for hire to Foodtown growers who would be directed to him by the Foodtown buyers. To differentiate his containers from FCC ones, Weck applied yellow paint to part of the box exterior. The decision to proceed with the creation of what eventually became known as the Weck-Pack system was taken in August 1989. The first produce packed in Weck-Packs entered the distribution centre on October 1st, 1989, the day the banana monopoly ceased to exist.

In 1990 I visited the UK and studied the produce supply chains of leading supermarkets Sainsbury and Tesco. I returned to New Zealand convinced that the future of fresh produce distribution revolved around shipping fruit and vegetables in plastic crates rather than wooden ones.

Graeme Weck was not entirely happy to hear that, as his core competence was the manufacture of wooden boxes. He was also of the view that he needed to gain an acceptable return on investment from his Weck-Pack venture first before abandoning his wooden boxes in favour of plastic crates.

I was keen to create as much competitive advantage as possible for his company and felt that converting to plastic crates would help to accelerate this process. An agreement was therefore reached with CHEP to import 30,000 plastic crates from the Sainsburys and Tesco supplier. These arrived in early 1991 and Foodtown growers were directed to switch to CHEP plastic crates.

This move was initially greeted with dismay by Weck-Pack and ridiculed by T&G, but within 18 months both companies had introduced their own plastic crate pools. Initially, there were substantial differences between FCC's and Weck-Packs 'deposit/ refund' systems and CHEP's 'daily hire' method, but market forces and competitive pressure prevailed, with gap closure and systems alignment occurring over a period of time.

There has been very little direct change in the crate industry since 1993. All three companies involved have introduced various computer systems, which ostensibly aid the process of hiring crates. After initially introducing a separate footprint for their crates, FCC and the Greenleaf Company were convinced by industry to adopt the common and more practical footprint used by CHEP and Weck-Pack. Greenleaf was eventually purchased by CHEP. Weck-Pack and FCC remained very much produce focused, whereas CHEP has branched out into the meat and wine industries in an attempt to establish a broader market for returnable plastic food packaging systems. In 2003, GE Weck was sold to CHEP.

One way packaging

The only viable one way packaging system for multiple produce units is cardboard. Cardboard packaging solutions are used as a solution of choice in the export industry, e.g., kiwifruit, apples and stone fruit. Cardboard will continue to play a role in the domestic fresh produce industry for several reasons, namely;

- Delicate fruit such as cherries or peaches, for example, do not travel well in plastic crates.
- Retailers have a tendency of wishing to use packaging material for in-store merchandising purposes, giving the impression that the produce on display is truly 'field fresh'. High quality printed material such as Visyboard is a retailer favourite.
- One way of not having to pay for this material is to insist that fruit is supplied in retail display ready containers.
- Despite all their obvious advantages, plastic crates continue to be an administrative problem. Once empty, they represent convertible cash due to their 'deposit refund' financial structure. Empty crates are also often diverted into unauthorised usage or stolen before the rightful receiver of crates filled with produce can return the empty crates to the relevant crate depot. The use of plastic crates between continents is not unheard of.

UK supermarket chain Waitrose has been known to send empty Iffco crates to New Zealand and insist that its kiwifruit is packaged into these containers in preference to Zespri's standard cardboard boxes, but this is by no means common behaviour. As is the case with other constraints, retailers are forever trying to stretch constraints to their limits in order to ensure they benefit from all possible aspects of competitive advantage that can be identified.

Who pays the ferryman?

Or more directly - who should be paying for what? Growers clearly incur the costs of producing their fruit and vegetables and getting the produce to the retailers' receiving points. Retailers are responsible for all costs associated with the sale process - including shrink and waste incurred at the point of sale. Then there are the bits in between; certification, quality control, packaging, advertising, etc. These factors will be discussed in detail elsewhere, but they all represent a constraint of sorts.

Costs are by default one constraint upon the profit a product can be sold for at retail, with another constraint being the value perception consumers have of produce. Retailers are therefore at all times focused on keeping the cost of goods landed at their stores as low as possible in order to gain maximum flexibility for themselves. Economies of scale, a limited number of suppliers each producing larger quantities of produce and modern technologies deployed at all points in the supply chain are all geared towards achieving the desired low cost base.

Technology requires investment though and is often associated with borrowing money from banks or finance companies. There is nothing wrong with borrowing money for the right reasons - but banks are usually quite keen to view documents like supply contracts and are looking for a certain degree of certainty that the debt they are asked to fund is based on sound decision making.

Written supply contracts are, however, not the norm in the fresh produce industry and supermarket suppliers often carry considerable risk based on a handshake and several price setting phone calls each week. A grower who is subject to retailers changing supply when it suits and at a drop of a hat is not considered to be a good credit risk by the trading banks.

Conversely though, once a retailer and grower/supplier have established a working supply relationship on the basis of a minimum amount of paperwork and a high degree of tactical communication, the retailer is faced with a few constraints of his own; the principal one being -where would he suddenly find another grower with similar capabilities?

The reality is that by the time a large retailer and a large supplier have aligned their respective systems in such a way that they are able to do business at a service level acceptable to both of them over a period of time, a mutual interdependency has evolved that neither party is able to extract itself from without incurring considerable direct or indirect costs.

I do not know whether I have already made the statement I am about to make elsewhere in the book or whether it appears here for the first time. It does need to appear in any event because it is absolutely critical. If it is a repeat - great, the points contained need to be re-emphasised anyway!

A grower needs to be able to earn an income as well as a return on his or her investment.

Why on earth would anyone want to subject himself to a way of operating a business if the dominant feature of the business was the production of negative cash flows and the disincentive to reinvest? At the end of the day, growing is a business, just like building or plumbing. Builders and plumbers will not stay in business for long if they are consistently being paid at a rate that does not allow them to cover their expenses and generate a profit. The same principle applies to growers.

The only difference is that one typically cannot walk onto a grower's property, see the produce lined up neatly on the shelves complete with a wholesale price tag as you can at a yard supplying the building trade.

What has that got to do with constraint? It is quite simple. There are natural constraints to what the consumer is prepared to pay for a head of broccoli, for example, unless, of course, additional value has been added. So, if the basic head of broccoli is experiencing purchase resistance based on rising production costs on the farm, increasing occupancy costs at retail and neither party being willing or able for that matter to live with reduced margins that keep the retail price below the consumer pain threshold, the ability of that crop to contribute positively to the economic mix of both grower and retailer is dwindling.

What should one do? Accept that constraint - grow less, sell less and get into an ever increasing economic death spiral? Maybe, if there are no other options. Constraints need to be identified and recognised, by all means, in order to cut one's cloth accordingly at a given point in time. Thereafter one has a choice. Accept the constraint as a permanent fixture or try to find a way around it by changing the goal posts, solving the puzzle that creates the constraint in the first place and by creating new realities.

That's my philosophy for what it is worth.

Recommended Reading

Reader, J.
Propitious Esculent: The Potato in World History
Random House 2008 ISBN 978-0-4350-1836-9

East, C.
75 Years of Market Gardeners Ltd
self published 1998 ISBN 0-473-05523-6

Stead, K. *One Hundred I'm Bid: A Centennial History of Turners & Growers* Kestrel Publishing 1997 ISBN 0-473-04169-3

Davies, P.N., Hope-Mason, D.
From Orchard to Market: An Account of the Development of the Fruit and Vegetable Trade in the UK
Lockwood Press 2005 ISBN 0-95398551-7-2

Conflict

Conflict is as old as mankind and needs to be managed. Not all conflict is bad. A degree of organisational conflict is healthy and aids in the development of a more robust organisation. The potential for conflict needs to be understood and the degree and nature of conflict needs to be measured in order to be able to deal with it. There is plenty of scope for conflict within the fresh produce industry at all points along the supply chain.

Consumer versus retailer

This is typically a covert form of conflict. On the surface, matters are pretty simple. The retailer has the goods and the consumer needs the goods. The minute they agree on a price and the consumer hands over the money, the sale is transacted.

If only it were just so easy!

Does the retailer open when the consumer wants to shop? Does the retailer stock what the consumer wants to buy? Does the consumer find the quality of the goods the retailer stocks acceptable? What about the level of service or the standard of cleanliness then? Or the product knowledge of the produce manager and demeanour of the checkout operator?

Consumers generally do not enter a store searching for conflict. They are typically keen to gather up their requirements, endure the checkout queues and get out. Unfortunately, conflict has a habit of finding them when things do not go as right for them as they expect.

Supermarket operations versus merchandise

A supermarket is a complex organisational being. Consumers typically only get to experience the store they are physically visiting at the time. One store often employs several hundred people. A store management team usually consists of a store manager and his deputy, an office manager, departmental managers for grocery, meat, delicatessen, produce, bakery, liquor and general merchandise, a checkout manager and in larger stores often a training manager. Each department has several staff with the number being determined by the size of the store and its opening hours; and then there are the checkout operators.

As a rule of thumb, managers are supported by a limited number of full-time staff, the rest of the crew more often than not work part-time. Numbers can therefore add up rapidly.

Each store operates as an independent unit but is usually tied into a wider store network. Store managers report to an area manager who is responsible for managing several stores. Area managers work for a regional manager who in turn reports to the operations director. How many layers an organisation has and what the roles are called varies depending on organisation size and location, but the principles apply regardless.

A supermarket business can easily be compared to a military structure. Think of departmental managers as platoon leaders, store managers as company commanders, area managers being in charge of battalions and the head of operations being the colonel commanding the regiment.

Regimental commanders and their subordinates are usually pretty competent people, otherwise they would not be holding the roles they do. Before they got promoted into their roles they tend to have completed a fair amount of training, so do they know what they are doing? You bet. Give a colonel an objective and enemy watch out! But who gives the colonel and his regiment their objectives? Where does the colonel get the battle plan from? Who ensures that colonel and troops are well briefed, up to the task, and most importantly, supplied with the right equipment to start with and replenished appropriately during the heat of the battle when it matters most?

This is usually the role of another group of officers, equally as well trained as the colonel and his men, but tasked to occupy themselves with the wider picture of the conflict at hand, rather than just with the state of today's battle. Within the military, the officers are referred to as the general staff or staff for short.

In the supermarket environment, managers in this role work for the merchandise department.

Store managers worry about every aspect of what is going on in their store.

Area managers do the same, just on a larger scale. These managers are generalists, which means they have a general, but not a detailed understanding, of how the various departments in their store function. Detailed enough to keep the produce department, for example, functioning over a number of days but not detailed enough to ensure that it is meeting all required hygiene, ranging and financial standards on an ongoing basis.

A merchandise manager, on the other hand, is usually based at the company's main office, head office or support office and his or her job is to worry about the way all produce departments in all company stores are performing and delivering service to the consumer. Merchandise managers are experts in their field and understand the produce, meat or delicatessen business in intricate detail.

Merchandise managers do not operate in isolation, but are supported by teams of subordinate managers and administrative staff. These subordinate managers are typically referred to as category managers or produce buyers.

On the surface the merchandise team's role is very clearly set out.

Keep the stores supplied and assist them to achieve the company's overall objectives of meeting sales, profit, wastage and market share targets. The potential for conflict relates to how much room there is for interpretation. Who has a better understanding of what a store is capable of selling, the store produce manager or a category manger working in the merchandise department? On balance, the answer is that neither has all the facts at his fingertips and that the optimum result can only be achieved through cooperation.

How much time though, is there for a debate between the two of them on every item in the range? And does this mean that every produce manager in every store has to speak daily to every category manager in order to optimise the range in his or her store? Logistically, this would be a totally unrealistic situation.

Supermarkets overcome this situation by creating rules. Rules such as,

- Merchandise staff determine the ideal store produce range
- Store produce managers must carry the range specified unless otherwise agreed to
- Store produce managers must place an order for new fruit and vegetables every day
- Stores must sell the produce at the prices set by the merchandise department.

Plenty of room for conflict here, don't you think? Does the merchandise department know the store demographics

better than the local store? Why can't the local produce manager decide whether broccolini will sell? Is it really necessary to order everything fresh every day? What happens when a local competitor sells a product cheaper? Should the store produce manager just ignore that?

Debates of this nature occur right across the world on a regular basis in any supermarket organisation that has separated its buying and merchandise function from the sales role - which means all of them, as logistically it would be an absolute nightmare for a supermarket chain to allow every store produce manager to buy his or her own produce.

The emergence of smart technology is now beginning to remove the argument in some of those instances. Store buying, for example, has just about been automated in some of the larger chains. Sainsbury's no longer allows merchandise and store staff to engage in the daily order argument. Once a store has been ranged by the merchandise department in consultation with store staff, an optimum stock level is determined and fed into the store computer. In establishing optimum stock levels factors such as the time of year, promotional periods, price, competitor presence and distance from the nearest replenishment point are taken into account. As customer purchases are scanned at the checkouts, sales are automatically deducted from the inventory. Once the inventory reaches a certain trigger point, the store computer automatically places a replenishment order. Some stores receive up to three fresh deliveries daily under that system.

Conflict is still possible. Managing a supply chain with the aid of complex algorithms becomes challenging when the product involved is non-standard or availability of supply is irregular.

Who decides whether a product should be ranged in the first instance? Surely not the computer, which has us back at the original question: does the store tell the buying team what it wants or does the produce buyer arrange for the store to receive what has been bought? Subtle differences that can make all the difference though!

Marketing versus the rest of the supermarket

Whilst operations manage the daily interface with the customers and merchandise is responsible for getting the goods into the store, the marketing team typically handles the communication strategy and to a varying degree wider strategic business issues.

Communication is the 'easy' part. Supermarkets are one of the print media's best customers. It would be frightening to even try estimating the number of trees it takes annually to satisfy the grocery industry demand for print space in newspapers, broadsheet flyers and catalogues. There are times when supermarkets also run radio and TV campaigns, but typically they stick to the basics - paper and ink.

Loyalty card programmes and customer magazines are also a standard domain for marketing departments, but I have yet to see the mobile telephone or podcasts being used to communicate with consumers.

A supermarket's operations and merchandise teams are usually quite relaxed about letting the marketing department get on with its work - as long as it does not interfere in what they perceive to be their domain. The real stuff. The coalface. Selling and making money. Marketing departments just spend the money; we make it. Everyone knows that, right?

Trouble therefore starts when the marketing department tries to influence the behaviour of the company.

There are two ways that this can happen.

Supermarket catalogues and advertisements do not put themselves together. A lot of planning and foresight has to go into those to ensure that the product is available and that the advertisement has the desired effect.

Like any business, supermarkets have budgets. There are sales and gross profits budgets for each department in each store, each store, each store region, each store format or type and the entire operations division which comprises all stores. Similarly, there are budgets for each merchandise department; i.e., produce, delicatessen, grocery etc.

There is also a marketing budget - typically an expenditure budget. Operations tends to be responsible for achieving the sales budget. The various merchandise teams are tasked with meeting the overall departmental profit objectives and marketing is not supposed to be spending more than their allocated budget.

Operations and Merchandise are very interdependent. Customers will not buy produce in a supermarket if the produce is of poor quality or too expensive. Merchandise relies upon store produce managers to ensure profit targets are met without being able to direct the behaviour of these managers who are all working for their respective store managers.

The atmosphere is therefore electric enough as it is without the marketing department suddenly suggesting that the catalogue due to be distributed in 6 weeks should feature Duck a la Orange to commemorate the start of duck shooting season and that the meat and produce departments should please come up with sensationally priced offers on roasting ducks and oranges.

At this point, the meat merchandise manager is likely to go red in the face and express in short sentences of few words and syllables that the company has never run a duck front page special in its forty year history and that he has no intention to start doing that now, given that

- there is not enough interest in ducks
- there are insufficient numbers of ducks in the market
- the planned special for that week is corned beef and that the way it is.

The produce merchandise manager by that stage has worked out

that the week in question falls within the gap created by the last US oranges being imported before the local New Zealand supply comes on stream. Supply will therefore be limited and advertising oranges would lead to embarrassing out of stocks.

Having just recovered from the meat man's response, the marketing manager now has to endure the produce man's lecture on why his idea won't fly - duck or otherwise.

Finally ready to re-butt, the marketing manager is being rudely interrupted by the operations manager who has just found his speech again and proceeds to remind the gathering that operators know what's best and can categorically state that Duck a l'Orange might be popular amongst the Ponsonby fairies the marketing manager frequents with, but the New Zealand heartland will not have a bar of such an offer. The company will therefore be doomed to absolute failure if it goes ahead.

And just as the also present heads of the IT, Human Resource, Grocery and Finance Departments had suspected, the meat and produce merchandisers who usually take it in turn to verbally abuse the operations guys, swing in behind the operator and support him to the hilt.

The second way a marketing department endears itself to the rest of the supermarket team relates to the environment within which the supermarket conducts its business. Stores are of a certain colour, display a certain brand, use a certain type of shelf fittings, display cases, lighting, freezers, etc. Inevitably, the marketing department has some views on what works best. Its opinion is heavily influenced by what looks best, whereas operations wants a fixture of optimum efficiency to save on labour whilst the merchandisers are looking for equipment that protects the stock on sales from the clumsy operators who destroy margin from the minute they set foot into the store. Try sorting that one out!

Perishable merchandise versus shelf stable

Supermarkets are divided into merchandise departments. These were not established with the consumer in mind, but on the basis of what works best for the supermarket operator.

The typical supermarket consists of these departments; grocery, meat, produce & floral, delicatessen, seafood, general merchandise and liquor. The seafood department is sometimes an extension of the meat department and larger stores can have a stand-alone floral department if turnover justifies it, but this segmentation is in essence standard across the globe.

Regardless of where in the world one visits supermarkets, one tends to find groceries in the centre of the store, together with general merchandise and liquor. The fresh departments and frozen goods are usually closer to the outer edge of a store, based on the fact that perishable merchandise ranges either require electricity or generate waste - or both.

The other requirement is usually working space beyond the area accessible to customers, where as dry or shelf stable groceries usually just need additional storage space.

Think about the local supermarket you shop at. Have you ever asked yourself the question, "How did the operators decide the size of the produce or meat department, and why is the produce department so often the first place I hit when I enter the store?"

Here is why:

The decision to build a store in a certain location is based upon whether it makes economic sense. Marketers and planners use the supermarket companies' own data sets as well as information available from organisations such as the Department of Statistics to establish the likely number of shoppers a new store will attract and the likely turnover the store will generate. Based on data collected by stores already trading, the company knows that produce departments, for example, generate on average, say, 12%

of total store turnover. The company can therefore assume an average weekly produce turnover for the store that has not been built yet.

The next step is to establish to what extent the new store is likely to over- or under achieve average store sales.

How many greengrocers operate in the area? How close is the store to the main horticultural production areas? What is the ethnic mix that is likely to shop for produce in the new store?

Armed with the answers to these questions the store development team consults with operations and merchandise to estimate a likely departmental size. At this stage other considerations are added.

Will the department fit-out vary in any way from that of the last new store built? New display cabinets perhaps - or refrigerated display tables rather than standard ones? What is the overall brief for the store? Are there any new store design features that could impact upon produce? A new lighting plan perhaps? Does the store have to accommodate a new department - video rental or a pharmacy to name just two options? What impact would that have on space allocation for the traditional departments like produce? Questions, questions, questions.

Meantime the produce merchandise team is faced with a few questions of its own.

What will be included in the store range? How should display cabinets and bins be configured from a practical perspective - never mind the funny ideas coming from the store development team. Should we ask for extra bin space or are we better off forcing faster stock-turns by running smaller displays? Do we really want to admit that we do not need all that space - it might be needed in the next store coming up and then we might have to fight for it. And this is just touching the tip of the iceberg.

The fact that produce departments can often be found at the entry to a store is not a coincidence of amazing proportions but a deliberate design. Supermarkets discovered quite a while ago that the quality of the fruit and vegetable offer can be a major influencing factor for consumers when they decide where to shop. The decision to have customers enter the store via the produce department makes perfect sense - from the supermarket operator's point of view! Unfortunately things are not as straight forward for the customer.

Bananas, tomatoes and peaches do not take too kindly to being squashed by canned soup, bags of dog biscuits and bottles of water. Accumulating one's shopping is already tricky enough in terms of trolley size, aisle width and the 'road rage' equivalent behaviour of some shoppers. Protecting one's produce from being flattened before one has even paid for it, is yet another task supermarket operators tend to leave to their customers.

Some stores offer their customers a compartmentalised trolley, but even that is not a sustainable solution. The alternative? Produce is bought on a separate trip to the supermarket - or elsewhere!

In any event and regardless of all considerations made by the produce merchandisers and operators, the greatest space scavenger in all supermarkets is the grocery department.

Fast **M**oving **C**onsumer **G**oods (FMCG) are developed around the globe at the rate of knots and for every item for sale in a supermarket there are at least five new ones trying to get onto the shelves. How suppliers and grocery buyers go about listing new products and killing off others is expertly told elsewhere. Suffice it to say within the context of this evolving produce story, grocers have an insatiable appetite for shelf space and the produce department is often at the receiving end of grocery space grab attempts.

Supplier brands versus private label

The arguments about whether a store should stock supplier brands or also develop private label product has now been around for at least thirty years. The produce department is a relative latecomer to this particular facet of the conflict between supplier and retailer. The issue is now heating up and conflict exists. Period.

In order to fully appreciate the topic at hand, we need to go back to the origins of the fundamental "job share" arrangement that had existed in the early days of supermarket retailing.

Suppliers and manufacturers were responsible for coming up with new products, packaging them, advertising them and getting them to the store delivery docks. It was the retailer's job to build the store, set it up, receive and price the goods, place them on the grocery shelves and ensure easy access for shoppers and their trolleys. In the case of meat, suppliers delivered half beasts, already skinned and gutted, for the store butchers to process further into mince, steak and chops.

Fruit and vegetables came in wooden boxes of their own, Hessian bags and later plastic ones and were "gotten ready" for sale by store produce managers and their teams swinging big knives.

As store numbers grew, supermarkets started to build grocery distribution centers and asked suppliers to deliver FMCG goods there instead of delivering them to individual stores.

Naturally, retailers with distribution centers expected a discount; after all, the supplier could drop off a whole truck load of goods at one location, rather than having to stop at six or seven individual stores. Makes sense, doesn't it?

Well with any economic argument, there are always two sides of the coin to consider. Whilst the cost the supplier incurred in delivering the goods to retailer A with a distribution centre certainly reduced, the supplier still needed to keep his trucks on the road to deliver goods to the ten stores operated by retailer B, who did not have a distribution centre. As retailer A was demanding his discount, retailer B was insisting on the same service as before an at the very least the same cost, but preferably a discount reflecting the one offered to retailer A on account of having a larger overall marketshare.

To top it all off, the supplier was forced to operate two dispatch systems, one based on bulk deliveries to a central location and the other for smaller deliveries to many locations.

At about the time retailers started to come to grips with centralised versus decentralised distribution, they also found the energy to tackle the issue whose brand name should be on the goods. We will shift our attention to that process now, but will need to return to the distribution a little later on. Readers will have noticed by now that nothing in the supermarket and fresh produce industries is simple and that most aspects are interconnected. This is the reasons why managers with a purely singular focus tend to fail

- a holistic approach is required to succeed in produce retailing.

When a supplier sells a retailer a can of peaches in syrup or a jar of instant coffee he is paid a price - commonly referred to as the wholesale price. That price is made up of several components, which, when amalgamated, make up the paid price. These components include the cost of the can, the cost of the label, the cost of the peaches or the coffee, the cost of processing the fruit or the beans, as well as a share of the manufacturer's total overhead cost for plant and maintenance, compliance, marketing, and logistics. Lastly, and most importantly, suppliers add a profit margin.

If anyone wants to conjure up an unkind image of a grocer, the pencil behind the ear paradigm comes to mind fairly quickly. Whilst one will not find many grocers with the aforementioned tool actually clamped behind the ear these days, the principle still applies. Grocers are trained to attend to detail, which includes focusing on the minute elements that make up a wholesale price.

Eventually, grocers figured out that suppliers often had another line item in their cost equation; one called brand equity.

The argument being that brand equity represented the good will consumers had built up towards a supplier brand over time and that the good will could be expressed as cents per stock keeping unit.

Retailers responded with two strategies. Initially they said, "Alright, we understand that, but this goodwill is being generated in our stores. We therefore deserve a share of the goodwill dollars generated. Let's call it a promotional allowance. And by the way, it costs us money to maintain your stock on our shelves. We are therefore also looking for a listing fee, carton discounts and a slotting allowance."

The second response was even more Machiavellian.

Retail margins are relatively low in percentage terms given the amount of investment required in operating a store. This is partly a fact of life in terms of the price of real estate, construction, fit-out and maintenance as well as a historic hangover of how things used to work in the past - when suppliers ruled the roost and determined wholesale and suggested retail prices.

Retailers now started to think like this: "Wouldn't it be nice, if we could eliminate supplier marketing costs and this brand equity component and just pay for the actual cost of goods and a reasonable amount for profit. Our margins would increase and that is what we are ultimately interested in, aren't we?"

And so the concept of private label products was born.

Today, there is not a supermarket in the Western World that is limiting itself to selling supplier brands only but all also sell a varying share of private label product, branded with either the supermarket name or a brand name the supermarket company has created for its exclusive use.

What impact did the development of private labels have upon relationships with manufacturers and suppliers?

Initially, relationships soured whenever a supermarket started mentioning the P-word. Suppliers interpreted the retailer's decision as straying onto supplier turf and many initially fought back by refusing to entertain the idea of supplying private label products.

This attitude generally did not last long. Competition to get FMCG products onto retail shelves is intense and many a second tier manufacturer started to take the position: "I might not be able to get my own branded product in there, but if the retailers are prepared to pay a reasonable price for getting a private label product, why should I not supply?"

The goods on the grocery shelf now represent a delicate balance between supplier goods which are typically sold for a lower margin, but generate other income from suppliers and private label product sold for a higher margin. The latter do not attract additional supplier funds but promote the retailer brand and position in the market place.

Fresh produce, of course, works slightly differently.

For starters, produce initially did not arrive in store packaged but "au naturel". Branding opportunities were therefore somewhat limited.

As late as twenty years ago, labels on fruit were something of a novelty and limited to bananas. Sunkist, the famous Californian citrus cooperative, was literally branding its oranges as they came across the packing line.

Sunkist, along with many other growers around the world, were early adopters of trade branding, by way of logos and information printed on wooden crates and later cardboard boxes. At times, boxes found their way onto the retail displays.

Other than that, very little printed material ended up in the produce departments or on the fruit or vegetables on display.

In the 1980s three things happened that are responsible for the way produce departments look like they do today.

Firstly, a couple of large produce companies which had started their business in the international banana and pineapple trade decided that it should be possible to manage produce along the lines of dry groceries. One of the consequences of their decision was that their company logos started to appear in miniature label form on any fruit marketed by these companies - Dole and Del Monte.

Secondly, consumers became more aware of food safety related issues and time poorer at the same time. Consequently they got used to the idea of buying prepacked produce and preprocessed produce such as washed potatoes and eventually ready to eat salads, which, of course, opened up branding opportunities. Thirdly, technology advances arrived with a hiss and a roar and enabled the upgrade of supermarket tills into in-store data systems. All of a sudden, it became important to retailers not only to record apple sales, but sales of Granny Smith apples versus Royal Gala, for example.

Checkout operators were perfectly capable of distinguishing between red and green apples, but what about telling Splendour and Fuji apples apart?

The answer was to introduce PLU stickers. PLU stands for *Price Look Up.*

These are the pesky little stickers consumers love to hate because they are often difficult to get off an apple or peach - but make the produce retailers' lives so much easier. All the checkout operator has to do is to punch in the four digit PLU number displayed on the sticker and, hey presto, the sale is recorded accurately, as long as the database capturing the information is being maintained accurately. PLU numbers are the produce department's barcode equivalent and have today become a vital part of the produce management information system. Life never stands still though. Neither does technology and a lot of work is currently underway to potentially replace PLU numbers with miniaturised barcodes.

As PLU stickers are now deemed a necessity on just about all loose fruit with confusion potential, the branding opportunities for produce suppliers have increased.

Retailers are very wary about any supplier attempts to brand produce. Given the importance of produce to the way consumers think about supermarkets, retailers prefer their produce to be as unadulterated by supplier brands as possible.

Produce margins are substantially higher than grocery margins. Shelf-stable grocery products found in the supermarket centre aisles contribute around 50% of store sales turnover and typically between 14-18% gross profit averaged across all categories. Produce on the other hand rarely exceeds a 12% contribution to sales, but can average a 25% gross profit margin.

A supermarket needs to be thought about as a finely tuned and delicately balanced organism whose equilibrium can become severely disturbed when base conditions and assumptions are challenged or changed. Now that branding is increasingly becoming an option in the fresh produce department, retailers are keen to see their own brands introduced, rather than leaving the field open to suppliers and having to claw 'territory' back painfully and over time as is the case with groceries.

The grower/wholesaler/retailer relationship

The relationship between growers, wholesalers and retailers is a complex one in the produce supply chain, as all parties have choice. The extreme choices are easy to describe.

Some retailers swear by procuring their produce purely from wholesalers and shippers and do not wish any contact with growers. Conversely, some retailers have a policy of only buying from growers and grizzle if they find that this is not possible in some produce categories. The positions at the extreme edges of the continuum are held by very few retailers. The majority of supermarket produce retailers occupy a middle ground, trending however towards the 'let's buy from the grower' end.

Why? What is going on here? How did these positions evolve?

The most common denominator is that these three links in the supply chain all want to make money from feeding the consumer.

The growers certainly deserve an income and a return on his investment, otherwise why bother growing? The retailer also needs to be rewarded for putting up structures like a supermarket and advertising his wares so that consumers come and buy them. Until recent years, the wholesaler was equally recognised as deserving a share of sales and profit dollars as he brought grower and retailer together through facilitating the transfer of goods and exchange of money.

The value of produce, in essence a commodity, is established through the balance of supply and demand. In short, this means there are no list prices. During the produce auction era, the price was established on the day based on what growers supplied and retailers bought - and possibly manipulated by the auctioneer through communicating with key growers about the volume they ought to supply as opposed to the volume they were able to supply.

Today, the auction system has disappeared. Some produce is still brought to the former auction facilities that have survived in the larger cities, but the product is traded rather than auctioned. A large percentage of the produce that used to be purchased by supermarkets at auction is now, however, delivered directly to supermarket distribution centre.

On the other hand, the farmers' market phenomenon has taken off in New Zealand and elsewhere which has growers selling directly to consumers. If that was not enough, some retailers are also trying their hand at importing products such as grapes, citrus and bananas and wholesalers are establishing strategic stakes in production units such as tomato properties. The boundaries are blurring and each part of the supply chain is busy straying into its partners' territory. Conflict is therefore inevitable.

How things changed

In their development phase supermarkets were very happy to purchase their produce from auction. The auction system was easy to access and the market quickly adapted to the changes large retailers with multiple outlets were requiring. Once supermarket produce volumes reached a critical mass, problems started to emerge and the flaws of the auction systems started to outweigh its advantages. It became very difficult to achieve consistency in terms of supply, quality and price. No single grower line available at auction was suddenly sufficient to cover all requirements in that category. Even when the right volume of cauliflower, for example, was sitting on the auction floor, there was no guarantee that other buyers would not try to get their share of the line. Some buyers were suddenly more equal than others in terms of volume required. Yet the supermarket buyer needing to buy four hundred cases of cauliflower was bidding on the auction floor against the green grocer wanting twenty cases and the citizens' veggie co-op buyer from one of the snooty inner suburb streets who was looking for five cases. The 'one rule for all' approach started to cause the supermarket produce buyers some considerable concern. Even if today's purchases could be successfully accomplished, there was no guarantee that the required volumes would be available on the next main auction day.

The 'main auction day' concept represented a problem in its own right. Main auction days were Monday and Thursday. On these two days the auction halls barely coped with the volumes of produce growers delivered during the preceding afternoons, during the night and right into the small hours of the morning. On Tuesday, Wednesday and Friday mornings only a fraction of the produce available on Monday and Thursday turned up. Buyers were therefore faced with the feast or famine concept and this approach translated into all processes associated with getting produce to the consumer. On Monday and Thursdays, the contract drivers responsible for transporting the produce into store after the auction had finished had to start at 6am, often ended up making more than one trip and had a very long day. On the balance of the auction days, fewer of them were required and those who carted that day could take things a lot easier. The same scenario existed in the stores. On Mondays and Thursdays, the stores were replenished to the point that it was difficult to move around and find the stock one needed in the rear-store produce departments. The produce managers and their teams were pushed to the limit, processing the green vegetables and ensuring some sense of order amongst all the stock that had been delivered. On Tuesdays, Wednesdays and Fridays, the deliveries were very light and often did not consist of the full range.

The whole supply chain from grower to retailer thus worked to a 'stop-start' model. The rationale behind the emergence of this inefficient process was twofold. Growers by nature occupy themselves with preparing the ground, sowing or planting, nurturing and harvest. Each step is vital and interdependent. It is tacitly understood that growers cannot spend their entire working week harvesting or solely concentrating on one of the other tasks. Some prioritisation is necessary, like setting a certain amount of time aside for harvesting. Once harvested, produce, and particularly green leafy vegetables, need to be moved through the supply chain fairly rapidly if condition and value are to be maintained.

Until the mid 1980s, New Zealand society moved at a steady pace. Just about every aspect of life was regulated. There was a limit to how much currency one was able to take out of the country. A government licence was required for any imported product. Bananas and oranges were imported by a government appointed monopoly holder and shops closed were closed on Saturday and Sundays.

Harvesting produce on a Sunday so that it could be transported to the auction firms later that day and during the night so that retailers could restock their stores on Monday mornings after being closed for two days made therefore perfect sense. As growers had spent all day Sunday harvesting, they needed to get on with the pressing farm matters on a Monday, which meant they sent no or very little produce to auction on Tuesday and so on and so forth.

The election of David Lange's Labour Government in 1984 had far reaching consequences for New Zealand society, the country's economy and our position in the wider world. It also changed the way the produce industry operates, although nobody would have been able to foresee all these changes at the time.

The critical direct change was that the government within five years of coming to power deregulated the imported fruit business and the domestic apple industry. All of a sudden anyone with the right connections and necessary small change was able to import bananas, grapes and citrus fruit. Even better, the New Zealand Apple & Pear Marketing board was told to focus on the export business and retailers were able to choose whether to buy apples from the board, a wholesaler or directly from growers.

The vital indirect factor impacting on the produce industry was the change to shopping hours. Stores were able to stay open for longer on the days they already traded and were able to open on the weekends as well. Initially that was restricted to Saturdays, but in the early 90s Sunday trading arrived with a hiss and a roar. The quaint 'stop - start' produce supply chain process was no longer adequate as supermarkets needed to change their behaviours to adjust to the new market place reality.

Stores no longer had to restock their entire range each Monday, as Sunday had become a trading day like any other, i.e., the range was already there, because it had been needed to serve Sunday's customers. All that was required was a reasonable sized top-up; more than what used to come on a Tuesday but certainly a lot less than on a 1970s Monday. In fact, with seven day trading, store volumes were never deliberately run down as used to happen from Friday lunchtime during the five day trading week. Instead, regular daily deliveries were called for, adjusted to the volumes set by daily store customer counts.

Longer store opening hours also meant that stores and their buyers based at a central office needed to be able to get hold of each other later in the day. In the days before mobile phone, that meant buyers needed to be in the office in order to be effective.

The only problem was that produce buyers typically started work at 5.30am, which meant they started to flag by 2pm. The altogether simplistic sounding solution was, 'let's stop buying at auction.' Buyers could start work at 8 am, put in a full day's work, buy over the phone and remain accessible to the store at all times.

Easier said than done. Apart from the fact that drastic change is never easily introduced anywhere, the produce industry had to overcome a few major paradigms in order to move forward. Paradigms such as:

- All produce needs to be physically inspected before it can be bought;
- The auction system is the only reliable and consistent price mechanism for produce;

- Retailers who do not buy at the auction will never be price competitive;
- Retailers will not know what is available and what is not unless they visit a merchant's trading floor.

The physical inspection paradigm was easily dealt with. Buyers did not mind staying in bed for longer on cold mornings. Quality specifications were written for all produce, which meant putting buyers' expectations carried around in their heads onto paper. Suppliers were told, 'supply to these specs, or else.' Yes, this rather crude system needs ongoing maintenance even today, but the principle was simplistic enough to overcome the paradigm.

If a large buyer announced that he has changed the way he sourced produce from buying off a trading floor to diverting it to his own premises on its way to town and then stayed away from town, the equilibrium of supply and demand would be maintained as long as trading floor operators and competitors had caught up with the retailer's message and understood it to be genuine. The real question was whether the retailer was able to find growers who were prepared to sell produce to the company direct? If all growers were happy with the auction system, then the answer was clearly 'no'. On the other hand, if the retailer was of a substantial size and it was financially rewarding to supply the retailer, product would find itself in that retailer's stores by the method the retailer preferred. As far as competitive pricing was concerned - yes absolutely important, though to a degree a red herring. One of the auction system's major flaws was its ability to produce price spikes and troughs at a drop of a hat and often several times a week. That was very disruptive to trade, consumer price perception and orderly merchandising. Retailers opting for direct purchasing mechanisms were usually interested in paying a realistic yet stable price that still took account of seasonality and availability but did not produce the extreme highs and lows the auction system was able to throw up.

An appreciation of the need for regular and current market intelligence and the skill to ask the right questions soon put any concerns over the 'don't know' paradigm to bed and on May 8th 1989 the writer took Foodtown Supermarkets off the produce auction floor.

Logistics versus merchandise

A supermarket is a viable organism, consisting of many parts which all need to sing from the same hymn sheet, more or less, in order to survive, prosper and grow. The degree to which the 'more or less' is managed will ultimately determine the success or failure of the organisation.

Let's imagine the following scenario for hymn sheet disparity, this time between merchandise, the people responsible for sourcing, and logistics, the team which manages daily store deliveries and operates distribution centres and trucks.

The grocery distribution centre sends a truck laden with shelf stable groceries from the company's logistics base to a provincial town with three stores two hours south. On the way back, the now empty grocery truck travels through the main vegetable producing area supplying both the city and the provincial town and literally past the front door of the company's main lettuce and broccoli grower who supplies his produce direct.

Thinking holistically, the grocery logistics team comes up with this brainwave. "Wouldn't it be economically sensible if instead of driving past the lettuce and broccoli grower we stopped off on the way back from the provincial town and backloaded all the produce and took it to the produce distribution centre. The grower would not have to drive into town to deliver his produce and could pay us a fee instead. We reduce our costs because we would have a backload and everyone is happy. Let's go and tell the produce merchandise guy about our great idea and that we want to start next Monday."

To the logistics team's surprise, the produce team is not jumping for joy and does not want to have a bar of it. When logistics insists that they have a mandate to pursue this matter, the produce merchandise manager throws the pushy warehouse guy out of his office as he cannot fathom how someone can be so stupid and ignorant in wishing to pursue a scheme right out of the Mad Hatter's tea party from Alice in Wonderland.

Logistics promptly enlists the help of operations by suggesting that merchandise is blocking a move that would reduce the transport cost of produce and translate into cheaper lettuce and broccoli.

Operations and logistics complain to senior management about merchandise and the edict is delivered, "explain yourself!"

The produce merchandise team thus has to take time out from their busy day and with the help of the grower who would be affected, proceeds to explain the following facts of life to operations and logistics:

- The grocery fleet consists of rear loading trailers; the grower's truck is a side loading curtain sider.

- The grocery fleet is configured to be loaded by via a loading dock; the grower's truck is loaded by forklift from the ground.
- The grower has no loading docks at his packhouse.
- At the time the grocery truck drives past, the grower is still harvesting his produce.
- Green leafy vegetables need to be held in a cool store for several hours after harvest in order to remove the field heat. Shifting them straight away would reduce shelf life.
- The grower has other customers who do not come to pick up their produce. He therefore would still be required to drive his truck into town, but at a higher operating cost.
- The grower also has a need to run his truck into town in order to pick up empty crates. He needs the empty crates to fill the supermarket orders for the next day. As the grocery team did not wish to involve itself in delivering empty crates to produce growers, the grower had a continuing need to come to town with his truck. The most economical way to achieve this was to bring a load of produce to the distribution centre and back load with empty crates. Any changes to that system means increased costs and therefore higher prices.

At this point the logistics manager suggested that he had not heard anything that would convince him his scheme would not work and that cost efficiencies for the transport fleet at large were more important than cost increases for lettuce and broccoli, just because an individual grower's efficiency was being marginalised.

Mr. Logistics was therefore shown the door for the second time in as many weeks, but the operations manager, to his credit, had seen the light and disassociated himself from his erstwhile ally.

Fact or fiction? Fact, unfortunately; and only one of many examples that could have been used to illustrate the various 'tectonic plates' in play within the supermarket environment.

Want versus availability

There would not be too many people who would when asked, "Would you like some strawberries for dessert?" respond with a resounding "No". Until a couple of decades ago, a question like this would only be posed in the strawberry season - for obvious reasons, i.e., dictated by common sense on the basis that both questioner and respondent had a fair idea that strawberries were a seasonal product available only in spring!

Today, seasonality no longer constitutes a constraint and most fruit and vegetables are available all year around because somewhere in the world it will always be strawberry season, etc.

Some would argue that it is not natural to consume fresh strawberries when they are not in season locally on account of upsetting the natural equilibrium. The fact that supermarkets and greengrocers merrily continue offering strawberries and other produce when it is not in season locally suggests that many consumers have abandoned the concept of local seasonality in favour of "I want it now, so let's have it."

More recently the food miles debate has erupted, at the centre of which is the position that fewer apples, flying strawberries from Western Australia to New Zealand or from California to Japan represents an extraordinary level of wasteful behaviour in relation to the carbon footprint generated.

New Zealand meat scientists managed to prove categorically that shipping New Zealand sheep meat to England produced fewer carbon emissions than growing and killing sheep in the UK, so one needs to be careful with such statements. And we had the case where hysteric British consumer elements were busy flagellating New Zealand for creating an enormous carbon problem through our airfreight exports of kiwifruit to Britain when the reality was that all our kiwifruit is shipped by sea! Another hint that the carbon debate is best left to the professionals.

Nevertheless, the debate exists and when interlinked with the views and opinions of the slow food movement and similar exponents of the notion that we need to slow down and get back in touch with our inner selves, we should not be surprised by the fact that even the large global supermarket chains like Tesco, for example, are suddenly rediscovering the 'locally supplied' and 'in season' aspects of their business models.

We will be hearing more on that front over the next few years.

Concluding comment - or just another place on the continuum?

This chapter was one of the earliest ones written and as my editorial assistant Kathryn pointed out to me, I had some finishing to do, to ensure readers had an easy transition to the next chapter. One can't just do that, of course, without reading what had gone before. Having therefore just reread what I had to say in this chapter, I am beginning to muse about the nature of conflict again and the way it can rear its ugly head in the most unexpected fashion.

I made a comment earlier in this chapter about PLU stickers. I said, "the branding opportunities for produce suppliers have increased" as a result of the increasing importance place by retailers on the presence of PLU stickers on the fruit.

How fast situations can change and how radically wrong perfectly sane statements can become is ideally demonstrated by the arrival of the databar on the scene. Many readers may still know the databar by its original descriptor, *reduced space symbology*, but regardless what you call it, the *branding opportunity* statement advanced here and elsewhere in relation to the PLU sticker is rapidly evaporating. Advances in technology and the need for greater traceability mean that supermarket retailers now wish to see a miniature barcode on what was known as the PLU sticker. The industry at large has said - and GS1, the global administrator of barcode systems, has agreed - that the human readable equivalent, the PLU number, will also be present on the fruit to assist those retailers whose IT platforms are not sophisticated enough to cope with the barcodes.

I give you three guesses what that means in terms of branding opportunities for producers! That's right, unless the sticker doubles in size, which is unrealistic, the brand presence will either be minute or gone totally.

Does that mean the tail has suddenly started to wag the dog? Yes, one could say that. More rational individuals would suggest that this is a natural phenomenon where the consumers' need for greater assurance drives the supply chain's behaviour in terms of ensuring the consumer gets what she wants.

I have also heard the view expressed that the demands of the supply chain have begun to get in the way of common sense - and that is certainly an attitude reflected by the fans of farmers' markets, with both fans and markets growing at a rapid rate.

Conflict is not all bad, as constructive conflict creates new opportunity. Conflict will not go away so we need to get used to it. The way to cope with conflict is to dissect it into its componentry, analyse it, learn from it and construct more robust business models.

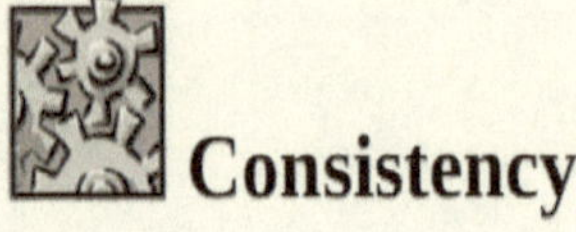

Consistency

Human nature does not cope well with change. We like our bananas yellow and our cauliflower creamy white. We also like to know that we can expect to purchase similar produce every time we visit a store and that it lasts for the same length of time when we take it home. Based on that consumer behaviour, the retailer does not want any surprises either. A food business therefore needs to be built around delivering a standardised consistent product in order to achieve operational excellence.

In the field

There is nothing a grower hates more than a paddock full of cabbages with inconsistent growth patches in it. Considerable effort is expended these days to analyse the soil nutritional profile of cultivating areas down to the last square metre and the wizards working for the fertiliser companies have become fairly competent in conjuring up a customised brew capable of bringing even the most stubborn piece of cabbage real estate into line.

At harvest time all these cabbages are expected to be standing in a straight file like a formation of soldiers at parade rest, ready to be inspected by a foreign head of state. Only, in the case of our cabbages the foreign component will most likely be a seasonal labourer imported from Tonga, the Fiji Islands or Indonesia - and hopefully in possession of a valid work permit.

Cutting cabbages, or cauliflower, lettuce or broccoli for that matter, is a skilled task and an awful lot of damage can be inflicted through careless handling or inconsistent performance.

Growers are not the only producers with an appreciation for consistency. Manufacturers across all product categories will sagely nod their heads when asked to confirm that consistency matters in their businesses. The critical difference between growers and manufacturers, however, is that the latter can influence the process of achieving a consistent product to a far greater degree than the former. Yes, growers perform a range of plant husbandry and associated tasks during the production cycle of their crops and aim at consistent outcomes. The operative word here is 'aim'. Manufacturers can achieve consistent outcomes through precision based behaviour, growers cannot.

Growers can anticipate what might happen or react to what has happened, but it would be a brave grower who guarantees an outcome months, weeks or even days from harvest. It is not that growers are reticent, unskilled or lazy - the opposite is the case; but regardless how hard a grower tries or how he skilled he is, at the end of the day, growers are not in full control of eventual outcomes, e.g., the degree of product consistency at harvest. Growers, unlike manufacturers, have to engage with Mother Nature on a very intimate and regular basis. Of course, the next hurricane coming through can demolish a factory - but the chances of hurricane damage are fairly slim, unless one knowingly operates in hurricane prone territories. A grower's crops, on the other hand, are vulnerable to far lower natural threat levels than a hurricane. A decent downpour at a critical time can make the difference between a sensible return and a disastrous outcome for the season.

Consistency from a production perspective is not a term that can be defined in absolute terms.

The demarcation line between unacceptable and acceptable produce quality is very fine and can change at a moment's notice. Consistency is therefore a moving target and the parties involved in striving for and requiring consistency need to be in constant communication with each other, so that the understanding of just what exactly 'consistency' means today, as opposed to next week or the previous season, is crystal clear.

The consumer

At the other end of the spectrum sits the consumer who has some quite specific expectations vis-à-vis consistency.

Can we relate to this? Of course we can. After all, we are consumers ourselves. When I go and buy Brussels sprouts, I wish to select from a display of even looking sprouts. I also have an expectation about the maximum diameter sprouts I would like to see on display and as a Brussels sprout connoisseur I naturally expect to be able to select from a line that was harvested after it has experienced the first frost, because that's when Brussels sprouts taste sweeter. To top it all off, I have this expectation every time I feel like purchasing Brussels sprouts.

Consistency thus is a multidimensional phenomenon at consumer and product level, involving all my senses. Monday to Sunday please, whilst Brussels sprouts are in season, from the first to the last day.

Freshness

Freshness, of course, is a given for Brussels sprouts. It is something I expect in any event. I might not know how to define it, but I expect it. I do not treat other vegetables I like and buy any differently, by the way. I have the same high demand for consistency. Seasonally adjusted, of course, and product specific.

Yet the concept of freshness is one of the most debated and most misunderstood concepts within the fresh produce industry. Does 'fresh' mean the apple has just been plucked from the tree? Does 'fresh' mean the kiwifruit has just been released from its controlled atmosphere storage facility where it has been slumbering for three months before taking its turn on the supermarket shelf? Does 'fresh' mean the sweet potato or kumara has just been dug or it was just taken from its storage pit where it had been placed 6 weeks ago to await further processing?

We have a strange relationship with 'fresh'. Walking through an orchard and taking some cherries from a tree for immediate consumption - that is fresh. Or is it? What about if the cherries on the tree are already past their prime on the day I am walking past and pick them? Are they still 'fresh'? Or how about apples which have been treated with a chemical compound that extends shelf life to around a year or more depending upon variety?

We may not give much thought to the freshness concept on a day to day basis, but it does influence the consumer mindset and contributes to shopping behaviour at a greater level than we might realise.

One of The AgriChain Centre's young fruit scientists, Rosanne Worsfold, came to this conclusion in a paper she wrote late last year for presentation at an International Society for Horticultural Science conference.

"Due to the perishable nature of fruit, time is always a constraint throughout the chain. The underlying function of the value chain is to get

fresh fruit to the consumer in a good quality state, so that they want to buy it.

The consumer associates time with the concept of 'freshness'. Historically time and freshness were directly correlated but now, due to advances in postharvest technology, the natural ageing process can be interfered with to give the appearance of freshness, even after long storage periods. Now 'freshness' is more related to quality than time, and can be maintained by using effective postharvest management. Postharvest management is all about avoiding the inevitable - ageing of the product."

So if Rosanne is correct in her statement that freshness these days is quality rather than time related - and I, for one, believe that she is indeed correct - what does that mean in terms of the requirement for consistency?

The big void between field and shopping trolley

Despite growers doing their utmost to achieve produce consistency and consumers expecting nothing less than the best in this area, there is unfortunately very little consistency in the process that takes place after harvest and before the consumer lays her hands onto the produce.

There are big differences on how growers treat their produce after harvest. Some product has the field heat removed through rapid cooling and some does not get treated to that necessity.

Some growers ensure their produce is travelling to market in refrigerated trucks with especially tuned suspension. Others bounce their produce along on the back of their pick-up trucks, gloriously unaware of the damage they are causing before the product even hits the packhouse. There is also nothing consistent about the channels available to get the produce to the consumer or how the produce is being treated whilst traveling in the channels.

The one thing I, as Mr. Consumer, will certainly not adjust is my expectation of produce consistency. It has taken me a long time to figure out what my perfect Brussels sprouts should look like and I would expect my requirements to be met every time, regardless of where I shop. And that goes for everything else I buy, naturally.

In the case of Brussels sprouts, we have a local idiosyncrasy here in New Zealand that illustrates my point beautifully. North Islanders prefer smaller sized and closed bud sprouts from Ohakune. Our Mainland brethren pull faces when presented with Ohakune Brussels Sprouts and opt for baby cabbage sized specimens from Oamaru instead. This preference is so ingrained that Auckland retailers prefer to import Brussels sprouts from Australia when Ohakune product is short as the Oamaru alternative would simply fail to sell.

A retailer's view

Retailers looove consistency! Just imagine - every produce line that has been ordered arrives. Every produce line that arrives does so to the correct specifications. Nothing is damaged, nothing is lost. We are not having a bad dream, we are not about to wake in a cold sweat, we have finally managed to tame the industry and tomorrow and the day after will see repeat performance of today's events.

The savvy produce buyer with a number of years of experience under his belt knows that nothing could be further from the truth, whilst his younger and impressionable colleagues still believes the impossible is achievable.

Yes, a certain amount of consistency is possible. Yes, give a grower a standard to work to, insist that the standard is met and it is likely that the grower will be able to deliver to the standard most times with a high degree of consistency - as long as there hasn't been a cold snap, a hail storm, a drought, a plague of locusts or an Act of God.

Achieving consistency in terms of produce availability and quality is a journey rather than a static target. Stomping one's foot will not alter the outcome.

Plans may have to change, advertised specials may have to be withdrawn, displays may to shrink and the better part of the produce department may have to be reconfigured if the failure occurred in a major crop and is systemic in nature.

Retailers love consistency because they know that the consumer responds to it. Inconsistent banana quality can see a store drop thousands of dollars in overall produce sale in one week. This phenomenon is called guilt by association. The rest of the produce might be OK, but if the bananas are too green, too spotted or the display is empty and looks picked over, consumers will rightly or wrongly make assumptions about the state of the overall offer.

Consistency of supply is therefore part of the retailer's mantra and the smart grower or supplier ensures that the retailer's need in this area works to his advantage.

The business of consistency

This is one of the most misunderstood concepts in business. Consistency is often portrayed as a secondary goal. "Ah well, I might not be able to be top dog, but at least I am consistent, so that's OK then." The reality is that consistency is a state aspired to either consciously or subconsciously by growers, service providers, retailers and consumers alike - and half the time without even realising that everyone is after the same objective.

Grower, retailer and consumer might be poles apart on their understanding about each others' perspective on the fruit and vegetable supply chain, but they certainly share a common business mechanism regardless of whether they are after sufficient fruit for their fruit bowl, are looking for enough bananas to meet tomorrow's demand in a busy supermarket or intend to corner the market on oranges for the season - globally.

This common mechanism is that a financial transaction will take place with the only variables being the size of the sum handed over and the way by which the money paid reaches the vendor's account.

All three parties share the expectations of receiving value for money and the need for the produce to last in their care for a specific period of time. The latter, time, is an easy property to measure. We have a system for that and what's more, the system is standardised and we all understand it. No one in their right mind will argue with the fact that an hour consists of sixty minutes, that a day has 24 hours and that there are seven days in any given week.

How do you measure value for money though? The fresh produce trade is still very much commodity based, regardless of the degree of fancy packaging solutions that are finding their way onto the shelves.

In the absence of an absolute measurement, mankind usually comes up with the best suitable substitute. The accuracy might not be absolute, but, hey - we are used to this with the one measurement we perceive as being perfect, time; despite our knowledge that the earth's rotation is not perfect, which is why we have a leap year every four years and February 29th appears on our calendars.

If we can live with that, surely we can live with a perceived value system based on observation of physical product in order to bridge the gap between uncertainty and defined knowledge?

Indeed we can, and the concept we refer to as consistency forms a substantial part of this substitute culture.

The consumer will look at a bag of apples and assess the number of apples in the bag, despite the fact that the bag is being sold by the each. The retailer will look at several crates containing apples being delivered into the distribution centre to ensure himself that each crate contains 18 kg of fruit. The grower will inspect the fruit coming off the packing line in his packhouse to make sure the grader is working correctly.

I might not be able to buy apples for the same price each week, but the reason for my decision to buy apples each week does not change from week to week. I am therefore demanding apples of the same quality, the same size, the same variety, the same standard and in the same pack type when I do my shopping.

And the customer is always right, isn't she?

There are several facets to achieving consistency. These revolve firstly around the produce itself, the way it is being produced, harvested, handled, packed and distributed and priced. All these facets are tangible. They can be observed, they can be measured and they can be adjusted.

There are a couple of intangible facets as well. These include the way the produce tastes, the time it lasts and the way it responds to being handled, packed and distributed.

These last three facets do not remain intangible ad infinitum. At some stage or other between harvest and consumption the taste, for example, will reveal itself. In the last few years, considerable effort has gone into developing new technologies such as Near Infrared Retroscopy (NIR) aimed at assessing fruit solids through non-destructive testing and thus establishing an accurate read for fruit sugar levels.

It matters little how fancy any process is to achieve consistency - and NIR would have to be one of the more complex ones. Ultimately, consistency will only be achieved through a full appreciation and adoption of quality management. Quality, however, lies in the eyes of the beholder and in our case, this is the consumer who purchases fruit and vegetables.

Readers will begin to get an inkling that these consistency and quality concepts are far more complex to succeed with than might initially be anticipated. There are several reasons for this.

Firstly, there are some quality aspects that are beyond man to manage. The quality of the weather, for example. No matter how good the seed, no matter how new the glasshouse is or how well a field has been ploughed, rain when none is wanted, drought conditions when moisture is needed, intense sunshine following a downpour are all capable of turning a promising crop into a disaster. We can aim to influence matters by way of taking sensible precautions, planting in areas that are known to be conducive to achieving expected results and deploying the best technology money can buy. At the end of the day, any horticultural producer takes a chance with regards to weather and climatic conditions.

Secondly, there are some aspects we can manage very well. We can buy the best seed money can buy. We can provide the best growing infrastructure, the smartest technology, the most amazing post-harvest facilities - as long as we have the money and actually know what is best for a specific crop. What we do not know, we can be taught. Even better, the missing knowledge can be bought in - it's called hiring a consultant.

Thirdly though, quality, and with it consistency, are determined by the skill we deploy in managing the processes involved in producing fruit and vegetables and getting to the point where consumers select the product and are prepared to pay for it.

Weather patterns are there for all to observe. Weather is not only forecasted, but analysed to death. A grower who skimps with equipment or fertiliser, a market gardener who does not operate a maintenance program for his glasshouse or 'forgets' to rotate his land between crops in order to optimise growing conditions is soon found out. Not by quality controllers necessarily, but his peers. Human behaviour being what it is means that anyone deviating from what colleagues and competitors deem to be the norm will soon be discovered and talked about.

Skills and processes, on the other hand, are closely linked to attitude; and poor attitude is not quite as tangible as a broken pane of glass or a rusted plough.

Poor attitude can crop up at any stage of the supply chain and growers, middle men and retailers are at times all guilty of displaying it. A grower who sends his produce to the market in overflowing crates, so that the produce gets damaged when the crates are stacked displays poor attitude. A trader who does not hold produce at the correct temperature whilst it is in his care during the time frame of transfer from seller to buyer is displaying poor attitude. A retailer who is collecting produce from his wholesaler and transports it back to his store on a flatbed truck without any cover is guilty of poor attitude.

The factors that contribute to the ultimate failure that is rejection by the consumer are plentiful and complex. Produce values will never rise to the levels the product deserves on account of its nutritional value until the entire supply chain can achieve a greater degree of consistency. Consistency will not be achievable without all participants in the supply chain taking responsibilities for their skills, their processes and their attitude.

Yet an awful lot of decisions are being made in the fresh produce industry every day in the name of consistency. The marketing concept referred to as a 'supply chain' is a perfect case in point. Supply chains emerged as a result of rationalisation in the retail sector and supermarket produce buyers purchasing ever increasing volumes, wishing these to be of a standard quality, regardless of volume, time of year or product season. The basic assumption made is that perfection can be achieved.

Surprisingly enough, perfection may just be possible - but at what cost? How do the Dutch manage to get one Bell pepper looking the same as the other 23 in the tray? Through rigorous breeding and generous applications of chemicals. Can a whole field of cauliflower really be trained to weigh 750 g each and be of the same height? Not quite, but if that's the standard, who says that every single head *grown* needs to meet that standard? The retailer is only interested in every head *supplied* meeting the standard norm.

Growers are therefore committing to grow extra volumes to ensure they are able to meet the rigid standards demanded by corporate retailers. What happens to the balance then; that part of the crop not purchased by the regular retail buyer? Well, there are three options. It either gets ploughed under, in the case of field crops (least likely); or, the surplus is committed to processing (possibly). Most likely though, the balance made up of product meeting the norm but surplus to requirement and product that is perfectly saleable but does not meet the retailer standard, is sold to other retailers!

Now, that causes a bit of a problem and highlights one of the self defeating weaknesses of the current system.

A retailer whose demand for a certain volume of produce presented to a certain standard has been satisfied, has absolutely no interest in the balance of a grower's product - unless and until it turns up on a competitor's shelves for a lower retail price than he has applied himself.

At this point the first retailer automatically assumes that his competitor had been able to purchase the produce at a lower price than himself and starts getting all bitter and twisted. In many instances his assessment will be absolutely correct, but unfortunately he only has himself to blame.

Due to the retailer's exacting standards, the grower is forced to grow 'extra' in order to ensure he can always meet expected volumes *and* grade. The extra volume will find its way onto the market. This is human nature as growers consider themselves successful when they have achieved a sale - not when they have ploughed a portion of a crop under.

The extra volume is most likely to be of mixed grade - precisely what our first retailer did not want. The cost price can therefore be expected to be less and is thus likely to lead to a lower end price in a competing consumer environment.

What will our miffed produce buyer do? He will pick up the phone and tell his grower that he, his preferred grower/supplier, obviously managed to read the market wrong which resulted in him, the buyer, being highly embarrassed in front of his boss - so the negotiated cost price will have to be retrospectively adjusted downwards.

That might be considered to be an extreme scenario but it and variations thereof occur around us on a daily basis.

Add to this micro economical spoof, the fact that modern plant propagation techniques these days ensure a greater percentage of a sown or planted crop makes it through to harvest today than twenty years ago, causing additional downwards price pressure, and one reaches the conclusion that progress and modern management practices may just cause more havoc in a commodity environment than that environment can robustly cope with over time.

Consistency is therefore a value that cannot just be applied to the produce but is of equal, if not greater, importance to behaviour and structure of the relationship between buyer, seller and/or grower. Consistent behaviour and consistent performance are critical to any business relationship but particularly those which exist within the 'handshake' environment where written contracts are the exception rather than the norm. Consistency is a prerequisite for confidence and inconsistent product quality, inconsistent process quality and inconsistent outcomes do not make ideal bedfellows of confidence building initiatives.

Recommended Reading

Goldratt E.M
The Goal. A process of undergoing improvement.
NORTH RIVER PRESS 1984. Massachusetts.

Confidence

Confidence in one's own product and process is an essential ingredient to ensure market place success. Confidence needs to be reality based, though, and not be 'blind'. Reality based confidence comes from understanding one's own business thoroughly, how it interacts with its customers and suppliers and through appropriate degrees of third party assurance; e.g., HACCP based management, food safety practices and accreditations.

What gives a shopper the confidence that the lettuce on the shelf in front of her is fit for purchase?

Well, for starters, it is there! In other words, the shopper is already conditioned to abdicating a substantial part of her judgment capacity to the professional who ought to know what he is doing - the shopkeeper or produce manager.

When she cannot find lettuce the shopper intuitively knows that it is either the wrong time of year for fresh lettuce or that the lettuce has sold out. Upon seeing the empty lettuce shelf she is likely to enquire from the first person she comes across who is vaguely recognisable as someone who works in the place whether there is any more stock in the rear store.

If, on the other hand, lettuce is available for sale when she approaches the shelf, our shopper will bring her senses into play to decide whether she can have confidence in the produce manager's core decision to place the lettuce on sale. She will visually examine the lettuce to check for limp leaves, brown edges, parasites and dirt. She is also likely to 'weigh' the lettuce in her hand to check whether it's dry, in a balanced state or totally waterlogged.

If she is examining a nectarine instead of a head of lettuce, she might give the fruit a slight squeeze to test ripeness. A product like a banana, however, does not need much squeezing. Green equals 'not ready for consumption just yet' and a full yellow colour with plenty of brown spots translates into 'overripe, eat me now'; all that is required for this test is good eyesight.

What gives the produce manager the confidence to place an order for lettuces? Produce managers do not usually get appointed into this position without several years experience. By the time a produce clerk or assistant has reached manager status he or she is expected to know the difference between a good head of lettuce and a bad one. These days, most of the guesswork is taken care of by the produce buyers or category managers. They determine how many lettuce growers they need on their books; how many hydroponic lettuce suppliers are needed versus conventional ones; whether to buy sleeved lettuces or conventionally presented ones; how many varieties are required and how the lettuce should be packed.

By the time the lettuce order reaches the store, all the produce manager has to do is to check that what was ordered has been received and that the quality the product displays upon arrival is acceptable.

What gives the lettuce grower the confidence to grow 10 hectares of lettuce?

This question cannot be answered in one simple paragraph and the reason for this will become blatantly obvious.

The underlying level of confidence all growers have is that their fellow men need to eat and as a substantial part of our population know lettuce as an acceptable food item, a certain percentage of that population segment will consume lettuce several times a week. A good lettuce grower will therefore stand a reasonable chance of being able to market a quality crop.

Our market economy being what it is, such underlying confidence can only be justified if the grower has made a profit and has received a return for his investment once the crop has been successfully sold.

The lettuce grower will therefore seek to achieve two outcomes. Firstly, he strives to operate an efficient market garden business which is capable of producing a quality product on a consistent basis. Secondly he will try to establish a relationship with one or more downstream partners in the value chain such as lettuce brokers and wholesalers, or even better, retailers.

Why? He is seeking to increase his degree of confidence of having a market for his product, because he has learned that even the most efficiently grown crop is worth diddly squat unless there is someone out there who wants to buy it.

Confidence is one of life's great intangible values. It is not available for purchase, it cannot be manufactured and it is invisible. Yet it shapes our behaviour and aids our decision making process even when we are not consciously aware of it.

In the days when marketing by auction was the norm for the distribution of fresh produce for public consumption, growers had the confidence to harvest produce and send it to auction, as they knew people with money wanting to buy their produce knew where to go and buy the produce.

Similarly, people needing to buy produce could turn up at the auction house at 5am confident that produce had been delivered there for purchase the night before. Growers and buyers would never admit it, but both had this core degree of confidence that the auction system would deliver for both parties due to a mutual need revolving around the availability of produce.

There were finer nuances, of course, such as the volume of produce available, the quality of the product, the way it was presented and the numbers of growers involved, but the principle worked well.

This confidence see-saw worked well as long as growers were assigning their produce by and large to the auction market and buyers were by and large purchasing their produce at the markets.

The system started to come apart at the seams when buyers were wanting to buy direct from growers. All of a sudden, the central point where buyers and sellers came together ceased being THE place where produce value was established, but became one of several mechanisms that set a price.

Unless it is in an entirely open forum, such as an auction, price information is typically not shared. Therefore no system is in place that brings the various prices set for lettuce on any day together in order to establish THE daily average price.

Does this matter? Not in an operational sense. Lettuce will still be sold and bought, placed onto the supermarket shelf and purchased by the consumer. Growers and buyers, however, lack the core confidence of knowing on any given day what THE price for quality lettuce ought to be at wholesale level.

What gives a grower the confidence to continue growing then? Actually before we tackle this question, we need to answer a simpler one: What is the definition of a grower? The Free Online Dictionary (who needs a hard copy these days) defines 'grower' as follows: "someone concerned with the science or art or business of cultivating the soil"

Growers are artists then? Not really. Scientists? Well, a basic understanding of science sure helps and some crops certainly need quite a solid understanding of scientific principles, but I would not call a grower a scientist. Are growers businessmen? Of course they are. A grower who does not get paid sufficiently for his crop cannot afford to buy the seed for the next crop. Most growers did not necessarily consider themselves to be businessmen in the past, but in reality just about all of them were.

Business was relatively simple though in the auction days. The direct purchasing regimes introduced by supermarkets have made the business of growing a lot more complex. The truly successful growers operating at the commercially viable and sustainable edges of the envelope are those who have in the last ten years rapidly developed all three facets of what constitutes a grower - artistry, science and business acumen - either on an individual basis or by way of expanding their business and establishing separate specialised roles for individuals but delivering as a whole.

In the pursuit of confidence, these successful growers - and we will probably need to define 'success' as well before long - have backed four key drivers to advance their businesses: technology, economies of scale, relationships and brands.

Technology

The technology applied to crop production is no longer advancing in incremental steps but rushing ahead in leaps and bounds. GPS positioning systems, wind turbine based frost protection and automated harvesters are just three examples of how growers have progressed rapidly from hand tools and cultivators. Micro propagation techniques have ensured that greater percentages of crops reach maturity and that these crops present more evenly and are therefore more saleable.

One of the challenges in this regard is that a grower wanting to produce, say, 1000 cases of cauliflower from a given plot of land will typically ensure that he plants the equivalent of at least 1100 cases in order to allow for partial crop failures and other eventualities. Old habits die hard and the practice persists although a greater portion of the crop now makes it to market.

Economies of scale

The number of retailers buying produce in the marketplace has reduced, both locally and internationally. Growers therefore have fewer customers to sell their produce to. These fewer customers have, however, increased in size and are requiring larger volumes of produce. They wish these volumes to be uniform, consistent, available on an ongoing basis, produced to either national or retailer specific quality standards and extremely price competitive.

Growers are therefore 'growing' as well. Creating economies of scale is no longer an optional activity or one that happens organically over a period of time. Rather, it has turned into a fight for survival, as satisfying the increasing retailer demands on the basis of suboptimal enterprise size is not a viable option.

Relationships

Supplying the auction system with produce was a quasi-anonymous activity. Whilst growers identified themselves by way of printing their name on the carton or writing it with chalk on the wooden vegetable crate, growers and retailers only met by exception. Today's retailers demand traceability from growers as they in turn need to satisfy increasing consumer demand for 'safe' produce. The need for interaction and communication between grower and buyer is therefore far greater than it used to be.

A further contributing factor is the fact that growers typically do not enjoy the security of a supply contract. Most domestic supply arrangements are conducted on an "in good faith" basis, which has the potential to cause sleepless nights for growers as well as their bank managers.

Growers are therefore keen to establish closer relationships with produce buyers. Similarly, retailers now view the ability to demonstrate a direct relationship with key growers as a viable marketing mechanism to convince consumers that the produce on offer in their stores is not only fresh but safe.

Brands

Whilst produce purchasing was auction/market centred, the produce department was the last frontier of the great commodity game. Product brands were non-existent, with the exception of banana stickers such as Dole, Chiquita and Bonita as well as the Sunkist brand.

Today's produce departments look somewhat busier. Branding is the norm for all pre-packed produce and even the single fruit PLU stickers tend to sport a supplier brand. The larger corporate retailers are busy trying to introduce their specific house brands at the expense of supplier brands and the produce department is in most cases no longer the oasis of natural colours it used to be.

The reason? Concerns around the 'confidence' concept are not surprisingly a major contributor.

Consumers have far more information at their fingertips today than ever before. The amount of data available to anyone who goes looking for it is frightening. Schools even at primary level are now focused on teaching robust information sourcing and assessment techniques rather than attempting to get children to absorb sets of static data for instant regurgitation.

We are all consumers and we are looking for anchor points and opportunities for validation of our views, values and opinions. We know the qualities associated with a pair of Levi's jeans, a bottle of Coke and Tommy Hilfinger eau de cologne. We crave consistency, yet our lives are getting busier. Product brands are the equivalent of bullet points in a business report. Short & sharp summaries of relevant data.

It is therefore no surprise that branding has established itself like a bad smell in the produce department. It was inevitable.

This realisation is compounded further by the retailers' determination to avoid supplier brand domination of their fresh food departments. Retailers have learned the hard way that owners of successful supplier brands need to continuously invest in their brands to maintain consumer awareness. These investment levels typically come with a price for retailers - the need to accept lower retail gross profit margins.

A supermarket is a finely tuned organism. A store's bottom line contribution is achieved through a careful balance between necessary operating costs and available product margins. These margins are managed on a category and merchandise department basis and not every item in the supermarket contributes at the same level. The produce department might only account for 10-12% of total store sales, but achievable margin can be as high as 27% without becoming uncompetitive. The grocery section by contrast, the long shelf life goods in the middle of the store, usually accounts for around 50% of total store sales - but at a margin of between 8-9%. It does not take an Einstein to figure out that the whole store margin model would collapse like a house of cards if produce margins or fresh food margins across the board were to suddenly drop to the level groceries are sold for. Retailers are therefore highly motivated to stem the relentless assault of supplier brands into their produce departments.

A by-product of this line of thinking is that the alternatives to branded supplier products are either non-branded products or retailer branded goods. Given the increasing trend of consumer preference for natural and fresh products rather than the highly processed variances, retailers see a sustainable opportunity to hitch the fortunes of their own store brands to the performance of their in-store fresh food departments.

Marketplace confidence - The direct import position

Confidence can be an underlying market regulator at every level in the produce trade. If the consumer does not like the look of a bunch of grapes or the oranges on display she will not buy them, regardless of price. Confidence can also be severely shaken at the macro level of the value chain. New Zealand is a long way from where its imported fruit comes from and with the exception of some Australian winter vegetables which tend to travel by plane, most other fruit and vegetable exports arrive here by boat. This requires a fair amount of planning in order to ensure a continuous supply during a product's season or even during the whole year for products such as bananas.

Importing produce by the reefer container costs money and importers are therefore attempting to sell their wares in such a way that they recover their costs and achieve a profit. Makes perfect sense doesn't it? Importers do not always get this right, but over time they understand the market needs in terms of volume, quality, frequency, seasonality, retailers' promotional aspirations and logistical constraints well enough that they get these matters right more often than they get it wrong.

There are typically several importers per product category in the market and whilst importers do not talk to each other about commercially sensitive matters, they usually have a pretty good understanding of their competitors' capabilities, sources and patterns by way of having fairly sophisticated market intelligence systems built around information available in the public arena, including shipping schedules, offshore harvest information, data requested/ distributed through government agencies and syndicated information drawn from market researchers.

The system relies on importers to get this right - the 'system' being the combination of consumer, retailer and food service operator desiring consistency when purchasing imported produce. Consistency of quality, availability and price.

Importing is a specialised supply chain function, it requires a specific set of skills as well as relatively deep pockets as imported produce in most cases has to purchased by the importer before it is sold. The days when exporters were happy to send produce to the importing country "on consignment" i.e., on the basis that the size of their payment will depend upon what the importer is able to sell the produce for, are long gone. Importing worked really well when every link in the supply chain stuck to its knitting and focused on its respective skills and competencies.

As it so happens, however, supermarket operators are past masters at getting involved in all aspects of the supply chain, something they are able to justify with the belief that they are the ultimate consumer advocates, given the number of people visiting their stores each week. It comes therefore as little surprise that supermarket owners are also increasingly getting involved in the produce import sector. The incentives are easy to identify from the retailers' perspective. Higher gross margin as the importer's margin disappears, increased certainty in terms of being able to communicate order quantities directly, better planning capability, promotional advantages against competitors who still rely on importers. Finding the cash to finance all of this is a bagatelle - supermarkets are blessed with extraordinarily positive cashflows.

So what about the risks?

An altogether different story indeed. Supermarkets are known to be risk averse when it comes to accepting responsibility for the merchandise they stock. Wal-Mart has managed to perfect the system to the point that in key categories the product actually remains the property of the supplier until the shopper places it on the checkout conveyor. New Zealand supermarkets do not have the purchasing power to achieve a similar risk model with imported produce and the same applies in most other mid-sized countries as well. The retailer involved in direct importing therefore ends up taking responsibility for the directly imported product a lot earlier than is usually the case - typically at the time of departure in the producing country.

Risk management of perishable produce that has yet to arrive in the country is not something supermarket buying departments were set up to manage.

Generally, suppliers have to put a fair amount of effort into relationship management when they have regular supermarket customers. To put it politely, supermarkets are not the easiest of customers to have. So when a supermarket decides to import its own produce, there is no supplier anymore who can act as a buffer between the producer/exporter and the supermarket. A entirely new way of supply management is called for - primarily because the supermarket already owns the produce as it arrives in the country. The adversarial buyer/seller relationship therefore has to be turned into a supply pipeline management concept.

Yes, other supermarket departments also buy their goods direct. Tesco, Sainsbury, Woolworths and The Warehouse, to name a few, all have buying offices in the Far East through which they procure manufactured goods. That works, doesn't it? Of course it does, but these goods are not perishable, they can be stored for months on end and even if they do not sell they do not smell!

Perishability is a risk supermarkets live with every day when they purchase produce, but when you own the goods and they have come from offshore by boat, you actually have to accept accountability for what you have bought.

Perishability and ultimate accountability are but two of the risks which come into play in the direct import game. Further confidence factors are market place intelligence and risk balancing and these two go hand in hand.

Supermarkets being risk averse to the degree they are, typically only import a proportion of any category once they decide to get involved in direct imports, based on the reasonable understanding that if something does go wrong with any one particular shipment of, for example, grapes, they have some traditional supply to fall back on. Sticking with the grape example for a moment, consumers purchasing a bunch of grapes from a store with a direct import programme may find that these grapes could be either directly imported by the retailer or procured the traditional way, via an importer. The consumer does not actually care, as long as the grapes look good, are priced competitively and taste sweet when she gets them home.

The supermarkets are thus relying on a mix of self sourced and importer sourced produce to satisfy the consumer demand. Part of that demand equation is the latent consumer expectation that if a product is in season, it is being presented for sale at their local store. What constitutes a 'season' is becoming very flexible terminology these days, but put in simple terms - a supermarket never wants to run out of grapes. Ever.

In days gone by, when every supply chain partner stuck to its knitting, creating and managing the required equilibrium between supply and demand for imported table grapes was the responsibility of the importers. They did not always get it right, but because they collectively had the same objectives, i.e., sell grapes for profit and minimise waste, a tacit understanding evolved through basic market intelligence that when translated into realistic shipping volumes and frequencies created a more or less stable market. Retailers who wanted to run grape promotions had to discuss this with the importers in advance which meant the importers began to understand promotional patterns, learned how to manage and even predict them and actually worked behind the scenes on not having too many retailers promoting grapes in the same week as it did not meet anyone's long term objectives.

These days, where retailers also act as importers, market management has become more fragile. Retailers who import their own grapes have less incentive to discuss their promotional plans with importers. Importers who now only supply part of a retailer's grape supply have less opportunity to develop reliable and robust market intelligence. Even if one could pool all importers' market intelligence into an industry model that would not cause confrontation with market regulators, one would still only have a partial picture of the market.

Partial pictures are not conducive to sustainable management of perishable product categories. There are consequences. Some of the consequences are uncertainty about the amount of stock in the country or on the water at any given point in time; uncertainty of supply source, i.e., are all importers still bringing in Australian grapes or has someone already switched to Chilean fruit; traditional importers trying to offload grapes at reduced prices as they miscalculated volumes brought into the country by importing retailers; massive retail price fluctuations; confused consumers.

The wholesale price for grapes in any given week is found by several factors aligning with each other, for want of a better phrase. These factors are the volume in the country, the volume expected in the next shipment, the timing of the next shipment's arrival, the quality of the stock still on hand, the promotional programmes in play in that week, the time of year, i.e. during the height of the strawberry season consumers buy fewer grapes, and the ability of the grape merchants to make the right call on these factors is critical. Not knowing the basics such as volumes on hand is a recipe for disaster.

Produce is seasonal and grapes are no exception. There comes a point, for example, in the supply window for Australian grapes, when it would be best for quality reasons to stop the import programme and switch to an alternative source, say Chile. If all importers achieve this switch within a similar time frame, the market will remain relatively balanced and retail buyers and consumers can compare like with like. There are differences between Chilean and Australian grapes in terms of variety, flavor intensity, time spent on the water, the way they are packed, etc. - having both in the market simultaneously creates problems.

All it takes, therefore, to create an underlying climate of reduced confidence is a combination of importers with a reduced ability to assess the market correctly, retailers who are importing sufficient volumes to unsettle the importers but not enough to dominate the market and consumers being presented with a glut of grapes one week at ridiculously low prices and not being able to find decent fruit the next week regardless of what they are prepared to pay.

Success

I commented earlier on the concept of a 'successful' grower and hinted that a definition was probably in order. Let's do that now.

Wikipedia, the newfound fountain of all wisdom on the web, is for once less than verbose. Success, it says, *"may mean, but is not limited to, a level of social status, the achievement of a goal or objective and the opposite to failure."* Very succinct indeed.

Charles Handy has this to say on the topic;

"Success, then, becomes the spur to our actions, but success, unfortunately, is more difficult to get a handle on than survival. We can buy the definition of that success from those around us or we can, more usefully, find our own definition. The search for that personal definition of success is what drives so many of us today. The more one thinks about it, however, the more it becomes clear that it is really a search for oneself."

Peter Drucker also had a view on success - *"Whenever you see a successful business, someone once made a courageous decision."*

And lastly, Reg Revans, the Father of Action Learning, who excelled at the indirect approach, *"those who are to change significantly that which they freshly encounter must themselves be changed by the changing of it."*

Wikipedia's brief comments are clearly outcome focused and for that reason very one dimensional. Handy suggests that success is very much a personal and highly individualistic journey. Drucker is convinced that success does not just happen, but is the result of a decision on the past, i.e. an action was taken at some point in the past, whilst Revans states that change (on the basis of action) not only alters the targeted situation, process or entity but also the 'actor'. So what does this mean within the fresh produce industry?

Here is an early produce supply chain example to illustrate the meaning of success.

Foodtown Supermarkets, for many years the dominant Auckland supermarket retailer but now a rapidly disappearing store brand of Woolworths Australia in this country, has its origin in the ambitions of Chinese green grocer Tom Ah Chee who dreamt of supermarket greatness US-style in the 1950s. His decision to push ahead with this concept against all the opposition he encountered at the time lead to the chain having 31 outlets across the North Island by 1987. Foodtown at the time was the ideal example to illustrate Drucker's definition of success. The company's success was very much focused around one man's determination and personal journey, Tom Ah Chee.

Turners & Growers, the then produce auction market leader, managed to satisfy the needs of greengrocer Tom Ah Chee more than adequately. This did not change as Tom added store after store, but by the early 1980s Tom no longer considered himself to be a greengrocer, success had changed him. Tom Ah Chee was now a supermarket operator and had created a new reality, as suggested by Revans. Old suppliers were being asked and expected to consider changing to fit the new reality and if that proved impossible old suppliers found themselves bypassed in favour of suppliers which could adapt.

Foodtown's success as a retailer meant that the company developed an ever increasing requirement for volumes of fruit and vegetables. Given the nature of the auction business, i.e., availability of product was not necessarily guaranteed, there came a time when Foodtown was no longer confident it could purchase the stock it wanted, in sufficient quantity, at the right price and of acceptable quality via the auction system.

This development had a profound impact upon what constituted a 'successful' grower and the reverberations are still being felt today. I should note that whilst the example is New Zealand based, the phenomenon discussed here is a global one and numerous examples exist around the globe.

As long as the supermarket continued to have confidence in the auction system, a grower was deemed successful if he managed to supply the auction floor regularly during the season relevant to his crop or crops with quantities of fresh produce packed into the wooden crates supplied by the auction house on a hire basis, dropped his crop off during the notified receiving hours with his crop being presented pleasing to the eye and without noticeable blemishes or defects. As the supermarket demands grew, the auction house encouraged its preferred suppliers to grow a bit more to meet the consistency needed in order to maintain the supermarkets' confidence.

Once the supermarkets started questioning the auction based supply model, the definition of a successful grower shifted drastically. By 2005, successful growers were growing produce on acreages of breathtaking proportions compared to what earlier generations managed to achieve. They were encouraged to achieve vertical integration through operating packhouses and were able to process not only their own crops but those of their neighbours as well. Their crops and products were in many cases marketed directly into the supermarket chains, bypassing the wholesale sector altogether. The term 'grower' was no longer sufficient to describe their activities. These 'growers' were employing business development managers, contemplating export opportunities and seriously discussing the possibility of becoming year round suppliers of their respective categories, even if that meant handling imported produce as well.

The industry literally ended up with a two class grower system - growers who participated in supermarket supply and those who were locked out of that supply stream. A grower who was a direct supermarket supplier was deemed 'successful' by virtue of that achievement. Everything else he achieved within that supply chain was an incremental enhancement. Success for growers who, for various reasons, were not able to supply directly to the supermarket had at the most basic level a very different meaning. Would the grower survive, given that a substantial and growing percentage of produce was finding its direct way into the supermarkets and the auction/wholesale system now had a reduced requirement for produce?

It is now 2010 and the goal posts are changing again.

Retailers, wholesalers and growers still exist and produce is still finding its way into consumers' shopping trolleys but we are seeing the confidence levels of all participants in the supply chain shifting significantly.

Control

There are elements of any business that need to be managed and controlled. The trick is to understand which are the ones requiring 'hands-on' control and which ones can be left to their own devices. The pursuit of operational excellence should not serve as the excuse to exercise control over every minute detail. There are processes, or parts thereof, where 'going with the flow' will generate better longer-term results.

Anyone who wants to succeed in the fresh produce industry long-term needs to understand this: it is virtually impossible to control all industry aspects or facets all of the time. At best, one can aspire to controlling some of what matters some of the time!

A profound insight? Well, common sense really. At the end of the day, produce is weather dependent. Even glasshouse produce that is relatively protected from the direct impact of the elements relies on an environmental factor like sunshine hours.

In order to avoid ongoing frustration, it is therefore vital to:

- understand what produce value chain elements can actually be influenced;
- create common sense based key performance indicators that are easy to measure;
- ensure one can react to the realities that present themselves with a high degree of reality. Influence is really the name of the game!

Value chain elements that can be influenced

In overview format, these include the production phase, time of harvest, harvesting method, post-harvest handling and transport, temperature management, retail handling and merchandising.

Retailers typically do not grow and not too many growers own supermarkets or city based greengrocer shops. It is therefore unlikely that any one value chain participant is in an optimal position to influence the entire value chain. That does not stop growers or retailers from trying though! Get a group of growers together just about anywhere and before long they will have settled down to a session focused on letting the retailer know about how they need to improve their produce handling and retailing skills. Naturally, that goes down like a lead balloon with any retailer who gets to hear about the growers' considered opinions. Similarly though, retailers are busy trying to extend their influence from their own delivery dock into the grower's paddocks and orchards. Retailers in their pursuit of control are attempting to define 'best practice' for growers, a situation not universally appreciated by all growers.

Neither party needs a lot of encouragement when it comes to letting their value chain partner know how he could improve his performance. The reality though is that neither grower nor retailer is able to achieve absolute control how ever hard they might try.

Production phase

It would be best if retailers did not try to tell grower how to grow. But hang on a minute - who is in the best position to understand consumer preferences? It tends to be the retailer. If a retailer detects a consumer preference for smaller heads of cauliflower rather than the large ones he is forced to cut in half - shouldn't he be able to communicate this to the grower without getting accused of interference?

Similarly, and as discussed elsewhere, consumers are increasingly worrying about the safety of the food they consume. Is it not prudent then for the retailer to insist that the produce he buys is free of chemical residues? It is interference alright, but for a good cause I would have thought.

How do consumers buy apples? They do not go into a store and ask for a kilo of red apples. No, they typically buy a variety. Royal Gala at the beginning of the season, followed by Red Delicious, Fuji and Splendour. All red apples and but all very different from one another. What about nectarines or peaches? I cannot recall ever having customers ask for summerfruit by name. Nor are retailers advertising peaches and nectarines by name. Is this important? No it is not, but what is important that consumers and retailers would appreciate some consistency in relation to the eating experience.

Growers have, for reasons best known to themselves, taken it upon themselves to plant an amazing range of peach and nectarine varieties over the years, to the extent that there are only a very few large blocks around that consist of the same variety. Retailers looking to buy, say, 3,000kg of fruit for a promotion are therefore likely to be presented with at least 3- 5 varieties of peaches making up that volume and, of course, consistency has gone out of the window. Retailers know they could sell more peaches if consumers could be ensured of greater consistency. Should retailers just keep that information to themselves or should they try to influence growers to make the necessary changes?

Time of harvest

Sticking with the stonefruit example for the moment. The worst thing that can happen to a produce retailer is that he does not have early season apricots (or peaches, plums or nectarines) available but the opposition down the road is already stocking them on their shelves. All hell will break loose and if the retailer is of any significant size, his wholesale supplier will have a lot of explaining to do.

Why the fuss though?

Well, it is simply inconceivable that the first of a season's fruit is stocked 'there' but not 'here' - or the other way around for that matter. It has something to do with the way a produce retailer perceives his relationship with the consumer to operate. Retailers, mistakenly in my view, believe that they must be absolutely the first cab of the rank at the beginning of a seasonal product's supply season, come hell or high water. In many instances eating quality is compromised in favour of just having the fruit available. If at all possible, retailers like to move from the position of 'no supply' to one of 'full supply' in as short a time as possible and at no cost to themselves.

Unfortunately Mother Nature does not work like this, which does, however, not stop retailers from trying.

The irony is that the early season fruit quite possibly has been taken off the trees too soon and is not fully ripe. It might look okay, but the taste has yet to develop. How does the consumer react to fruit that might look good but only tastes average? Certainly not with heavy repurchases! Wouldn't it therefore be better for retailers not to vie for the early fruit and thus not encourage growers to rip into the harvest too soon?

The harvest

It was not all that long ago that harvesting method simply was not a topic for debate. The only sensible way to get fruit off the tree or the vine and spuds out of the ground was by picking it. Hand-picking, to be precise.

Today, this can no longer be taken for granted. Mechanical harvesting is the norm in the potato industry and the grape industry and growers of crops with high labour intensity during the harvest season look longingly at their grower colleagues who worry about digger damage and oil changes rather than sore backs and staff not turning up.

There is something very primal about harvesting. When everything works well, harvest is the culmination of a season that has run well. There is nothing worse for a grower when the harvest is disrupted, when the crop is damaged or destroyed prior to harvest or when it is known that the price achievable for the product is barely able to cover the cost of production or worse. In some cases it is possible to abort the harvest or not start it in the first place, but for other crops this is simply not a practical option. Leaving apples hanging on the tree to rot is not a smart move, even if the prices are down. The fruit needs to come off and the trees need to be pruned in order for the grower to stand half a chance for a better season next year. Ploughing three quarters of a field of cabbages under, on the other hand, presents no problem. Not that many growers do so on a regular basis - it is not the first thing that comes to a grower's mind when they need to deal with balancing supply and demand, there is always the hope that "I might get a little bit" for the crop "somewhere". Sometimes though, the plough is the only sensible option but emotion does have a habit of getting in the way of common sense.

That is the way it works in free market economies. In the old Soviet Union and many of its East European satellite states, the system was a bit different. Land was owned by the state and collectively farmed by farm workers pulled into a cooperative known as a *kolchos.* The workers were paid a wage regardless of the crops they grew, the yields they achieved and the price their produce sold for. They had little incentive to care. Crop failure therefore was the norm rather than the exception as crop production was viewed as 9-5, Monday to Friday activity. Too bad if the apples were ready to be harvested, but a hail storm was forecasted for Sunday afternoon. Initiative, accountability and drive were not called for in those days.

Luckily we do not have to contend with these issues here in our economy.

Can anyone other than a grower control better how the harvest process should be managed? I do not think so. Growers through necessity continually try to improve and retailers luckily seem to be keeping their sticky beaks in a direct way out of this step of getting produce to the consumer, supplier accreditation programmes notwithstanding.

Post-harvest handling & transport

Here on the other hand, lively debate rages between grower and retailer. In principle, the situation works like this. Growers realise that how the produce is treated during and after it is being removed from its growing environment is critical to the value they can achieve when the produce is sold. It is therefore their natural inclination to do the right thing. A common misconception of retailers is often that the right thing to do would be to rush the crop as fast as possible to the retail premises so that the, at times, outlandish point of sales claims about freshness are physically supported.

That is not necessarily the smartest way to go about achieving an acceptable shelf life as removal of field heat from green leafy crops, for example, is not achieved by rushing bins of produce from one place to the next.

Retailers see the post-harvest step in the supply chain as the obvious point where they are most likely to succeed in influencing how growers manage the produce. This is best illustrated by way of two anecdotes from my time as produce merchandise manager from the early nineties.

The Blackfriars Gang

During a visit to the UK, I was stopping off at the London head office of Sainsbury's, then situated south of the Thames in Blackfriars. After a cordial lunch with my opposite number during which we exchanged professional courtesies and discussed common suppliers such as Sunkist and Bonita, I was invited to accompany my host into the building's basement. In answer to my raised eyebrow and the unspoken question, the head of Sainsbury's produce laughed and said, "Don't worry. We have given up running this place as a torture chamber a few years back. We use it these days to educate our buyers."

It transpired that I was visiting on the day the distribution centres located around London were scheduled to send samples of the produce received the night before, so that the buyers could familiarise themselves with the goods growers and suppliers were delivering. This was apparently a once a week event.

It was truly fascinating to observe the produce buyers in their shirt sleeves and colourful braces with the goods they were responsible for buying. I soon discovered that this was not just about checking grades and quality but also about acquainting buyers with produce they might not necessarily have seen before. Sainsbury's buyers were procurement specialists, trained in negotiating techniques rather than product knowledge. For this aspect, Sainsbury's used a team of in-house post-harvest scientists and agronomists. It was the latter who selected suitable suppliers based on their ability to assess farm based processes. Buyers were simply told, "Here are the growers we have selected as suitable. You can buy from all of them or negotiate a deal with one - what ever makes commercial sense. But you are not authorised to buy from someone else, unless you have asked us to check them out first." It was the role of the science and technical staff to 'accompany' produce and its growers as it moved along the supply chain and they often did so for several seasons in a row. The buying staff were just that, professional buyers who, for example, might have been in hardware/ general merchandise last year and slotted to move to frozen goods at the end of their two year stint on produce.

Banana farming near Guayaquil

On another trip I visited Bonita banana farms near Guayaquil in Ecuador. Bananas are harvested green and ripened once they have reached their destination. Bruised bananas do not ripen well and finding ways to avoid bruising prior to ripening is a favourite past-time for growers, shippers and retailers alike.

Two of the farms I visited during my trip stood out, each for its own reason! We were traveling into the Ecuadorian countryside on a well maintained and tar sealed highway. The same highway in fact the green bananas were taking on their journey from the farms to the port. It was not rocket science to deduce this fact - there was a constant stream of loaded banana trucks coming towards us.

Eventually, we turned off the main highway on to the first farm property. The highway changed to a narrower road, which was, however, equally as well maintained and after a smooth ride across the plantation we eventually arrived at the farm's main packing station. We observed the process of fruit coming in from across the plantation and the bananas being graded, washed, dried and packed into their 18kg cartons, before we set off to the next plantation.

Back we travelled the way we had come to the farm's main gate and then back onto the highway. A couple of kilometers down the road we turned into the drive of the next plantation. By the time we had arrived at that plantation's packing station, I was sporting a bump on my head and I was cautiously feeling my ribcage to check whether anything was broken. No, we did not have an accident; we just travelled on a collection of potholes loosely strung together and being referred to optimistically as a 'road'.

What do you think my second reaction was? Dead right; I announced that under no circumstances was I prepared to accept bananas from this plantation, unless the road was fixed quick smart.

The retailer is always right - bananas

That is obviously debatable. With bananas in particular, there is a tendency for retailers to attempt exercising control due to the strategic importance of that particular crop.

Best practice in their own behaviour or ability to control the fruit in their own environment is certainly not how retailers obtain the assumed authority of being able to tell growers and shippers how to look after bananas during the production and shipping phases.

Here are the ten most common banana sins committed by retailers:

- in summer, banana cartons containing ripe bananas are not stacked down and opened after arrival at store;
- conversely, in winter, bananas are stacked down and opened after arrival at store;
- bananas are piled onto the retail fixture seven or eight layers high;
- the banana display is stocked at the beginning of the trading day and then left to its own devices;
- hands of bananas are taken out of the boxes, placed on display and not

separated into customer friendly size bunches;

- bunches are separated by being ripped apart rather than cut with a sharp knife;
- bananas are placed on display the wrong way - curvature up;
- green bananas are on display whilst ripe bananas are in the rear area;
- single bananas are spread all over the display unit;
- there are no produce bags at the banana display.

Some of these points are self-explanatory; some deserve to be expanded upon. I would like to demonstrate by way of this example why it would be helpful for retailers to regain control of their produce departments. Unlike in the grocery department, where retailers are in a constant clinch with suppliers over brand and shelf supremacy, the produce issue is very simple.

Perishable produce is entering the store at one end, the rear store delivery dock, and leaving by the other end, the checkouts. The retailer's objective is to have as much of the produce that leaves the store doing so at full price, keeping the mark-downs to a minimum and avoiding the third way by which produce can leave the store - via the rubbish bin.

Bananas rear store - summer

In order for bananas to arrive in store ripe they are commercially exposed to ethylene gas, a job typically carried out by the banana wholesaler. Each cardboard box of bananas has a plastic lining in which the bananas sit and each box is capped with a lid. The ripening process is stimulated and advanced in the ripening rooms into which ethylene gas is pumped.

Once the fruit is removed from the rooms, the ripening process continues and is still in progress once the fruit arrives at the store. Stores are trying to sell the fruit in its best condition - which is not overripe!

By stacking the pallet of bananas down and opening the boxes, the ripening process is slowed down and stores can avoid having too much overripe stock on their hands. The two pre-conditions to this situation are that the bananas have been correctly ripened and arrive at the store in the right condition and that the air temperature is at least 8° Celsius.

Bananas rear store - winter

In winter, when air temperatures can range from 8° Celsius to below freezing point, the opposite practice needs to be applied. The cartons stay closed, as each represents a unique microclimate which protects the ripe fruit from chill injury.

The trick, of course, is that the produce manager needs to understand the basics of post-harvest banana physiology and be prepared to act upon his or her knowledge.

Bananas - piled high

Bananas are one of the fastest selling items in the produce department. The temptation therefore exists to really fill the display up to ensure that it does not have to be restocked every half hour. This habit does unfortunately cause considerable problems. Bananas are soft fruit and by the time the fourth or fifth layer gets added, the bottom layer will have become thoroughly squashed. Not that this injury is initially visible to the eye, as the skin affords a certain degree of protection, but latent damage is unavoidable and by the next day, the markdowns will be going through the roof.

Produce managers need to realise that a banana display causes work. Handled positively, the extra time invested into managing the banana display correctly and not having more than two layers on display at any one time will lead to extra sales. The flipside of the coin is that a "pile them high and watch them fly" approach will cause more work for a reduced return, as the labour hours will go into bagging bananas from the bottom layers of the pyramid and putting "reduced to clear" stickers on the bags.

Bananas - left to their own devices

Not only are bananas one of the fastest selling items in any produce department, they also serve consumers as an indicator product for the rest of the department. A well maintained banana display therefore suggests to customers that the rest of the department is also well looked after.

A poorly maintained banana display will raise doubt in the shoppers' minds about the entire produce department - which of course has consequences for the overall store.

Time spent maintaining the banana display should therefore be considered to be a strategic investment rather than an unnecessary cost.

Bananas - not separated

At the point of being unpacked from the boxes they have travelled in, bananas undergo the transformation from agricultural commodity to fresh product. The state in which they were packed, in whole hands, was very suitable from a packing point of view, but now the focus has to shift to selling.

The typical consumer does not want to buy a hand of between eight to twelve bananas. She prefers a bunch of between four to six fruit. Unless the hands are separated into bunches, sales will be lost and some customers will take matters into their own hands (pardon the pun) and rip hands of fruit apart.

Bananas - ripped apart

Banana hands should be separated into bunches with the aid of a suitable knife that produces a clean cut. A ripped hand is not only ungainly, but there is the potential for banana crowns to be damaged as a result, which may lead customers to reject the bunch or attempt to doctor it by ripping undesirable fruit off. Not a pleasant sight and very unprofessional.

Bananas - curvature up

The best way to avoid damaging bananas is to present them to customers in such a way that a bunch can easily be picked up. The best way to pick up a bunch of bananas is by the crown.

A bunch that is being displayed curvature up cannot be easily picked up as the crown is out of sight and out of reach. It therefore makes no sense whatsoever to pursue such a display policy.

Bananas - green

There is a place for green bananas. It's on the green banana display aimed at ethnic consumers who use green bananas in the way we use potatoes. There is no need for green bananas on the main banana display. Supplying green bananas should be a sacking offence for banana ripeners. Produce managers have been known to compound the problem by putting green bananas on display, the excuse being, "this is all which was delivered today."

That may well be the case, but the consequence is that sales will come to a screaming halt, as consumers tend to want bananas with at least a yellow tinge rather than the grass green version.

An even worse offence is leaving the green bananas on display and allowing the new delivery of ripe bananas that came in early the next morning to languish in the rear store because it is "not their turn yet."

Bananas - single

Despite a produce manager's best efforts, some customers will rip single banana fingers off the bunches on display. Do not leave them lying around. It makes the place look untidy. The best solution is to place a small basket near the main display and sell single bananas to the lunchtime trade.

Bananas - no bags

Bananas, and all other fruit and vegetables for that matter, need to be kept together in the shopping basket or trolley to make the passage through the checkout easier. Some produce also gains a little protection from being in a bag and keeping like produce in the same bag reduces any confusion about what type of produce it is and how much it should sell for.

The natural prerequisite for that is that bags are placed near the produce displays for customers to use and that the bag size on offer corresponds to the size of the produce a customer wishes to bag.

And lastly on the topic of retail control over the banana category: consumers and growers alike should be wary of any retailer who regularly sells a product called 'salad bananas', complete with a professionally executed point of sale ticket, just like for all the other produce on display. All this fancy way of dealing with the banana markdowns shows is that the store does not have its banana category under control.

Control - tactics or strategy?

In the banana example I have just discussed, the focus is clearly on instore behaviour and the tactical issues surrounding banana sales. These elements can be single store related or a concern for a multiple site retailer across his entire range of stores. Regardless of scope, the problems and their likely solutions are tactical in nature.

As retailers increase in size, they inevitably aim to create leverage within their respective supply chains in order to benefit at a higher and thus strategic level. Most produce retailers of any size are constantly aiming to improve their strategic and tactical control over their respective supply industries.

I will discuss strategic control by way of New Zealand examples, but readers need to be aware that very similar examples exist in other countries as well. New Zealand is not unique in that respect.

Control in a strategic sense is not an outcome but an ongoing process. Control increases as existing processes are incrementally improved, re-engineered, abandoned and/or replaced with new ones. Existing processes are often habit based and can at times bear little relevance to the purpose and outcome they are trying to support. The availability of the fax machine, for example, did by no means lead to an immediate cessation of the spoken word when trying to establish produce prices with a direct supplier for the coming week. Produce buyers missed the finer nuances of a verbal exchange and the ability to read between the lines of what was being said. Similarly, when produce buyers were initially told that visiting auctions was no longer a part of the job, that what mattered now was that quality produce was available on the shelf and a telephone call to the supplier could suffice, major angst broke out amongst the buyers as they used to place a extraordinary degree of emphasis on being able to view the produce prior to purchase and being able to look the auctioneer or merchant in the eye!

Auction

The existence of produce auctions had made it relatively easy for supermarkets to grow their fruit and vegetable business - up to a point. Any greengrocer or produce buyer visiting a produce auction could always be *reasonably* confident that the fruit and vegetables needed to fill the retail shelves could be procured. The elements the buyer had no control over were the source of the produce, the quality of the produce, the volume of the produce available, the number of growers supplying on any given day, the way the produce was packaged, the time the produce had been harvested, the way the produce had been managed during its growing phase, the way it had been handled during harvest and the price the produce was going to be sold for.

In short, other than finding the answer to the core question of, "can I buy cauliflower at auction today, yes or no?" the buyer had no organised method at his disposal to generate answers to those more in-depth buying process related questions.

Supermarkets tacitly understood and accepted this until they reached a level of scale, which saw them questioning initially their own business practices and eventually those of their trading partners.

What lead to the change of heart that caused supermarkets to actively attempt to change the market system? There is no single direct answer, just a series of circumstances coming together and turning into the critical mass needed to induce change. Circumstances such as:

- the number of stores having grown to the point where availability of suitable supply could not always be guaranteed,

- bottom line growth becoming dependent upon improved business practices rather than growth in store numbers,
- the desire for consistency guiding a different type of thinking related to supply matters,
- the sheer volume of business being written each day creating an environment where all given processes and behaviours were constantly being challenged.

Eventually, this combination of circumstances led to supermarkets first supplementing auction or central market buying with buying part quantities of some crops directly from growers, and eventually switching to buying all their requirements from producers rather than middlemen.

Equilibrium gone - withdrawal from auction

When all produce grown is directed to auction and all produce buyers turn up to buy their fruit and vegetables, an equilibrium exists. Sure, there are a myriad of daily adjustments between volumes and quality available and prices buyers are prepared to pay, but both parties soon learn how to manage the relationship from a distance. Growers look at their returns and understand how much produce to send on what day to which market to optimise results. Buyers learn to associate certain grower names with specific quality expectations.

Each market day therefore reflected a more or less true state of supply with all information, i.e., volumes, quality and values being accessible to anyone who cared to attend the auction.

The circumstances listed in the previous section eventually culminated in the supermarket chain I worked for, Foodtown, withdrawing from the auction floor.

We simply announced that from a certain date our buyers would no longer purchase produce by sight at the central market but from named suppliers via telephone for direct delivery to our new distribution centre.

The first day of this new regime (8th May 1989) was the day the New Zealand fresh produce market equilibrium was severely disturbed and it has yet to recover.

What do I mean by that? Did the market actually get out of control? And whose control would that be - if it did at all?

The consumer noticed very little difference. Cauliflower, tomatoes, kiwifruit and all other produce continued to show up on the retail shelves. It was a different matter further up the supply chain. Those growers who had received direct orders were now consigning less or no produce to the market. The Foodtown produce buyers had dropped out of sight and the remaining floor buyers had to adjust their bidding dynamics with one of the largest purchasers gone.

Suddenly two markets co-existed. The established one, albeit with less produce and one less corporate buyer and the new one, revolving around that corporate buyer and his chosen suppliers. Whilst both mechanisms worked in as far as getting produce into retail stores was concerned, the critical element that was now missing was the daily creation of fair market value. Instead, two value equations emerged.

These value equations were ostensibly created in isolation from each other, but they certainly merged together again at the point when competing retailers were spotting each other's retail prices in the public arena- or even worse, when the consumer started noticing variations in the retail prices.

The traditional elements within retail management structures feared that they had lost control over their produce business, a sentiment echoed by many growers who felt totally manipulated by retailer systems.

So - where should control sit and who should exercise it?

In the purest sense, the answer is "there simply should be no control". An effective market system works to everyone's advantage when the parties involved are able to resist attempts to manipulate the system in any way shape or form. Reality is often different.

One of the consequences of Foodtown's decision to withdraw from the auction in May 1989, for example, was a six month glut in the cauliflower market.

The central market operators had underestimated the retailer's ability to follow through with his decision to buy produce direct and wherever possible had discouraged its suppliers from reducing volumes grown. The assumption being that the produce would find itself to retail somehow, as the consumer demand had not been reduced at all. Produce would therefore either be purchased directly or end up with the "renegade" retailer by way of complex brokerage transactions.

In the case of cauliflower though, the market operator had overlooked the fact that the retailer had for a number of years expressed his dissatisfaction with the quality of the crop for sale and had therefore taken the opportunity provided by this fundamental change in purchasing practices to appoint a non-traditional cauliflower grower, i.e., an individual who had never grown cauliflower in any quantities before but had all the makings of producing a consistently high quality crop.

The cauliflower market was therefore totally oversupplied and the value of the crop at wholesale went below harvest and packing cost; clearly not a sustainable long-term position.

I sincerely hope that I have made my point in this chapter. Namely, control is a strange bedfellow in an industry that is perishable, weather dependent and so diverse as the produce industry. Do we need to increase our influence when it comes to producing, packing and marketing quality fresh fruit and vegetables? Absolutely. Can we hope to control all industry processes and outcomes? The realistic answer is "up to a point." Anyone who actually thinks total control is achievable is dreaming.

Thought pieces

These pieces aim to provoke readers to think critically about the produce industry and were published between 2000 and 2009. Undoubtedly some of my views have shifted during that time.

Do not treat any inconsistency you discover as a negative, but please view these as a part of your own learning journey.

Beyond Fresh Produce Supply Chain Management

An Introduction to Action Learning inspired Fresh Food Converging Forces Theory

Abstract

Describes the key fresh produce industry drivers. Discusses the Action Learning context within which the theory emerged. Explores the link between supply chain management and operational excellence within the context of supply chains evolving into demand chains. Introduces Fresh Food Converging Forces Theory and the seven element CON-Factor Construct as enablers to achieving demand chain competence through the pursuit of operational excellence. Discusses the construct elements - CONsumer, CONstraint, CONflict, CONsistency, CONflict and CONtrol whose mastery is a prerequisite for CONvergence.

Keywords

Fresh produce, supermarkets, Action Learning, supply chain

Introduction

"No man is an island...
every man is a piece of the Continent, a part of the main..."

John Donne (1624), Emergent Occasions

The same is true for the participants in the fresh produce supply chain. Each participating organisation has its own particular set of expertise and competencies and therefore the ability and potential to add value. Not every organisation can necessarily be part of every chain, due to competitive circumstances and conflicts of interest.

Competent organisations will create their own future within the chain that is right for them. No one supply chain partner can in the long term expect to control the entire chain, as chain complexity will grow beyond one link's ability to dominate the others (Maurer, 2000).

The fact that supply chain management is seen as the only sustainable form of generic value chain management in the corporate retail environment is already well documented (Grimsdell, 1996; How, 1993; Hughes, Merton, 1996; Larson, 1997)

Similarly, the need to provide leadership and advance the fresh produce industry through innovation and the application of leading edge knowledge are also frequently discussed and explored (O'Keeffe, Fearne, 2002)

Yet - how can we advance at a better rate? How do we improve our understanding of the drivers that establish sustainable value in successful fresh produce demand chains? What will it take for identified drivers to deliver a robust implementation process for consistent application across the multitude of sectors making up the fresh produce industry?

The Action Learning context

"The mark of the person is in the questions they pose, not the statements they make."

This profound statement by Reg Revans, the 'father' of Action Learning is equally as applicable to organisational 'persons' as it is to individuals. Revans' goal right throughout his life was to encourage managers in the workplace to manage their own learning - which inevitably leads to questions being formulated in relation to the problems the learning managers settle on for resolution.

If the right questions are being asked, problems will be resolved. Problem resolution is often achieved through innovative new ideas being generated through the integrated questioning/problem solving process.

Revans obviously also experienced one of the negative consequences of new idea generation, which he exquisitely expressed thus,

"Unless your ideas are ridiculed by experts they are worth nothing."

The ideas behind 'Fresh Food Converging Forces Theory' have their origin in the writer's practical application of Action Learning during the course of his doctoral studies with IMCA in the 1990s and specifically arose as a result of a subsequent explication of published work in 2002/2003.

Key industry drivers

As is the case with any other industry, the fresh produce industry contains a number of key drivers that ultimately determine organisational success or failure of industry participants. There has been a lot of debate in recent years about what constitutes success in the fresh produce industry, and more importantly, how success can be sustainably achieved. This section lists the critical industry drivers and discusses their impact.

Supply

The most critical industry driver is supply. Supply attracts attention from the market place. How supply is moved to the market place is dependent upon the degree of leverage market place participants are able to exercise. The highest degree of leverage will usually achieve the greatest degree of success in attracting and processing supply.

Supermarket Buying Power

The natural growth supermarkets underwent as a result of consumer behaviour changes has been further accelerated by the availability of modern technology, the convergence of various technology strands into one, e.g., the Internet and globalisation in general. Supermarkets have thus gained increased leverage over supply and are able to influence and shape virtually every element of their supply chain to suit their circumstances, including the type of packaging used and determining the packaging supplier.

Retailers are merging across continents and are getting fewer in numbers. At the same time, the quantities of produce purchased and quality levels expected by these continuously growing multinationals is increasing.

Supply chains supporting these companies are now realigning themselves in order to better serve their customers and to maintain and hopefully grow their business.

More produce will in future be purchased in larger consolidated amounts from fewer but larger growers, packhouses and brokers.

One of the consequences of consolidation is that supermarkets, through necessity, are placing 'larger eggs into fewer baskets' and are becoming more dependent upon their key produce suppliers than they care to admit.

They are attempting to manage that risk through extensive communication programmes with their key suppliers, which in some cases includes an 'open book' policy with regards to the entire cost structure, inclusive of packaging costs. In any event, supermarkets and their preferred suppliers are talking to each other more than ever.

Bananas

Bananas represent approximately 10% of average produce department turnover. Produce buyers preferably purchase their requirements from as few sources as possible, in order to reduce administrative workload and maintain a degree of consistency. Relationship based buying is both a strength and weakness of this industry.

A supplier with access to large quantities of quality bananas will always succeed in establishing and maintaining a significant produce wholesale market share - as long as he has a good working relationship with at least one large supermarket chain in need of a reliable banana supplier (Maurer, 1999).

Distribution

When produce was purchased at auction, distribution was relatively simple. The auction house, by way of being the mechanism that brought grower and retailer together, ensured all produce was physically present on its site on the auction day. After the sale, company drivers would locate the purchased produce, sort it into store orders, load it onto their vehicles and take it as one consolidated order to the designated store.

As supermarkets abandoned the auction in favour of dealing direct, they had two choices: let every supplier deliver direct to every store or establish a distribution centre that would attract all produce purchased, similar to the way an auction floor attracted all produce available for sale.

Supply chain evolvement & operational excellence

Supply chains are evolving into demand chains. Demand chains are viewed as being a structure to be aspired to. Yet a number of authors (Brooks, 1995; Looseby 1997; Kaufman et al, 2000; O'Keefe, Fearne, 2002) go as far as stating directly or indirectly that demand chain management principles will not take hold unless retailers develop an interest in true supply partnerships.

Achieving constructive true supply partnerships within the area of fresh food retailing is only as robust as the supplier's ability to deliver "tomorrow's" order on time, to the right place, in the correct quantity, at the right price and to the right quality specification. The argument for loyalty to a supplier wears thin very quickly when the retailer is faced with empty shelves due to inability to deliver, reduced volumes, uncompetitive prices and unacceptable shrinkage.

It could therefore be argued that rather than worry about supply chain "improvement", the real issue is the need to achieve operational excellence in order to maintain the right to prove every day that one's supply "contract" was awarded with just cause and should be allowed to continue.

Achieving operational excellence is by necessity a predominantly inwardly focused process. Demand chain competence will arise as a result of achieving operational excellence. The ability and requirement to adjust one's own processes in order to achieve compatibility with the next link in the chain should not become a topic for discussion until internal processes have been mastered.

How does one go about achieving operational excellence within one's core fresh produce or fresh food business?

Demand chain management is about the convergence of interests of individual market orientated organisations all involved in satisfying a common consumer.

A theory is therefore proposed that results in a practical framework for use by market led fresh food organisations to create organisational excellence and demand chain compatibility.

Fresh food converging forces theory

Fresh Food Converging Forces Theory states that:

- The interests of several organisations directly or indirectly engaged in providing a fresh food based product or service to a common end user are able to converge into a demand chain once more than one individual organisation reaches a threshold level of operational excellence.
- Operational excellence is best achieved by implementing successful change strategies within individual organisations over time.
- Change strategies should be based on the six core elements of the CON-Factor Construct and delivered through Action Learning methods for meaningful and sustainable results.
- Successful implementation of the six core Construct elements will result in the seventh element being achieved - Convergence. Convergence drives competent demand chain creation and ongoing management.

The CON-Factor Construct

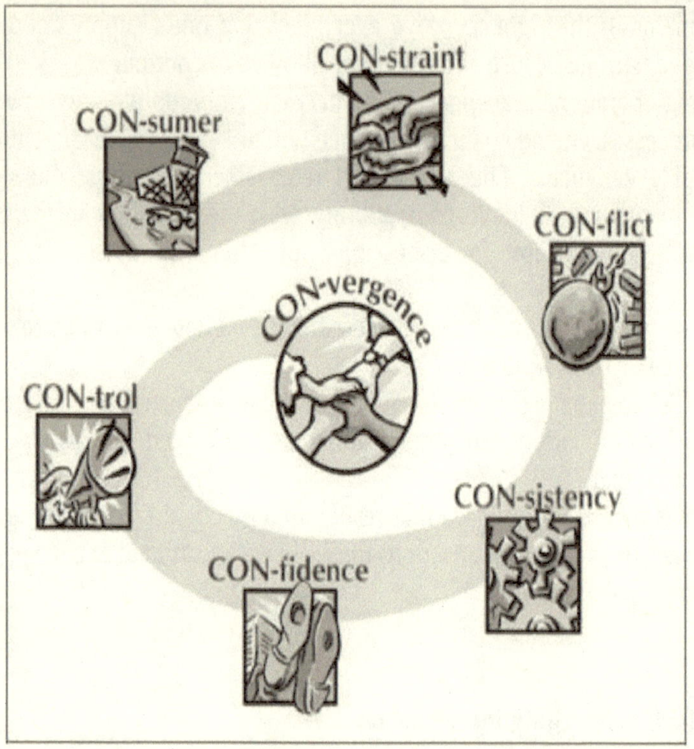

The Construct is based on several elements, referred to as CON-Factors.

Each CON-Factor represents an area of knowledge that needs to be acquired, a business segment that needs to be understood and an organisational behaviour that needs to be implemented

The CON-Factors

CONsumer

The purpose of achieving operational excellence within the fresh produce and fresh food environments is to satisfy the consumer. Period. It is irrelevant how many levels separate an organisation and its ultimate consumer. Organisational excellence is unattainable unless a consumer focus is adopted and consumer needs are better understood.

CONstraint

Food businesses operate under constraints. Constraints vary, but may include distance to market, seasonality, capacity, crop compatibility, financial scope and others. The key is to identify the constraints relevant to one's particular business and the degree of 'stretch' the constraints are able to tolerate before quality is compromised.

CONflict

Conflict needs to be managed. Not all conflict is bad. A degree of organisational conflict is healthy and aids in the development of a more robust organisation. The potential for conflict needs to be understood and the degree and nature of conflict needs to be measured. There are typically three areas of conflict that occur within a fresh produce/fresh food environment.

These are related to

§ timing, on account of produce perishability and the need for swift and timely action;

§ position, on the basis of whether the produce/product in question is the 'main event' on a plate or a member of the 'orchestra', i.e., there is a difference between managing a piece of steak and Brussels Sprouts or potatoes required for the main course or a pineapple destined for dessert;

§ role, by way of differentiating between those people in the organisation procuring the product and those tasked to sell.

These types of conflict need to be tackled differently from each other. The 'one cure for all' approach does not work.

CONsistency

Human nature does not cope well with change. We like our bananas yellow and our cauliflower creamy white. We also like to know that we can expect to purchase similar produce every time we visit a store and that it lasts for the same length of time when we take it home. Based on that consumer behaviour, the retailer does not want any surprises either. A food business therefore needs to be built around delivering a standardised consistent product in order to achieve operational excellence.

CONfidence

Confidence in one's own product and process is an essential ingredient to ensure market place success. Confidence needs to be reality based, though and not be 'blind'. Reality based confidence comes from understanding one's own business thoroughly, how it interacts with its customers and suppliers and through appropriate degrees of third party assurance, e.g.; HACCP based management, food safety practices and accreditations.

CONtrol

There are elements of any business that need to be managed and controlled. The trick is to understand which are the ones requiring 'hands-on' control and which ones can be left to their own devices. The pursuit of operational excellence should not serve as the excuse to exercise control over every minute detail. There are processes or parts thereof when 'going with the flow' will generate better long-term results.

CONvergence

Convergence will occur as a result of achieving operational excellence in the areas defined by the preceding six CON-Factors. It is an outcome, rather than a process. By achieving operational excellence in CON-Factors 1-6, organisations will either be ready to become effective demand chain leaders/ builders or be more flexible in how they fit into a chain put together by others.

In a practical sense, each CON-Factor is developed within the learning organisation through answering a specifically designed set of Action Learning questions. Answers generated constitute the organisational action plan.

Fresh Food Forces Theory and the Action Learning based CON-Factor Construct are enablers for demand chain improvement. Demand Chains are organisms that require ongoing nourishment in the form of both intellectual rigour and practical application. These two need to be applied hand in hand to achieve sustainable improvement.

References

Brookes, R. (1995) "Recent Changes in the Retailing of Fresh Produce: Strategic Implications for Fresh Produce Suppliers", Journal of Business Research, Vol. 32, pp. 149-161

Grimsdell, K. (1996) "The supply chain for fresh vegetables: what it takes to make it work", Supply Chain Management, Vol. 1 No 1, pp. 11-14

How, B.R. (1993) "Marketing System For Fresh Produce In The United States", Academic Press, pp. 1-26

Hughes, D., Merton, I. (1996) "Partnership in Produce: The J Sainsbury Approach to managing the fresh produce supply chain", Supply Chain Management, Vol. 1. No. 2, pp 4-6

Kaufman, P., Handy, C., et al. (2000) "Understanding The Dynamics Of Produce Markets", Consumption and Consolidation Grow, Agriculture Information Bulletin No 758, Economic Research Service, United States Department of Agriculture

Larson, R.B. (1997) "Key Developments in the Food Distribution System", Working Paper 97-08, The Retail Food Center, University of Minnesota

Maurer, H. (1999) "Comprehension of Cost Considerations during, before and after Deregulation of the New Zealand Retail Banana Business", Management Literature in Review, Volume 2 Issue 2, pp. 203-210

Maurer, H. (2000) "Improving the (New Zealand) Fresh Produce Supply Chain", Action Learning Outcomes Journal, Volume 1 Issue 1, pp. 21-31,

O'Keefe M., Fearne, A. (2002) "From Commodity Marketing to Category Management: Insights from the Waitrose Category Leadership Program in Fresh Produce", Vol. 7. No 5, pp. 296-301

Revans R., "ABC of Action Learning". 1990. Chartwell-Bratt. Bromley, UK.

Some thoughts along the chain

The phrase "Let them eat cake" is commonly attributed to Marie Antoinette, the last French Queen whose life ended on the guillotine during the French Revolution. The historians are still debating whether it was really the unfortunate Marie Antoinette who was responsible for coining the phrase or not. What is not up for debate, however, is the fact that "qu'ils mangent de la brioche" has generally been regarded as the epitome of the French decadence which sparked the revolution.

There is no revolution of the French kind occurring in New Zealand and Horticulture New Zealand certainly has issues to be concerned with other than cake consumption.

What is happening though in this country is a quiet revolution and the battle lines are being drawn on several fronts at once. Briefly these are:

1. Global commodity values are in very turbulent waters, with the main drivers being the contracting US economy, China's insatiable hunger for resources and its emergence as an economic powerhouse;
2. The diversion of arable land from food to biofuel production;
3. Rationalisation at corporate retail level not showing any signs of slowing down;
4. The 'Australianisation' of New Zealand picking up pace since Woolworths Pty Ltd purchased Progressive Enterprises Ltd;
5. An increasing number of consumers are choosing to buy from specialty stores and farmers' markets;
6. Consumers and their various advocates (self-appointed or legitimate) wanting to understand the food supply chain better, with the focus being put on two factors; food safety and margins.

All of these issues have been on the agenda at one time or other. Many of them are underlying and dormant and have been with us for a number of years and we have managed. As a collective bundle, however, these issues have reached the strategic equivalent of a water jug's boiling point and the hot liquid is about to spill out over the edge.

The grower body Horticulture New Zealand, in its own words,

"represents 7,000 commercial fruit and vegetable growers, providing strategic direction and focus, building strong relationships with product groups and associations and working at both a national and regional level."

The issues outlined above are, and will continue to be, impacting upon New Zealand growers in a very strategic fashion - and some of the consequences are quite painful. The industry therefore needs to ensure that it is able to live up to the expectation it has set for itself

- *the ability to have strategic direction and focus.*

What can grower organisations do about such issues?

Directly? Nothing!

The first issue, the state of the global commodity market, is beyond anyone's control. New Zealand as a primary industry focused export dependent nation will continue to work hard at developing value added products, identifying niche markets and creating innovative supply solutions.

Issues two to five are both global and local in nature and every grower is affected by these one way or the other. These topics are also very closely related to each other and are already receiving plenty of attention in other countries in the form of parliamentary commissions or inquiries by regulating bodies focused on governance, compliance and competition.

What grower organisations therefore can and should do in these topic areas is to increase their knowledge on those industry and economy drivers, to ensure the *strategic direction and focus* truly adds value and maintains relevancy.

Who are the growers then?

Undoubtedly, organisations such as Horticulture New Zealand have their own membership categorisation matrix.

Here are grower segments we have identified:

A. Growers who grow for the local market and exclusively supply through wholesalers.

B. Growers who grow for the local market and supply through wholesalers as well as directly to one or more supermarket chains.

C. Growers who are primarily export focused and who only supply a small volume into the local market.

D. Growers who have a balanced approach to supplying export and local markets

E. Growers who are in essence small family businesses.

F. Growers who are extended and complex family businesses.

G. Growers who work within a co-operative structure.

H. Large growers who have in the past questioned the value that is added by grower organisations.

I. Small growers who often think a grower organisation can fix anything on their behalf.

J. New corporate growers who can't quite see how they benefit joining a grower association.

K. Growers who have until recently had surety of supply to a supermarket chain and no longer can be so sure.

L. Growers who prefer to stick to selling their produce at local farmers markets.

M. Growers who are purely focused on growing.

N. Growers who have extended their activities into brand development, packhouse management and retail merchandising.

O. Growers who export their own crops.

In other words, the matrix is quite complex - which means so are the needs of growers. However, regardless of a grower's size or the number of matrix categories that describe him or her, the common thread across all the categories is that they are affected by rationalisation at retail level, the "Australianisation" of New Zealand, the growth of speciality stores and farmers markets and increased consumer demand for information.

And it goes without saying that all growers want to and need to have the ability to generate an income as well as a return on their investment in order to remain in business.

With all this in mind, grower organisations are today compelled to ensure they have up to date strategic knowledge of the entire fresh produce supply chain, not just the grower related elements.

The behaviour of retail supply chains, in general is no mystery nor is the behaviour of markets. Fresh produce has also been a topic that has attracted various authors over the years, both here in New Zealand and elsewhere. There have also been several attempts at analysing supermarket buyer behaviour, recording the evolution of the wholesale produce trade, and understanding related consumer behaviour. The various texts referenced here are just a small selection of writings that exist. It will therefore not be necessary to reinvent the wheel. The New Zealand market is not unique in the way it generally behaves and the drivers that impact on the state of our horticultural industry are largely international. (Having said that, allowances have to be made for our unique geographic structure and location which do create certain idiosyncrasies.)

Growers market their produce either directly or through wholesalers and retailers. Growers require strategic insight into the minds of those supply chain participants further up the chain with whom they work to satisfy the consumer.

A better informed horticultural production sector with the ability to improve its strategic focus on value chain optimisation as it works with its supply chain partners can add substantial value to its own industry and the country at large.

References

i Blackwell, R.D. (1997). From Mind to Market. Reinventing the Retail Supply Chain. HarperCollins. New York.

ii Gattorna, J. (1998). Strategic Supply Chain Alignment. Gower. Aldershot.

iii McMillan, J. (2002). Reinventing the Bazaar. A Natural History of Markets. W.W. Norton & Co. London.

iv Maurer, H. (1999). Improving The New Zealand Fresh Produce Supply Chain. Doctoral Thesis.

v Maurer, H. (2003). Beyond Fresh Food Supply Chain Management. Explication. Submitted towards Distinguished Professorship Award with IMCA UK.

vi Maurer, H. (2003). A Produce Industry Perspective. Report for the Commerce Commission in relation to Decision 495 (Brambles NZ Ltd & GE Capital Returnable Packaging Systems Ltd)

vii Richards, T.J. & Patterson, P.M. (2003). Competition in Fresh Produce Markets. An Empirical Analysis of Marketing Channel Performance. Economic Research Service. USDA.

viii Thompson, G. (2001). Supply Chain Management. Building partnerships and alliances in international food and agribusiness.

ix McLaughlin, E.W. & Perosio, D.J. (1993). Fresh Fruit and Vegetable Procurement Dynamics. The role of the supermarket buyer. Cornell University. New York.

x Seth, A. & Randall, G. (2005). Supermarket Wars. Global Strategies for Food Retailers. Palgrave MacMillan. New York.

xi Stead, K. (1997). One Hundred I'm bid. A centennial history of Turners & Growers. Kestrel Publishing. Auckland.

xii East, C.C. (1998). 75 Years of Market Gardeners Limited. MG Marketing Ltd. Christchurch.

xiii Davies, P.N. & Hope-Mason, D. From Orchard to Market. An account of the development of the fruit and vegetable trade in the UK. Lockwood Press Ltd London.

xiv Kahn, B.E. & McAlister L. (1997). Grocery Revolution. The New Focus on the Consumer. Addison-Wesley. New York.

xv Underhill, P. (1999). Why We Buy. The Science of Shopping. Touchstone. New York.

Sustainability, carbon neutrality and all that jazz

A discussion of the challenges faced by the produce supply chain

2008 has been an interesting year: a produce related salmonella outbreak in the US; a financial crisis of global proportions that will not bypass the produce industry either; elections here and elsewhere with watershed results; and a travel schedule for me that has meant I needed to revisit how I allocated my time. One of the 'victims' was my monthly FMCG column. Editor John Corbett and I managed to arrive at a compromise solution - you will be hearing from me less frequently from now on, but in greater depth.

I managed to get into two countries last year I had not previously visited before: Finland and Vanuatu. At the time of my visit the papers in both countries were full of labour issues. Finland's strawberry industry needed to import seasonal labour from Thailand of all places, as Finns and other assorted Scandinavians are not inclined to take menial jobs of that nature. Vanuatu, on the other hand, had just joined New Zealand's seasonal horticultural labour scheme for Pacific Island nations and was busy preparing to dispatch cohorts of harvest workers to the Land of the Long White Cloud.

Meanwhile, at the business end of the supply chain, supermarkets were busy testing and rolling out their various marketing strategies, changing produce packaging solutions in the name of sustainability and engaging to a greater or lesser degree with issues such as carbon neutrality, local buying as well as the legal process in connection with who might be allowed to own The Warehouse and how much longer a perfectly well positioned Pak' N Save store on Auckland's North Shore has to remain closed on account of planning consent interpretations.

Amongst these myriads of issues which took me very little time to list, are one or two that are likely to matter to the consumer of 2009 and beyond.

I am looking here particularly at sustainability and local buying concepts. Both concepts sound very plausible, both concepts are difficult to avoid and both concepts are right little minefields when examined in close proximity.

Is it sustainable, for example, to cut heads of cauliflower in the field, the way we have for generations, outer leaves slightly trimmed but leaving enough cover to completely encase the white florets until the product has arrived at retail, where it gets trimmed 'retail ready'?

At first glance, the answer is yes, because exposing the head already in the field (there are no cauliflower packhouses in New Zealand) would lead to damage by the time the crop had reached the supermarket delivery dock, given the way the crop is packed. The leaves trimmed off at retail are these days chucked into the waste bins which are regularly removed from stores by commercial contractors. Twenty years ago we were less sophisticated. Stores were equipped with industrial wastemasters and all produce waste was washed down the drains.

So there has certainly been some improvement. The current practice still means that growers are using packaging capacity, transport capacity and cooling capacity to move a crop through the supply chain that generates avoidable waste as it reaches the consumer. Couldn't these cauliflower not just be trimmed properly in the field and the green waste generated be turned into compost there and then? Yes, but the packaging methods would have to change. So, what's wrong with that?

Cauliflower is but one example. Just about every product on display in the produce department could do with some re-engineering in terms of sustainability.

Local buying is also a topic that causes considerable interest. But what is the definition of local?

It is certainly not importing fruit in the off season from Australia or California. Local, for instance, means grown here, in New Zealand. Pursuing this line to the logical conclusion, we would not import any fruit or vegetable that can abundantly be produced during a defined season here in the country. In practical terms - bananas would still be allowed in but strawberries or summerfruit better stay where they belong.

Let's stick with strawberries for the moment. Auckland growers typically manage to get sizable volumes to market from mid October. South Island growers, and there are not any who produce consistently in volumes comparable to what their Auckland counterparts harvest, come on stream later. If local is very tightly defined, Christchurch consumers will need to wait until Nelson and later in the season Geraldine crops come into production. Until then, no strawberries for our Canterbury cousins because they prefer to buy locally. Can you imagine the uproar that would cause?

In many ways therefore, 'local' is nothing other than yet another mini trade barrier warped in the respectable cloak of politically correct behaviour in whatever particular locality one wants to create an issue in.

Have I got you wound up yet? How about we throw the issue of achieving a neutral carbon foot print into the mix as well.

What is better then - buying local lettuces from your local market gardener in Ashburton, New Plymouth or Whangarei, shipping them in by the truckload from Gisborne or purchasing bagged ready to eat salads from a South Auckland vertically integrated salad producer who has managed to achieve carbine neutrality to your delivery dock?

Ah, what a choice to make: local variation versus national consistency. Wholesome like granny used to grow in her garden or minimally processed? Natural versus scientifically produced? 'Who gives a ...' or politically correct?

I am glad I am not a retailer anymore, this is getting far too hard. In reality though, you will be lining up your volume mainstay lettuces alongside a few heads of the local crop and right next to it will sit a range of bagged salads because you have learned by now that every customer is different and each customer therefore has different needs. The parochially minded will get satisfaction being able to by lettuces produced by a grower who is in the same rotary club. Mum on a budget wants to be able to buy a reasonably sized head of lettuce anytime she enters the shop and it had better be of reasonable quality and at the same price as it was last week. The time poor want to get in and out of your store faster than you can say 'advertised special' or 'wall of value' and these customers will thank you for having the bagged kind in stock. And if there is a sachet with dressing in the bag as well, even better.

So what can we do to come to grips with those environmental concerns which are driving our customers' shopping behaviour, be it consciously or subliminally? One industry player who is not just talking about sustainability but has already achieved a remarkable milestone in this area is Ashley Berrysmith, the Governing Director of New Zealand Fresh Cuts.

Twenty-five years ago Ashley was growing bean sprouts in bathtubs in the backblocks of Avondale. Today, based in a modernised factory in South Auckland, the business has expanded to also include baby peeled carrots, bagged ready to eat salads, salad shakes, a model farm where the salad ingredients are produced, as well as a joint venture aimed at commercialising hempseed oil production.

Get the feeling that Ashley & Co are into natural foods? Not only are you right - Ashley is a vegetarian from way back and visitors to his premises are served green tea!

The flipside is that Ashley has one of the brightest business brains in the industry and represented New Zealand at the Ernst & Young Global Entrepreneur of the Year event in Monaco.

Check out *www.nzfreshcuts.co.nz* for more info.

NZ Fresh Cut is a really good example of where we need to move towards as a supply chain. In order to really make a difference on a day to day basis, we need to understand and measure our carbon emission and energy consumption, we need to mitigate our outputs by either reducing them or buying carbon credits and we need to manage our behaviour which determines how we reduce our carbon foot print. Sounds simple enough, doesn't it?

Stephen Dench, NZ Freshcuts' CEO puts it this way: "In order to succeed in a sustainable fashion, a business needs to first develop a carbon mentality and then adopt that mentality as its philosophical business platform."

Here we have a supplier to the industry who demonstrably has both a healthy level of business acumen and the philosophical mindset to be credible in this whole sustainability arena.

A supplier though, does not have responsibility for the entire supply chain. NZ Fresh Cuts might be growing their own raw ingredients, drive low emissions cars, have staff quality circles constantly reexamine business processes to ensure all options to reduce the carbon foot print are acted upon and have self-dimming light switches in the board room - but their accountability for carbon neutrality by definition stops when the retailer takes delivery of the product.

Now that is an interesting concept. Retailers, and remember I used to be one, are usually quite good at extending the suppliers' responsibility right into their stores. Wal-Mart has truly perfected that by negotiating supply contracts with its key suppliers which have the suppliers owning the product right until the consumer takes it out of the shopping trolley and places it on the checkout counter.

But this concept does not work when a customer looks you in the face whilst holding a head of lettuce or a salad bag in her hand and asks, "Excuse me, Mr Produce Manager / Store Manager / Store Owner, is this product carbon neutral?"

It might only be Sue Kedgley and assorted other tree huggers asking this question today, but tomorrow this will be a mainstream demand which requires an answer.

And answering, "Yes madam, we insist our suppliers are carboNZero certified before we agree to buy their product," will only satisfy a handful of shoppers. The overwhelming majority will follow through with, "Great; now what about you? What is your company doing to ensure this product is still carbon neutral, given that you took delivery a day ago, had it sitting in your cooler out the back, possibly trimmed some leaves off which you didn't really need to bring all the way from the farm to the shop in the first place, and are selling it to me from this refrigerated cabinet in this brightly lit department, using up all this energy?"

Oh, boy! Did I mention I am glad that I am no longer a retailer?

Seriously though, it seems to me that the burning issue of better managing the planet's finite resources will do more to achieve efficient supply chain management in the true meaning of the term, than all the financial business drivers used as justification to date put together.

'Doing your bit' and doing it well will in future no longer be good enough. 'Your bit' will have to be coordinated with the activities others are undertaking within the supply chain - and that includes growers, wholesalers, importers, packaging companies, service providers and retailers.

Supply chain management as a discipline will become more holistic, complex and rewarding than it is today.

If I were a retailer today, I would be talking to the savvy suppliers out there who are already on the journey and understand what leverage can be created by supporting and or building upon their efforts.

Sustainability within the fresh produce context

My attempts to look at sustainability from a 2010 perspective land me back in 2000 and 2004.

The concept of sustainable agriculture can be described as a "three legged stool", the three legs being economic viability, environmental soundness and social acceptability. When one leg is weak, the farming system is likely to be unstable and not sustainable in the long run (Granatstein & Kupferman, 2006).

This statement is equally as applicable to horticulture. That is all very well - but this definition opens up a causality dilemma that is a close relative of the "what came first - the chicken or the egg?" question. Given that this particular question has been around since Plutarch's time (46-126 AD), and has also been debated by everybody from the Roman philosopher Macrobius to the wheelchair tied theoretical physicist Stephen Hawking, as well as you and me, I fear that the sustainability argument may suffer a similar fate. What comes first then - economic viability, environmental soundness or social acceptability?

With my tongue firmly pressed into my cheek, herewith a few comments with the respective perspectives.

<u>The Economist's view</u>

Surely it must be economic viability that comes first. We can't afford the luxury of environmental claptrap or all that social stuff without money in the bank. Yes, there is a need to look after our planet and people have needs too - but really, who is going to pay for all of that?

<u>The Environmentalist's view</u>

Unless we look after the land and stop using chemicals and anything else inorganic, we are likely to implode any time soon and dollars and wider social acceptability will no longer matter anyway.

<u>The Social Acceptability Advocate's view</u>

At the end of the day we need to focus on the communities we live in and these communities deserve our support. Supermarkets should only be allowed to source locally gown food from a radius of, say, 50km around their store. And all imports should be banned.

Admittedly, I chose to be extreme and confrontational in my above impersonations, but extremists who hold such views do indeed exist. Even without taking such a confrontational approach though, the similarities between the sustainability debate and the chicken and egg argument are scary.

The production oriented ones amongst us will always pursue the 'economics first' approach. The environmentally active segment will argue that unless we get serious about taking care of the planet we run the risk of economic collapse anyway, if not now then certainly at some point in the future and social acceptability has certainly become the new buzz phrase, haunting us every day until late at night.

So let's take the pragmatist's position on sustainability. The notion that the planet we live on is a finite resource is understood by all sides in the sustainability debate. The arguments around how the remaining resources should be used typically fit around one or more of the following conceptual strands:

- The developed world has had its time plundering Earth. It's now the time for developing nations to catch up and for the developed world to reduce its exploitation so that there is something left to exploit for the others.
- We should be worried, but we simply can't adjust our lifestyles to the extent advocated. So, let's leave the fixing to the next generation. We just do the research so they know what needs doing.
- We have been talking about running out of oil, for example, for the last 20 years. And look - we still have some. It is therefore not going to happen.
- Let's compensate - someone can plant trees on our behalf, etc.

Around the world, governments are attempting to introduce emission trading schemes, companies are trying to position themselves as environmentally friendly and individuals are largely bewildered about what is going on.

In Australia, the Leader of the Opposition in the Federal Parliament was toppled in December 2009 because he had the audacity to support the Government's proposed emissions trading scheme legislation.

Companies such as Air New Zealand, for example, offer customers the option to ease their conscience at the time of booking their flight by donating a certain amount of money towards environmental purposes aimed to offset their carbon creation by deeming it necessary to fly.

Consumers are watching with incredulity as scientists are taking opposing sites on the climate change debate, the Prime Minister being coy about whether he should attend the Copenhagen Climate Summit or not and radio talkback hosts promoting their particular views not only on air but also on associated websites.

What is our position on all of this? What does the fresh produce industry have to say for itself on the topic of sustainability?

Well, how many readers know of the existence of the **Sustainable Agriculture/Horticultural Management Systems Network (SAMsn)**?

I, for one, had to plead ignorance until I started researching for this article. The Network was apparently formed in 2000 and according to its website funded by MAF's Sustainable Farming Fund. On its website the network describes its function thus;

"The establishment of the Network was based on areas of 'commonality' across the agriculture and horticulture production sectors and has an objective to more efficiently develop commonality and build on the known NZ advantage of high quality and environmentally friendly production - the NZ 'clean and green' image.

Implicit in this is the ability to produce and develop agriculture and horticulture products in a sustainable manner. Productivity and good resource management are interlinked.

The Network developed a focus on Sustainable Management Systems, which encompasses the 'pillars' of environment, economics and social responsibility, and the interactions between the 'pillars', in an on-farm context, because of the recognition that the future of the New Zealand primary industries depends on both sustainability and profitability.

SAMsn has undertaken to develop a framework that could form the basis of any agriculture or horticulture industry Sustainable Management System (SMS) now, and in the future. It has also identified information and a wide range of possible resources that could be used by organisations to develop and refine SMS systems which may lead to the evolution of common approaches and elements across programmes. The purpose is to add value to producers, sectors, industries and businesses with a focus on both productivity and sustainability."

The website also identifies 27 key issues of relevancy to sustainable land management.

<u>Key Issues:</u> Identified on the Sustainable Agriculture/Horticultural Management Systems Network website:

- Air Issues, Pollution
- Animal Welfare, Animal Disease, Stock Shelter
- Biodiversity
- Biosecurity
- Cultural/Maori
- Dust and Smoke
- Energy Efficiency
- Fertiliser Run-Off, Contamination
- Food Quality
- Food Safety
- Genetically Modified Organisms
- Greenhouse Gases, Climate Change
- Ground Water Contamination
- Hazardous Substances
- Health and Safety
- Heavy Metals
- Irrigation
- Land Management
- Noise
- Odour
- Soil Erosion
- Soil Structure
- Solid Waste, Waste Management
- Spraydrift
- Water - General
- Water Quality
- Weeds and Pests

Further investigation suggests that VegFed, Pipfruit NZ, Zespri and Summerfruit NZ had some involvement as they are listed in a section entitled *"Supported Industry Groups"*. Another section of the site contains a 2004 Research Report in pdf format.

A quick glance at the topics suggests that they are as relevant today as they were in 2000 or 2004. How are we tackling them then? Whose job is it? Where do we start? Do we work by ourselves or within our product groups or regional grower associations? Where does Horticulture New Zealand fit into all of this?

May I suggest that you start by visiting the website and either refamiliarise yourself with it or learn more if you are a first time visitor. This is a classical example of where we can avoid reinventing the wheel, build on work already done and draw on resources already in place.

So what are you waiting for? Don't get tied up in the chicken versus the egg debate but get a wriggle on.

References

Granatstein, D., Kupferstein, E. (2006). Sustainable Horticulture in Fruit Production. ISHS Acta Horticulturae 767: XXVII International Horticultural Congress - IHC2006: International Symposium on Sustainability through Integrated and Organic Horticulture

Advancing Sustainable Management Systems in Agriculture and Horticulture. http://www.samsn.org.nz/ website, accessed 4 December 2009.

Wharfe, L., Manhire, J. (2004). The SAMsn Initiative. Advancing Sustainable Management Systems in Agriculture and Horticulture. MAF Sustainable Farming Fund.

Parallel universes and the fresh produce industry

It does not matter where in the developed world one lives nor whether one is male or female, straight or otherwise, of European descent or already part of the cultural & ethnic mix that our descendants will turn into - supermarkets are never far from our mind. The hunter/gatherers of prehistoric times pursue these activities within supermarkets today. Supermarkets have, depending whom one wishes to believe, a market share of between 60-85% of the total food business. Yes, I know that there are variations and fluctuations based on store departments, store location and the competence level of store management, but I am talking averages here.

My favourite source of semi-reliable information, Wikipedia (*http://en.wikipedia.org/wiki/Supermarket*), suggests that,

*"a **supermarket** is a self-service store offering a wide variety of food and household merchandise, organised into departments. It is larger in size and has a wider selection than a traditional grocery store and it is smaller than a hypermarket or superstore."*

Whilst one usually has to take Wikipedia with a grain of salt as all and sundry are able to edit contributions on-line, I am sure that most readers would agree with this description as being fairly accurate. Let's see what else Wikipedia has to say on the topic to help us better understand what a supermarket is - and equally as important, what it is not!

On the matter of why we shop at supermarkets, Wikipedia feels,

*"Its basic appeal is the availability of a broad selection of goods under a single roof at **relatively low prices**."*

As a possible reason why relatively low prices should be achievable, Wikipedia offers this explanation.

"The stores often are part of a corporate chain that owns or controls (sometimes by franchise) other supermarkets located nearby

- even transnationally - thus increasing opportunities for economies of scale."

Wikipedia also thinks it has got the answer to the fundamental question on supermarket economics.

*"Supermarkets usually offer products at low prices by **reducing their economic margins**. Certain products (typically staple foods such as bread, milk and sugar) are occasionally sold as loss leaders, that is, with negative*

profit margins. To maintain a profit, supermarkets attempt to make up for the lower margins by a higher overall volume of sales, and with the sale of higher-margin items."

Hmm, let me sum up here.

Supermarkets are food outlets that achieve economies of scale which enable them to sell food at relatively low prices and in the process often reducing their economic margin.

I have spent the last few days contemplating the Wikipedia article which appears to have been put together by perfectly sane and sensible people. Yet the supermarket world I see is somewhat different to the one described by the Wikipedia authors. How can this be? What is happening here? Who has gotten hold of the wrong end of the stick? The answers to these questions, valued readers, are actually very exciting because we may just have reached the point where the good old supermarket business is at the verge of proving and confirming a theory that has fascinated mankind for hundreds of years.

I am referring, of course, to the theory that parallel universes exist!

No, I have not gone completely of my rocker but I know that consumers and growers alike are experiencing a totally different supermarket-related reality than the one described in Wikipedia. In our reality here, supermarkets with established and unquestionable economies of scale are, for example, selling Royal Gala apples for around $1 per kilo more currently than a greengrocer down the road. Suppliers are being asked to buy space in supermarket catalogues in order to have their produce advertised whilst reducing their own economic margins is typically a totally abhorrent concept for supermarkets because that is not in their shareholders' best interest. On top of that, regular suppliers are being asked to implement complex food safety programmes whilst supermarkets reserve the right to buy from whomever they like regardless and when it suits them, food safety system or otherwise.

This all fits with physics theories involving parallel universes, *"which form a natural four-level hierarchy of multiverses allowing progressively greater diversity."* (Tegmark, M. 2003).

In his somewhat challenging paper, Tegmark (2003) introduces multiverses as a conceptual hierarchy that is peppered with Hubble volumes, chaotic inflation, unitary quantum mechanics and mathematical structures unknown to us that give rise to different fundamental equations of physics.

The key question, by the way, for Tegmark is not whether parallel universes exist, but how many of them there are!

So, you can see it is perfectly simple. We do not live in a universe but on several multiverse levels all at once. That would explain why what the supermarkets are saying and what they are doing is often barely related to each other. It seems that supermarkets have developed the ability to cross from one multiversal level to another and back so rapidly that we don't notice and perceive them to be locked in one spot because of the brick and mortar needed to build them. Another possible explanation is that supermarkets are able to be simultaneously present on more than one level of our multiverse without themselves realising that this is so. If I have thoroughly confused you by now, forgive me. My excuse is that the topic is very complex. I will try to explain it in a nutshell.

Common economic principles related to economies of scale no longer apply because the economic unit size of supermarket chains has grown exponentially and disproportionally compared to the economic unit size of supermarket suppliers.

We started off in the 1950s and 1960s with New Zealand supermarkets buying their produce at auction, alongside all other produce retailers. In the 1970s first attempts to buy direct from growers emerged. This trend became more robust in the 1980s and snowballed in the 1990s. By 2000 then separately owned Woolworths and Progressive had their respective systems sorted out, often sourcing whole categories from just one supplier. This in turn changed the nature of some of these suppliers from growers who packed, to packers who grew and purchased from other growers. Subtle difference, eh. Foodstuffs in the meantime followed its own evolutionary path on produce supply.

Then two events occurred in relatively short order. Firstly, Progressive purchased Woolworths. No sooner had the dust settled, the tables turned for Progressive. It became the successful takeover target for Woolworths Australia. Now we have a substantial volume of New Zealand produce being procured every day under Aussie rules. The intrinsic costs of running a produce buying operation, the additional costs of complying with Woolworths Australia requirements in this market, the costs associated with funneling all produce through a centralised distribution centre, the impact of corporate accounting policies on distribution costs as well as associated regulatory or self-inflicted compliance costs and the produce department margin expectation all add up to negating the benefits of being able to buy attractively due to enjoying economies of scale. To be very clear here - I am not blaming supermarkets or anyone else for that matter. Running a buying team costs money and, of course, one wants to play by one's own rules if one is big enough to achieve it; centralised distribution provides more control and accounting policies exist for a reason; compliance costs are a fact of life and positive margins are needed in order to justify the capital intensive nature of being in the supermarket business.

Every single aspect listed here can be vigorously defended and justified up to a point.

My point is that the sum of these aspects when added to the fact that our industry markets and sells commodities and not 18 karat gold jewellery, and compounded by the imbalance in economic unit size between buyer and seller, is tipping the balance and no longer makes it possible for a supermarket to do what Wikipedia says a supermarket should be doing - offering *"a broad selection of goods under a single roof at relatively low prices."*

And none of the above is purely a local New Zealand phenomenon.

This brings me back to the multiverse theory, which obviously deserves closer investigation than many of us have realised until now.

Reference

Parallel Universes. Science and Ultimate Reality. From Quantum to Cosmos. Cambridge University Press.

Views on reusable plastic crates

The market for reusable plastic crates goes beyond fresh produce. Evidence from the UK suggests that the market expands considerably into other 'fresh' areas, once an efficient and effective produce system is in place.

"In the United Kingdom returnable shipping containers are widely used for grocery products, ranging from produce and meat to chilled prepared foods."

A report by Twede[1] containing the above statement goes on to predict a doubling of UK supermarket use of returnable plastic crates by 2004 across all fresh food categories.

The fact that the market has not expanded to the same extent in New Zealand is a function of the current system of three operating companies not being economically viable in the long term. Operators are therefore focusing on the short-term objective of market survival rather than market development.

Limiting the market to "the hire of reusable plastic crates" is too narrow a definition and not reflective of market place reality.

As pointed out in an earlier report[2] , one way cardboard packaging is a viable option and a robust shipping solution currently in use. It is also worth noting that in the US and Australia cardboard packaging of a similar footprint to that of returnable produce crates has been developed to facilitate smoother interaction during the distribution process, a factor that will most certainly provide increased competition between the two packaging solutions.

A more realistic market definition would therefore be *the national market for one way and reusable variable materials containers for the transport and storage of fresh New Zealand produce.*

Barriers to entry

A view has been expressed that "the current volume of crates in service is sufficient to serve the market." This view is open for debate. Of particular interest is the Dutch[3] experience.

The Dutch, when setting up a national crate pool for the produce industry, experienced that "the initial target was to produce a minimum of 4 million crates within three years. But already within 18 months of the introduction there were 6 million crates being used. This number is expected to rise to about 10 million. Nevertheless thus far the new crate has only been introduced systematically in The Netherlands."

This suggests that when an efficient and effective reusable crate system is put in place, the market will expand.

It would be fair to ask at this point - 'why has market expansion not occurred at a similar rate in this country?'

The simple answer is that our reusable hire crate system is anything but efficient and effective. It can be argued the presence of three crate pool providers to the produce industry in a market of our size is creating inefficiencies of a scale that discourage natural market expansion.

The contradictory behaviours of the two supermarket chains in terms of providing direction on packaging specifications to suppliers are further contributors to the inefficiencies of the system.

Produce is not purchased against firm contracts but on an indicative basis, which usually firms up 6-24 hours before the crop is expected to arrive at a Progressive supermarket distribution centre. Market supply or supply to Foodstuffs is less regimented, with merchants managing 'the slack' in the supply chain.

In any event, a 6-24 hour gap between order receipt and fulfillment is for many crops insufficient time to commence harvest after order receipt. There is literally no grower who just supplies Progressive. All Progressive growers have secondary supply channels.

With harvest regularly commencing prior to order receipt and limits imposed by Progressive in terms of the crate type accepted, i.e., Weck Packs only, knowing how much produce to pack into which container is a grower's daily version of playing Russian Roulette. This is further complicated by the fact that whilst Foodstuffs accepts all packaging types, its major supplier and grower agent, Turners & Growers, does not.

Growers are therefore required to hold and manage sufficient volumes of at least two crate types and possibly three, depending upon which supply channels they intend to utilise.

In addition to costs related to that exercise, there is the matter of re-packing. It is a regular occurrence that growers or merchants end up re-packing volumes of crates from one system to another in order to meet the specific channel requirements after the produce had been harvested.

A rationalisation of crate suppliers would improve overall crate pool effectiveness and efficiency and assist in creating an underlying climate within which natural market expansion can occur.

A further issue is the assumption that any new entrant must, by definition, be a national entrant. I have made referencet to the smaller 'closed loop' systems that exist already, e.g., systems that move crops such as tomatoes from growers to their packhouse.

Two other possibilities that create a different perspective on are these:

- A cross-category supplier with a strong financial relationship with supermarkets establishes a cross-category internal pool that is physically compatible with the current produce crate footprint. He then negotiates access to retailers by way of an attractive supply package based on the usual grocery industry financial incentive, but linked to the use of his own crates. The 'sunk cost' scenario is a lesser issue, because he also requires a crate washing plant in place for his internal needs. One example of a supplier who could conceivably move into this direction is a supplier, who supplies canned product, fresh and frozen poultry, frozen vegetables and chilled pasta and soup to supermarkets and other retailers.
- Other than stonefruit and mushrooms, there is very little produce that moves from the South Island to the North Island. Produce grown in the South Island tends to stay there. Foodstuffs (South Island) Limited is rapidly embracing modern supply chain management practices, which includes the public stated desire to establish and operate their own produce distribution centre. At the same time, the company is looking for closer relationships with growers, wishing to reduce its dependence on produce merchants. It is entirely feasible that Foodstuffs establishes a 'South Island only' produce crate pool. This would not take $5 million to establish, but could be achieved for considerably less.

A $5 million benchmark appears to be based upon the assumption that a new operator would have to, in any event, establish his own crate washing system.

This is not necessarily the case. If one of the current crate providers were to be faced with the reality of a supermarket wishing to establish its own pool and therefore affecting the provider's revenue stream substantially, commercial pragmatism would probably lead to the erstwhile crate provider washing the retailer's crates under contract, in order to preserve at least a portion of revenue.

Mature technology

The view has been expressed that "reusable crates are now a mature technology and there is sufficient existing capacity to meet market demand".

It could be argued that crates are anything but mature technology. One of the critical problems the crate business faces is the leakage of empty crates out of the pool system. This problem is being experienced by all parties. It is not a New Zealand problem, but one experienced in the UK and the US as well. European suppliers and retailers are therefore keen to measure leakage by way of using new intelligent chip technology into the returnable crate supply chain. Industry solutions can no longer be classified as 'mature' or 'new'.

A piece of 'mature' technology can turn 'leading edge' over night by changing a minor facet of operation, based on 'new' technology.

The following segments concerning Heineken and Sainsbury's are excerpts from presentations made at a conference on "Recent Impacts of IT on the Supply Chain", held in Holland in October 2001u.

Chip in crate

Dutch brewer Heineken saw RFID tags as a way of monitoring more effectively the rate of non-returns on crates from their distribution operations. Put simply, "what you do not measure you cannot manage", said Jan Teeuwen, Logistics Consultant, Heineken Technical Services. Heineken's level of non-returns in fact amounted to between 0.5% and 4% of its total park of 40 million crates in Europe. The company decided to pilot a RFID system, known as "Chip in Crate" (CiC), to establish a clearer pattern of non-returns. The key requirements for the chips were that they be invisible to the customer (i.e., positioned discreetly on the crate), visible to the project team and also removable for recycling purposes. A pilot involving 9,600 crates at one brewery offered data as to where the 1% of non-returns were being lost. The advantage of the chip system was that it was simple to install and provided valuable information for overall supply chain management.

Non-returns are a critical issue. Suppliers are keen to reduce supply chain costs. A crate pool operator that can offer a cost effective solution will gain favour with suppliers and supermarkets alike. This has implications for existing providers. They must grow the market in order to be able to afford the technology. Whilst existing providers attempt to grow the market, they are vulnerable to other parties able to offer the new technology solution entering the market.

A further example relates directly to the supermarket industry, Sainsbury's in this instance, which had two particular issues of concern; crate losses and the need to optimise crate flows between growers and retail.

Tracking perishables

For Sainsbury's, RFID represented a potential tool in pursuing its goal of a "simple, stockless, paperless, accurate" supply chain. The main problems affecting implementation, explained Andy Banks, Supply Chain

Development Director, were the relatively high cost (US$2 per chip in 1996) and the fragmented state of the sector, with a range of manufacturers and solution providers not linked by clear standards. Sainsbury's opted to go ahead with a pilot in 1998-1989 using chips to pallets and trays to track perishables both at distribution centres and at stores. The main benefits promised by the innovation were better information, which could be applied to whole supply chain, labour savings, reduced stock loss & more cost-effective supply chain management. However, the retailer decided not to proceed with the project as the market was not then sufficiently developed to make a major investment worthwhile. The key then for Sainsbury's in the future is to "implement proven solutions, which address specific business issues".

It is a matter of time before 'mature' technology crates will travel with imbedded chips. The cost of chips had come down to $US1.60 per chip by 2001. Is this then 'new' technology, 'upgraded' technology or 'mature' technology with a twist?

Therefore it is the writer's view that there is every prospect future technological developments will occur that will see new entry or expansion.

However, I do not agree that new entry will only occur if there is technology change. The produce industry is highly competitive and if one of the supermarkets became, either directly or indirectly, dissatisfied with one of the two incumbents, in the event of an acquisition going ahead, then it can be expected consistent with past experience that new entry will be encouraged. This would most likely involve Progressive, as it has in the past.

In closing, I would like to comment on two underlying strategic issues that emerge from the correspondence reviewed:

The Dutch produce industry felt that the Dutch market was too limiting in size to introduce anything but a standard crate managed by one industry body, the Freshcrate Foundation in which producers and retailers cooperate. The suggestion here now is that in order to keep an adequate degree of competition in the New Zealand market place, maintenance of the status quo is required. New Zealand consumers are quite price conscious, particularly when it comes to purchasing commodities. The consumer does treat produce as a commodity and has scant regard for the costs involved in producing fruit and vegetables. Supermarkets operate on slim margins which generate huge

$ returns based on volume. There is no room for 'slack' in the packaging system and supermarkets will not tolerate inefficient or uncompetitive crate providers adding unnecessary costs. Uncompetitive behaviour will cause a supermarket reaction. This will either be an invitation to another existing party to provide the service, or encouraging the creation of a new provider to take up the position.

This brings me to the second issue.

At the end of the day, supermarkets are more interested in the contents of a produce crate, than the crate itself. The crate is the means to an end. I do not believe that we will see speculative entry into the crate market without that party having received sufficient encouragement from a retailer - or another key player like a leveraged wholesaler - with sufficient market share. This encouragement is however unlikely to take the form of a formal contract. Supermarkets are notorious for not signing supply contracts for goods or services - an indication of the significant market power they exercise.

Any arrangements a perishable supermarket department enters into will only be treated as such - arrangements that are prone to change.

Having said that, I see no difficulty in a new entrant securing such an arrangement especially if the supermarket - like on the previous two occasions in the New Zealand market- wants to encourage a new entry. Provided the new entrant supplies a competitively priced product, i.e. crates, and service, then it can be reasonably confident that such an arrangement will manage any sunk cost risk. Given that the capital costs are not high, that cost would be able to be recovered within a reasonable short time span, even more so if the crates are also used in areas other than produce.

[1] Twede, D. (1999). Reusable/Returnable Plastics: European Influences and Trends. Returnable Packaging Trends in Great Britain. Promat 99. School of Packaging, Michigan State University.

[2] Maurer, J. (2003). The Brambles Application to the Commerce Commission to acquire GE Capital returnable Packaging Systems. An Industry Perspective. p13.

[3] Koehorst,H, de Vries, H., Wubben, E. (1999). Standardisation of crates: lessons from the Versfust (Freshcrate) project. Supply Chain Management. Volume 4. Number 2. pp. 95-101. MCB University Press.

[4] Maurer, J. (2003). The Brambles Application to the Commerce Commission to acquire GE Capital returnable Packaging Systems. An Industry Perspective. p17.

[5] http://www.ciesnet.com/programmes/it/executive_summary.html

Country of origin labelling & fresh produce CPR

CPR is the commonly used abbreviation for Cardiopulmonary Resuscitation, an emergency medical procedure for heart attack victims. CPR is performed in hospitals, or in the community by laypersons or by emergency response professionals. I have decided to borrow the term CPR for the purposes of this article. Only in this case CPR stands for Concern, Perception and Reality.

Country of Origin labeling is one of the hot topics that have emerged in the fresh produce industry during 2007 and are likely to stay on the forefront of debate in 2008.

Consumers are far more inquisitive today than they were a generation ago and, of course, they - or should I say *we* - have every right to know where the products on offer in a supermarket come from.

The Internet has brought the world into most suburban households at the touch of a couple of keyboard buttons and anyone with an opinion on any topic under the sun is busy blogging away, sharing his or her views, whether the rest of us like it or not. Little wonder then that our interest in just about anything has increased drastically, thus increasing our vulnerability to the machinations of 'special interest groups' exponentially.

And boy, have special interest groups been having a field day with the origin debate. This whole topic actually looks fairly innocent until once starts breaking 'origin' down into the various components that contribute to the subject matter. All these components are clustered around one driver; this driver being *concern*.

The interesting thing about *concern* is that it is not necessarily reality based. *Concern* arises when we believe we have grounds for it. These grounds may well be arising from how we perceive things rather how they actually are, but it does not matter. *Perception* is nine tenth of *reality*, isn't it? So, there.

The concerns that underpin the country of origin debate relate to wellness and the environment, seasonality and cost, the emergence of functional food and taste, as well localised economy issues.

Every one of these topics, taken on its own, is highly charged from an emotional perspective. Combined they are lethal.

What are the issues then from a horticultural/agribusiness perspective?

Seasonality

Left to their own devices, food producing plants go through a consistent and predictable cycle, regardless of where in the world they have been planted. The arrival of spring is heralded by the appearance of foliage on trees, the rising of new growth from the ground and the production of flowers. Fruit or risps will set and develop, receive nourishment during late spring and early summer, and all things being equal, harvest will take place in summer or early autumn. This sounds possibly a trifle oversimplified, but readers will get the picture.

Over the years, consumers have learned that Asparagus and Strawberries arrive at around the same time in any given season, cherries are the first stone fruit in early summer, followed by peaches, nectarines and plums. Apples are harvested from midsummer whilst Kiwifruit stay on the vine until autumn. Consumers also know, for example, that apples can be stored for a few months, whilst strawberries need to be eaten fresh or have to be turned into jam.

Seasonality used to have its limitations when someone developed a taste for fresh strawberries in winter - but the condition was not lethal and life went on.

Today, seasonality has gone out of the window, as modern storage and shipping technology has made it possible to extend shelf life with minimal conditioning loss and to airfreight fruit between continents in different hemispheres within natural shelf life parameters. Then there is SmartFresh™ - but that is a different story altogether.

Wellness

Intuitively, consumers have always been concerned about their health. In former times, when survival was the primary name of the game and choice was limited or non-existent, food was eaten and consequences were dealt with after the event; i.e., when one became sick.

In today's ultimate consumer society where the choice of food solution is enormous, the focus has switched to staying well and food choices are evaluated accordingly.

Maintaining one's wellness has become the ultimate goal and eating strawberries from Uganda, for example, is in the mind of many consumers more likely to compromise wellness than eating the 'local' equivalent.

Functional food

This topic is closely related to the wellness theme. Wouldn't it be neat if a regular feed of blueberries means I no longer have to take an Aspirin a day to reduce the risk of a heart attack? Or how about carrots which turn myth into reality and improve my failing eyesight? But wait a minute - how is functionality achieved? Better not through genetic engineering because I would not like that one little bit. And didn't I hear somewhere that some countries are a lot further down the track with this than we are in New Zealand? So, can I really trust these Californian oranges, Chilean grapes or South African asparagus?

The functional food concept is still raising more questions than it answers.

Taste

I want fruit and vegetables which taste as good as the ones my grandmother used to grow in her kitchen garden. Yes, I know the world has changed, but hey, I am the customer and that is what I want. Okay?

Well, it is and it isn't.

Of course, it is okay to have expectations based on childhood taste experiences and general perceptions. The reality, however, is that the fresh produce available in supermarkets today has to be "supply chain proof". In other words, the time and process of getting fruit from harvest to consumption is a little more complex and something has to give. What tends to have given is taste. Huge efforts are under way globally to re-inject taste into produce but the very idea has those consumers with definite ideas about the perceived risks of genetically modified food heading into the other direction. And then there are those who associate taste with origin, of course.

Environment

Environment and sustainability are also two trigger concepts that contribute to the origin debate. Let's grow more maize to produce ethanol and other biofuels to reduce our dependency on the evil black gold - oil. But, hey, what about the thousands of hectares of Amazon rainforest which are burned each year to grow more maize? And what about the shortage of stock feed in the US that is driving pork and poultry prices up? And grain farmers preferring their crops go into the biofuel supply chain rather than going down the traditional stock feed routes?

Does produce really need to be sprayed? How about growing it organically? And what about this Demeter concept I am hearing about? You know, filling a hollow cattle horn with dung and burying it in the soil at a full moon?

A more structured level of environmental protection relates to legislation like the Resource Management Act, the existence of which has spawned numerous positive schemes like the Pukekohe Sustainability Project but also creates an enormous amount of red tape.

One of the perceptions held in consumer country is that companies which are able to put produce consistently onto retail shelves must be complying with at least a base line of regulation and best practice

- and yet we know that not every country has the same tough rules as we have, don't we? Therefore..., and that is where the trouble often starts.

From a carbon foot print perspective, a lot of nonsense has come out of the UK in 2007, not least the statement that New Zealand kiwifruit are a major polluter by virtue of all the air miles they clocking up being shipped to the UK.

That ridiculous statement was easily dealt with, as Zespri categorically is not airfreighting kiwifruit. A Lincoln University report went further and conclusively proved that even shipping New Zealand lamb carcasses to the UK produced less carbon emissions that farming sheep in the UK due to different climatic conditions and consequences related to that fact. The argument will not go away though - it suits parties with vested interest!

Localised economy

Buy Kiwi made! Right - but is it 'Kiwi'? Can't tell with the salad, but, hey, I'll get a can of Heinz-Wattie tomatoes. There is a local brand if ever there was one. Actually, the Heinz bit of the brand is global and the brand balance has been compromised to the extent that the tomatoes in the can are more likely to be Spanish, Greek or Thai. What is local anyway? A twenty kilometer radius around the Central Post Office in Putaruru?

So where do these courgettes come from again? Auckland? Get out of here! I want local produce - here we go again! 'Local' means different things to different people.

Cost

Does everything really come down to cost in the end? Shouldn't Hawke's Bay tomatoes be preferable to Thai ones because they are growing just here on my doorstep for goodness sake? That may be so

- but the local Hawke's Bay harvest picker is likely to earn $12 an hour where as her Thai equivalent earns 500 Baht a day - US$15 more or less. What is more cost effective? Shipping Gisborne lettuces to Christchurch or shooting them across the Tasman?

And if I insist on only buying organically produced fruit, can I really expect to pay no more than a pittance per kg, because the crop is in season right now and plentiful?

Concerns, perception & reality

Consumers are clearly rushing around their daily life with an abundance of concerns floating around in their heads. Unfortunately, these concerns are not pursuing single trajectories but are multifaceted and in many cases interrelated. That represents a problem when it comes to addressing these concerns in order to alter perception. Focus too much on cost and any concerns for the environment will have to go out of the window. Rigidly supporting the local economies will cause a reduction in food choice which in turn heightens awareness and concerns about wellness and health related issues.

Ask for better tasting fruit and you may well have to modify your stance on genetic activity.

The reality is that the debate related to country of origin labeling is nothing but window dressing for a bundled group of underlying concerns which not every consumer is prepared to articulate up front. Will moving to country of origin labeling address all these concerns and satisfy every consumer?

Of course, not - but it would be a good start towards performing comprehensive fresh produce CPR!

I am an advocate of country of origin labeling for a very basic reason. The fresh produce industry faces enough substantial challenges without providing grandstanding politicians with profiling opportunities which have the potential to cause confusion, disruption and mistrust in the produce value chain.

An industry where business transactions are still largely based on handshakes rather than contracts cannot afford uncertainty, a decrease in trust and more confusion.

What we really need to do so, as an industry, is to find solutions to the real consumer concerns hiding behind the country of origin debate.

Fresh produce CPR will therefore hang around as a topic of mine, so watch out!

A retailer's summerfruit reflections

I was Produce Merchandise Manager for Foodtown 1989-1993 and held the same role for the wider Progressive Enterprises Group 1996-1998.

<u>The environment</u>

The year is 1988. September, to be precise. The Internet, Sky TV and Palm Pilots have yet to be invented. Fax machines are proving their worth as a marvellous new communication tool. Mobile telephones are available, expensive and best transported with the aid of a wheelbarrow.

Foodtown has 30 stores. 3 of these are in Hamilton, 1 each in Tauranga, Palmerston North and Wellington, the balance are in Auckland.

Produce buyers will shortly be introduced to computer systems and major behavioural change is on its way.

The company is about to stop relying upon the auction system for its Auckland produce purchases, although the practice will continue for a year longer in out of town stores.

Foodtown's produce buyers are taking a day-by day approach to the purchasing patterns for most domestic produce, but there are exceptions.

Summerfruit is one such exception. Or to be more specific - Hawke's Bay Summerfruit. It is possible to be even more specific - Yummy brand Hawke's Bay peaches and nectarines.

Yummy's owner and co-creator, a third generation fruit grower called John Paynter, was - and still is - an intelligent, visionary, commercially focused individual with an eye for opportunity.

John had realised in the mid-eighties that direct grower/ retailer relationships were needed to secure the future of his annual crops and assure stable return on investment. He also understood intuitively that consumers were looking for fruit that consistently looked good, tasted good and was priced attractively and with a degree of predictability.

<u>The deal</u>

The business model that had evolved by 1989 looked like this:

- Foodtown was purchasing early and late season peaches and nectarines on the open market.
- During the mid-season, i.e. through January and most of February, Foodtown purchased Yummy fruit.

- Yummy fruit wholesale prices were set by the Yummy team.
- The retail prices for Yummy fruit were also set by the Yummy team.
- Yummy handled the Foodtown relationship directly but used Turners & Growers to facilitate supply.
- John Paynter spent a considerable amount of time during the season travelling around Auckland stores, interacting with store produce managers on all aspects of fruit handling, including storage and merchandising.
- During the weeks John was unable to do so, a selected Turners & Growers account executive was tasked with that job and equipped with a camera so he could report back instantly - as instantly as was possible in those days.

<u>Why did it work?</u>

There were a number of reasons why this rather unique arrangement worked for several years:

- Foodtown buyers viewed this deal as a solution to a problem. Peaches and nectarines are a substantial part of the fruit business during the summer months and the Yummy deal represented a saving in time and energy.
- John's fruit was of high quality and his attention to detail in terms of post-harvest handling was substantially ahead of its time. Harvested fruit was moved faster into cool stores than was usual grower practice and the entire process of shifting fruit along the supply chain was carefully thought through, before the term "supply chain" became the buzzword of the nineties. Even the tractors used to move field bins had been fitted with a softer suspensions to reduce damage during the initial journey into the cool store.
- The fruit lived up to its promise in terms of taste and appearance and the consumer responded through repeat purchase. Foodtown was therefore prepared to back Yummy fruit through advertising, which drove sales further. The fruit was however not discounted at loss-leader level.
- Yummy was the first grower brand of any significance that featured prominently in the retail produce area and consumers started asking for the brand by name.

<u>What has happened since?</u>

- Foodtown decided to discontinue the Yummy supply agreement in 1990. The company had passed from local ownership into the hands of

Australian retail giant Coles Myer and the notion of a supplier setting fresh food retail prices was unacceptable to the new management team.

- Yummy built on the strength of its brand and started to supply New World instead.
- The brand was subsequently migrated into pipfruit and Yummy markets its own fruit on the Auckland Turners' floor.

<u>What went on in Foodtown's mind at the time?</u>

- The company wanted to expand its direct purchasing agreements with growers but needed a common platform. Having individual suppliers set retail prices was not seen as a desirable way forward.
- Similarly, Foodtown was looking for a total Summerfruit supply solution, which included other parts of the season, other fruit that formed part of the category and a different supply region.
- Pipfruit and banana deregulation were the major strategic initiatives of the day. Summerfruit was not perceived to be in the same league.
- The Foodtown team was not entirely comfortable with the intensity and depth of Yummy's desire to influence the behaviour of its trading partner.

<u>What can be learned for 2004 and beyond?</u>

- Growers, Wholesalers and Retailers are components of a supply chain, which ends with the consumer who decides whether to purchase or not.
- A consistent consumer success experience is only achievable when the supply components involved cooperate.
- Retailers prefer "package solutions" which make their life easier.
- Taste and appearance are the key criteria by which the consumer judges Summerfruit.
- Fruit needs to be treated "right" in order for it to taste and look "right".
- Shortcuts will eventually backfire and should be avoided at all costs.
- There needs to be regular and focused interaction between grower and retailer, ideally wrapped into a communication package that caters for the different learning styles - visual, written and oral.
- Retailers don't want to be told what to do.
- Branding and advertising works.

The great kiwifruit debate

Is there room for alternatives to bunker mentality and scorched earth approaches?

In September 2009, I gave the keynote address at a Dutch Produce Industry Conference, my topic being fresh produce value chain economics. One of the questions I was asked at the conclusion of my presentation by a Dutch produce importer was, "why is it that weeks before the onion export season from New Zealand officially starts, I receive unsolicited offers from at least eight different New Zealand onion exporters, each trying to offer the lowest price to secure the business? I don't understand why your country is prepared to leave so much money on the table. Of course, I'll take it, but is this really necessary?"

I did not know how to answer that question honestly without opening myself to libel suits back here in God's own - but I certainly was not unfamiliar with this topic.

I had spent a fair amount of my energy in the twelve months leading up to August 2009 on being part of the strategic advisory group that worked with Horticulture New Zealand and Deloitte on the development of the industry strategy aimed at creating sales of $10 billion in 2020. Some vigorous debate had occurred during advisory group meetings on the amount of money (thought to be at least $200 million annually) the horticultural industry as a whole was indeed leaving "on the table" through lack of foresight and internal competition in trade matters.

One of the debates that was rekindled in 2009 relates to the single desk selling activities of the kiwifruit industry.

One of the business strategists I have admired for the last quarter of a century, Kenichi Ohmae, wrote in The Mind of a Strategist (1982) that "long study of communist and socialist regimes has convinced many observers that detailed long-range planning coupled with tight controls from the centre is a remarkably effective way of killing creativity and entrepreneurship at the extremity of the organisation, the individuals who make it up."

No one in their right mind could accuse the New Zealand kiwifruit industry being communist - kiwifruit growers understand the law of profit far too well to make such an accusation stick. It can however, not be denied that the kiwifruit industry follows several principles that could loosely be described as socialist in their nature, including the single desk concept itself, the ownership of the single desk vehicle; i.e, Zespri, the allocation method of the crop to vessels, the payment pool system, as well as the overriding criterion by which all collaborative marketing proposals are judged - namely, "will the proposal add value for growers".

And the industry is not exactly the fastest in the innovation stakes, Kiwi Gold notwithstanding.

Is it possible to apply a label to the single desk selling system Zespri is enjoying? It is certainly not market socialism, as I have heard it repeatedly referred to, as the means of production; i.e., orchards, are not publically or collectively owned.

A study into the single desk phenomenon by the Provincial Government of Alberta, Canada (Carter & Loins, 1996) expresses the view that single desk selling is comparable to "new trade policy" in economics, which suggests "the possibility that government intervention in trade may be in the national interest". The study identifies a number of theoretical rationales offered in support of the single desk selling concept, but deems all but one rationale offered as "spurious".

The one exception is the suggested rationale that a single desk operation is able to increase revenue through price differentiation as a result of wielding market power.

Closer to our shores, an Australian researcher determined that "nominal food product marketing margins had increased over time." At the same time, "retail prices increased more rapidly than farm prices and the farmers' share has declined." (Griffin, 2004).

The researcher than proceeded to examine whether a relationship existed between the ability of food retailers Woolworths and Coles to grow exponentially the way they have and the decline of margin share available to farmers. As one would expect, he did not come to a clear cut conclusion. His data however showed that "for a wide range of food products real marketing margins have remained stable or risen slowly but real retail prices have fallen, implying real farm-gate prices have fallen at a greater rate than real retail prices" (Griffin, 2004).

Why would farm gate prices fall at a greater rate than retail prices? Numerous theories have been advanced on that topic over the years but they all come back to a single argument - market power, and in particular, the concentration of market power on an unprecedented scale in the history of global trade in the hands of a dozen or so players (supermarket chains) around the world.

On that basis, one can understand the reluctance displayed by the majority of kiwifruit growers to see their single desk approach tampered with.

On the other hand, the concept of national interest is a double edged sword when it comes to international trade negotiations. The New Zealand kiwifruit single desk appeared to have survived scrutiny by the WTO, as an STE, a state trading enterprise, because it does not receive government subsidies. That all changed in November 2009 when a WTO "please explain" notice was issued which also involved the US White House.

Turners & Growers do have a point. Not only is the company a grower in its own right, albeit a corporate one, but it is of a size that it feels it can add value to its own crop and that of others without being tightly bound into Zespri's collective approach which does not allow it to harvest the fruits of its investments in research and innovation.

Companies have directors and the role of directors is fairly clearly spelt out in the Commerce Act. Directors of companies such as Turners & Growers which are zeroing in on the kiwifruit single desk are actually doing nothing other than acting in the best interests of their own company, which is something they are compelled to do under the provisions of the Commerce Act.

Yet, if letting market forces prevail means I get asked the same question I was asked about onions with regards to kiwifruit in a couple of years - is it really worth it?

Can we really afford to tamper with the industry's consistently most successful export crop which in many ways actually underpins the entire industry?

Anyone who looks at the high and lows of the New Zealand kiwifruit industry over a period of time and who has maintained his or her ability for rational thought will reach the conclusion that there is no right or wrong answer if the only two options on the table are 'single desk' or 'total deregulation'.

Could there be another possible answer?

Let's briefly revert to the concept of market power. The market power of global retailers is clearly understood. Another supply chain link with increasing market power are shipping companies, which is particularly relevant for a country sitting at the cold end of the South Pacific trying to send perishable produce to Europe, Asia and the Americas. It makes sense therefore, to optimise freight rates by way of a consolidated approach.

So, if the need to exercise market power from a shipping and offshore retail perspective requires no extended debate because the benefits are evident to all concerned, is there a model that could work better than the single desk in place currently and the ones already tried and cast aside?

Changing what appears to be a successful model is always accompanied by risk, regardless of the industry in question. But the fact that the current Zespri single desk model is the envy of other local primary producers such as meat and wool growers is no guarantee that it can survive in its current format. This is especially so as the traditional boundaries between growers, packers and exporters are beginning to blur in other fresh produce industries and kiwifruit is no exception.

I could see a model succeeding that is based on

- Zespri being maintained as the common New Zealand kiwifruit brand,
- The fruit being marketed offshore by an integrated exporters' collective which is also responsible for single desk shipping negotiations,
- The exporters' collective determining the best approach for each market based on pooled intelligence made available by its members,
- Innovation, research and development being a core commitment expected from all export collective members for the greater good of the industry.

And in order to avoid reinventing the wheel, the simple commercial solution to achieve this model is for New Zealand Kiwifruit Growers Inc, the owners of Zespri, to sell 45% of the company for a solid commercial consideration to suitably qualified and responsible free market produce exporters; e.g. Turners & Growers and others, and export capable commercial entities such as Zespri's current onshore supply managers.

In conclusion, I offer these comments:

We cannot consider anything set in concrete these days. The only certainty we have is that the pace of change will continue to accelerate. Black and white answers based on 'yes' or 'no' or 'do' or 'don't' cannot always solve complex issues. Graduated solutions based on workable compromise may therefore need to emerge - and this means graduated proposals need to be articulated in the first place so that they can be debated.

It is in this spirit that this contribution should be considered.

References

Carter, C.A. & Loins, R.M.A. (1996). The Economics of Single Desk Selling of Western Canadian Grain. Department of Agriculture and Rural Development. Government of Alberta. Canada.

Griffith, G.R. (2004). The Impact of Supermarkets on Farm Suppliers. Australian Economic Review. Vol. 37 Issue 3, p329-336, 8p.

Ohmae, K. (1982). The Mind of the Strategist. Business Planning for Competitive Advantage. Penguin. New York.

New Zealand short story icon Frank Sargeson was actually a bit of a produce marketing expert as well

Where to in 2008? Where I discuss the fundamental differences between New Zealand and Australian produce supply structures with the help of Frank Sargeson.

New Zealand short story master Frank Sargeson summed up the essence of the risk involved in supplying produce markets in 1941.

"If you grew something for sale, he found out, particularly if it was something that would not keep, you mainly had to take just what people would pay for it, even though you might get a lot less than would pay for the work and expense it had cost you."

Sargeson made these comments in a story entitled " A Man of Good Will" - a story that described the relationship between the writer as a boy and *"a tomato grower who was supposed to be eccentric."*

Sargeson's comments are as relevant today as they were in 1941. A little further on in the story Sargeson's eccentric tomato grower takes matters a bit further.

"Well, the world was a funny place, he said, you'd strike people who'd grumble over the price of tomatoes when it hardly paid you for the work of picking them, yet if you'd ask those people to work for such little return they'd had properly hit the roof."

Little has changed today, 67 years later.

Growing tomatoes, or any other fresh produce for that matter, without having a market for the produce is a big risk and invariably growers end up having to take what buyers are prepared to pay for it. Yet by the time this produce for which no one can determine a firm price until the buyer is prepared to offer one reaches the supermarket shelves, a price ticket has miraculously emerged and on the basis of the cost price paid to the grower, the retailer has created a price for the consumer which very much so tries to make sure that all costs the retailer has incurred in handling the produce are covered and accounted for.

And a profit needs to be made as well, of course.

Sargeson had figured this inequality in approach out as well and that was before supermarkets had become the dominant force they are today.

"And this was a different thing from the big store he had worked in", said Sargeson, "where you usually managed to buy at one price and sell at another that would always keep you on the right side. You did not wait until you were offered a price, no, you mainly got the price you asked for."

Sargeson died in 1982 and the world has moved on since but not sufficiently enough to make his comments irrelevant.

The produce industry is still very fickle. New supply channels have opened up, consolidation has occurred in the production and retail sectors alike, and growing produce is no longer a marginal land based activity hovering at subsistence level. A 10ha size glasshouse complex is considered an economic production unit and as a consequence, consumers now have access to New Zealand grown tomatoes 52 weeks of the year which had not always been the case. It is easier for retailers to predict consumer demands because local tomatoes are on the shelf all year around and price fluctuations are moderate by comparison.

Similarly, the influence of the domestic produce wholesale sector in writing domestic supermarket business has reduced. Supermarket buyers are forever trying to get closer to the grower, partially in their desire to optimise margins and partially due to indirect consumer pressure in relation to product knowledge. That's how things work in New Zealand - or at least that how they used to work here.

One of the country's supermarket chains, Progressive, has now been owned by Australian connections since 1987. Melbourne based Coles Myer bought Foodtown and 3 Guys at that time and, boy, were they going to set the world on fire. What a wonderful opportunity they said, for the New Zealand grocery industry to benefit from the superior skills of the Australian retail mindset. And off we went on our roller coaster ride. Six years down the track, with the New Zealand experiment having failed to deliver the required the corporate returns and after having totally mismanaged Progressive's marketplace position vis-à-vis Foodstuffs, Coles Myer sold out to Foodlands. A short while after withdrawing from New Zealand, the then Coles Myer Managing Director Brian Quinn resigned from his position to take up a new role: inmate of Her Australian Majesty's Loddon Prison in central Victoria after having been found guilty of misappropriating company funds for private gains - specifically, having his mansion in one of Melbourne's exclusive suburbs renovated by the Coles Myer stores maintenance division and having a heated swimming pool installed on the property, all to the tune of A$4.5 million!

Foodlands merged its newly acquired Foodtown and 3 Guys supermarkets initially with the already owned Countdown chain and a few years later, in 2002, merged it with the New Zealand Woolworths supermarket group, freshly purchased from the Dairy Farm group when that company decided to exit Australia and New Zealand.

Throughout the years under Foodland ownership, West Australian fresh produce business models were being investigated, trialled and rejected at what must have been at considerable cost to Progressive.

Rejected, interestingly enough, for two reasons. Firstly, there was an absolute limit to the ability of what amounted to a bunch of Perth and Hinterland based provincial owner/operator grocers, who only came together under the Foodland banner for the purpose of grocery wholesale benefits, to direct the fortunes of a substantial corporate New Zealand food retailer by remote control from WA.

Secondly, by now the New Zealand model had started to actually work quite well. It was generally understood which grower was targeting which market. There were still no supply contracts in place, the produce industry is not too keen on those, being commodity based and all, but the system worked. Larger growers were establishing packhouses and coordinating the activities of other growers as well. The supermarket retailer committed to direct supply was benefiting through knowing that its demands for consistency in supply, grade and quality were being met without causing a logistics nightmare in the distribution centre. The supplying grower/packer benefited by enjoying a degree of certainty related to supply, which generated the confidence for capital investment needed to satisfy the demand of the retailer who had by now grown to 185+ stores.

Now the company is owned by its third Australian owner in 20 years. This one is from Sydney. Not surprisingly, this one also believes that the Australian fresh produce supply model is the cat's whiskers and far superior to anything developed locally in New Zealand.

But unlike the previous two, the Woolworths Group is neither inept nor preoccupied by the CEO's swimming pool or similar activities. This one is determined to bring the Australian model into the New Zealand, come hell or high water.

Is this a bad thing? Don't they have a right to do what they like - after all, they own the joint?

Ownership does, of course, grant certain privileges, but ownership needs to be seen within context. The context that matters in this particular equation is that New Zealand is not a state of Australia but an independent nation which operates an economic model that has evolved separately from its Australian counterpart. The New Zealand economic model is based on several facts that fundamentally define the difference between New Zealand and Australia.

New Zealand has 4 million citizens compared to Australia's 21 million. We are an island nation, with the largest two islands separated by a 4 hour ferry ride, whereas Australia is a continent and the distance between Sydney and Perth is covered by a 4 hour jet plane ride. New Zealand's wealth (or lack thereof…) is based on an agricultural commodity producing structure geared for export, whereas Australia's wealth is mineral resource based. New Zealand's tangata whenua are somewhat more integrated into main stream society than Australia's Aborigines, although there is always room for improvement. New Zealand's climate is a Mediterranean island climate where temperature extremes are the exception rather than the norm. Australia is far closer to the Equator and temperature extremes are the norm rather than an exception. New Zealand imports its bananas, whilst Australia bans the importation of bananas in order to protect its inefficient domestic industry.

I could go on but readers will get my point.

How many suppliers per crop category are needed, in order to ensure competition principles are in play? The answer is - it depends. It depends on market size, the nature of the category itself, the level of investment required to turn out quality produce on a consistent basis and the degree of sophistication demanded by the consumer.

There is a limit to how many tomato packhouse and production complexes, for example, the New Zealand economy can sustain, given the size of the market, the cost per m^2 of glasshouse, and the way demand is spread across the country.

Forcing the local horticultural industry back into an outdated central market based business model just because it is believed to work well in Australia - an opinion which this writer would beg to differ with in any event - is not only shortsighted and unwise, but also detrimental to the New Zealand economy as a whole. So why should we be subjected to this? On the basis of foreign ownership?

I never thought I would find myself in agreement with the Rt. Hon. Winston Peters, but I must say I am rapidly coming to the conclusion that he has a point in his campaign to expose the folly of foreign ownership of New Zealand assets.

Growers, including tomato growers, have the right to earn an income from their work on the land as well as a return on their investment. When they can't and lose hope, they rebel. Here is Sargeson again:

"He should have been nailing up cases in the packing shed but I didn't hear him, though when he called me to lunch I noticed as I went past that the tomatoes we'd picked the afternoon before had all disappeared. He was drying his hands off outside on the verandah and straightoff he said, Come and tell me if I have made a good job. So we went down the length of the glasshouse to the front of the section, and there, just inside the gate, he'd put all the tomatoes in a heap. Not just an ordinary heap though, he'd built them up into a sort of pyramid, the way you see them in shop windows, only this one was a monster."

If Woolworths persists with its determination to change the way the New Zealand produce industry operates - and there is no indication to suggest otherwise - there will by necessity be a realignment of how the various supply channels in existence across the industry will source the produce required to keep the supply lines humming. And, of course, the industry will survive, although some participants may not and some supply channels will dry up or become unrecognisable.

The New Zealand produce supply system will, however, never work the work the way it works in Australia, because this is New Zealand, not Australia and even big supermarket chains cannot change some of the key geographical, demographical and economical differences that exist between the two countries.

Sargeson's tomato grower was a determined fellow:

"And besides leaving the heap of tomatoes there, he was all the time making it bigger with every lot that we picked. One morning I turned up for work and struck him having an argument with our carrier. It was our main market day, and the carrier had made his call to pick up the cases we'd normally have been sending into town. My boss was saying he wasn't sending anything in, and the carrier was pointing to the heap and asking what the big idea was. I stood listening, and my boss just laughed and said, No my friend, until the carrier got annoyed, and drove off after shaking my boss's hand from his arm, and telling him he was clean off his rocker."

Most growers have their own trucks these days, typically temperature controlled and efficiently loaded and unloaded, a benefit of having certainty of supply and being able to make capital investment decisions with a degree of confidence. Asking the truck driver to deliver the produce elsewhere in future will be the easy part of any new way of doing business.

Change is inevitable and there is nothing more certain than change. Robust businesses are able to manage change, survive and prosper, but change needs to make sense in order to be embedded and become the new norm - and change needs to benefit the entire value chain from consumer to grower in order to be sustainable.

Opinions

Where I have pulled together a number of short, and at one time or other topical views, expressed in weekly newsletters or monthly trade publications between 1998 and 2008.

5+ A Day on a Saturday?

The soccer season has started again in earnest. As the boys are getting older, their games are no longer at the crack of dawn. I had also managed to talk my older son out of playing for the school as well as the club on the same day. He would have probably been able to handle it - but there is a limit of how many places one can be at the same time. That's before one starts factoring netball and the demands of the daughter into the equation. She doesn't just want to be taken places, but she wants to drive there herself - in my car, naturally.

Anyway, there I was standing at the sideline with all the other parents. Believe it or not, I am actually not one of the rowdy ones - but I got a bit noisy today.

My 'performance' had nothing to do with the activities on the soccer field, but with a half-time occurrence.

Thomas is playing in a different team this year. New coach, new manager, new faces all around.

Those of you with kids playing team sports would be familiar with the half time ritual of orange segments being handed out to the exhausted players to revitalise their energy levels. This is particularly popular with junior teams and I had not seen it happening with my guys for the last couple of years or so.

I got to the game a little late and whilst the sun was shining there was a chill in the air. I was therefore wearing my sleeveless "5+A Day" vest. The logo really stands out on the black vest and it always causes a comment or two when people see it. It surprises me just how many people are actually familiar with the "5+A Day" message, given the advertising onslaught we are faced with each day.

At halftime one of the mothers rushed onto the field to hand out what I presumed to be orange segments to the players. The team had not come to the sideline. The half time 'pep talk' was happening near the penalty area.

When the mother returned, I noticed to my sheer amazement that she had not been handing out fruit, but lollies.

I am afraid I lost the plot at that point. I purposefully approached the lolly dispenser and asked her what she thought she was doing. To which she replied, "providing the boys with an energy fix".

As you can imagine, I was not impressed with that response, but I won't bother you with the exchange that then took place.

Some things better remain unprinted.

5+A Day has until now focused its attention on schools and health professionals to get its message across.

Parents of sports playing children and teenagers appear to be an untapped 'market' if my experience is anything to go by.

Where are they best reached? On the sideline. How should the message be transmitted? Possibly by way of the 5+A Day bus making the rounds on a Saturday morning, stopping at major sports venues and offering free fruit snacks to sports playing children and parents alike.

Has anyone got a better idea?

Compromise

I have been focusing on silly things this week. You know, trying to answer questions such as:

- Why do company vehicles suddenly qualify as 'places of work' and need first aid kits? Don't drivers of other cars need first aid kits as well?
- Why does the Airport Authority bother issuing licences to shuttle operators if it has no intention of enforcing them?
- How do you teach someone the difference between strategy and tactics, if the individual in question thinks Darth Vadar was one of the twelve apostles?

Here is another one that fits into the same league.

- Why would a retailer want to advertise something that he does not have for sale?

Well, the short answer is - he probably does not want to. It usually happens when there is a glitch in the planning cycle, human error or in the case of fresh produce - the produce is not where it is meant to be.

It does sound silly, I admit, but consider this.

- Supermarket catalogues are planned weeks in advance.
- Baked beans, frozen chickens and dishwashing liquid can be called upon with relative ease.
- Even the butchers will manage to slaughter a beast and turn it into steak, as long as they have enough time to move the animal through the process.
- What options does a produce buyer have, though, when the lettuce that is advertised at 99 cents a head is suddenly frosted - without replacement in sight?

Sure, customers can be sent home with a 'rain check', but things are often not quite so simple. The worst case scenario involves stock being around, but in short supply. It is not unheard of that supermarket buyers in those instances end up with very unhappy suppliers who are held to previously negotiated prices or they manage to blow a substantial part of the department's gross profit on just buying enough stock to honour the advertised special.

Or both.

Does this have to be the case? Not necessarily, but it will continue to be a problem for as long as supermarket marketing departments have unrealistic expectations of their produce divisions in terms of working to deadlines.

Four week deadlines to confirm product and price is often not realistic in an industry which is still very much commodity based and the supply situation can change overnight.

Producing a catalogue is all about achieving compromise - balancing the needs of all departments, selling an allocating space, getting the product mix right, avoiding conflict and repetition and taking account of seasonal requirements and consumer taste.

Compromise needs to be extended to timing, deadlines and flexibility. The Cauliflower crop may, for example, be hit by a hailstorm, 24 hours before cut-off - it might not suit everyone involved to pull the product, but this might just have to happen to avoid damaging long-term relationships or losing money by the bucketful.

And before I forget - compromise is all about talking and listening to one another's points of view and constraints.

Instant accessibility - curse or opportunity?

The Internet provides fascinating opportunities, apart from being able to have instant access to information from around the world. People also use it to play games. You can find a fabulous game server at *www.yahoo.com*. I use it from time to time when I need to clear my mind from clutter, especially when I need to shift gear between my three roles - business adviser, teacher and journalist.

The range of games found on that server is endless. I only play two games there, 'Go' and 'Literati'.

Go is an ancient strategy game played predominantly in Japan. Literati is basically 'Scrabble', but it cannot be called that because of trade mark issues.

There are no trademark issues with Go. It is at least a thousand years old and Go scholars believe that it originated in China.

To compare Go with Chess would be doing both games an injustice, but the roles both games have played within their respective societies is indeed comparable.

Being a Kiwikraut based in New Zealand with an interest in playing a game of Chinese origin that was predominantly played in Japan did cause me certain logistical difficulties for many years.

There is actually a Go Club in Auckland, but I just found that too restricting.

The Internet has sure changed my life in that respect.

I can play Go now when the mood takes me - no need to find a partner who is willing and able and available 3 nights from now. No more driving across Auckland to a dingy community hall. I don't even have to go to the cupboard to find the box that contains the game and I am certainly no longer dropping game pieces all over the carpet in my excitement at the next possible move.

Major change, wouldn't you say?

And you know, the frightening thing is that this change has so easily become absorbed into my life that it is now second nature. As long as I can find my computer, I can play games - and do all the other things I use my computer for.

Only - this also means I have become instantly accessible as well. Not just to other game players, but also in the wider sense.

It used to be that when one hopped onto a plane out of New Zealand, one literally became incommunicado for 36 hours. A good time to gather one's thoughts, plan the next strategy, review the year to date, etc.

No longer possible I am afraid. Anne-Marie Arts is in Holland at present, attending a conference on post-harvest quality assurance issues in the produce supply chain. She is our financial director and prior to her take-off she sent a flurry of instructions to me relating to our financial and treasury activities.

Once I knew she was on that plane, I thought, "Now I can get on with things for a couple of days before she gets me to do something else."

Wrong.

She can't have been off the ground for longer than 90 minutes and I suddenly received another e-mail from her. This time courtesy of Singapore Airlines, which has equipped its fleet with e-mail capable personal entertainment centres for every passenger!

George Orwell's 'Big Brother' concept, as laid out in his famous novel '1984', has well and truly taken hold and we don't even register it any more.

Coffee or peaches-the principle is the same

Regular readers of the Sauerkraut Corner already know that I don't like the coffee on offer at the Millenium Centre. The choice there is Nescafe or Nescafe.

This morning I therefore decided, having dropped my son off at the Centre for his morning's surf life saving winter training, to venture into Brown's Bay and combine the consumption of a decent cup of coffee with stocking up on groceries.

Brown's Bay Foodtown has a franchised coffee shop on its premises; managed by an independent operator, not by the supermarket chain itself.

I had just ordered a latte for take-out and was watching the barrista going through the brewing motions, when my phone rang.

The friend at the other end wished to know what I was up to. Having received the desired information, she said, "What are you doing buying your coffee from [that outlet]. Their coffee tastes like &%#@ !"

As we live in a free and democratic society where everyone is entitled to their opinion, I couldn't really do much about this statement, delivered with clarity, conviction and a decibel level that lent itself to this damning verdict being broadcasted to anyone standing within a two metre radius of the phone - which, apart from myself, unfortunately also included the barrista, whose facial features changed in an instant from 'sunny' to 'storm clouds approaching fast'. My coffee was shortly thereafter placed in front of me with a certain degree of firmness and I beat a hasty retreat, whilst making a mental note to recommend the master class at Swiss Finishing School to the caller at the earliest possible opportunity.

The coffee wasn't actually half bad (make of that what you like) - but perception is often 9/10th of reality. If you think you won't enjoy the taste experience, you obviously won't go anywhere near that particular coffee brand. At one stage or other the taste had not been enjoyed and a negative memory anchor had been created. The mere mention of the coffee brand triggered instant recall, which manifested itself in the opinion proffered.

The same principles apply to the consumption of seasonal fruit. Summer fruit is a classic example.

Every year supermarkets are trying to outdo each other in getting the first of the new season's peaches and nectarines into their stores.

Quality and taste are often relegated to the 'bench' with availability being the overriding concern. Growers of early varieties know that supermarkets are often not so fussy at the commencement of the season and can aggravate the situation by harvesting too soon, ignoring acceptable brix levels and fruit flesh pressure in favour of the chance for a higher return.

How many customers are likely to come back for a second bite of the cherry, pardon the pun, if their initial taste experience has them running to the oral surgeon to have their teeth prized apart again, the sour taste of the fruit having removed their spittle in a nanosecond and their mouths feeling like they had had stand-alone epileptic fits?

Not many I would suggest. May be we can get this right this year

- given that the consumer will have high expectations after this winter's high impact Californian summer fruit season.

Read the book

I don't get to see the news very often during the week. 6 o'clock is just too early for sitting down for half an hour and watching the box. On the days I do watch, I usually get annoyed three or four minutes into the bulletins. Some of the stuff presented as "news" is, at least in my view, totally insignificant and a waste of time and money. The critical bits of information one ought to know get hidden between the irrelevant, superfluous and politically correct elements.

I was therefore delighted to discover a condensed summary of weekly New Zealand news on the Australian Sky News network. It presents the real newsworthy stories of the week gone by as screened on TV3 and is well worth watching.

I certainly learned something from watching this morning and I didn't like the implications.

The couple of disturbing things I am referring to were:

- the Prime Minister had not read Nicky Hager's book on the alleged genetic corn cover-up when she started attacking book and author so energetically prior to last year's election.
- When this fact emerged during the select committee hearing on the genetics and the moratorium last week, Helen Clark responded in a televised press conference to the question whether she would read the book now with, "Why should I? I have better things to do."
- Well, Ms Clark, you can't have it both ways. Politics is a dirty game and all too frequently do political conflicts turn into personal mud slinging, which can be very unpleasant and should ideally not take place. At the same time, I find it difficult to understand what gives the elected leader of this country the authority to refer to an interviewer (TV3's John Campbell) as 'the little twerp' or words to that effect, when she didn't like his line of questioning. He, at least, had bothered to read the book!

On matters of authority more specifically aimed at the practical issues in the produce industry - a store produce manager should be given the authority to ban certain grocery items from 'being slipped' into the produce department merchandise area. It doesn't matter how appealing the department looks, a display of Persil washing powder in a prime location at the entrance to the produce department is not a smart idea and will negatively affect produce sales. Customers do not want to see this type of merchandise when they are busy selecting the contents of their fruit bowls. Please relocate this stuff ASAP.

And while you are at it, what is the point of taking Bobby Bananas out of their bags and selling them loose for 10 cents per kg more than what you get for an 850 gram pre-pack? The combination of that brain wave and the rotting Californian cherries selling at $12.95/ kg ensured the store made a lasting impression on me.

Store managers and owner/operators might want to do from time to time what the Prime Minister clearly has no interest in:

Read the book! In your case, it's the merchandise manual issued by your respective support office. Trust me - reading does pay off in the long run.

Why produce managers need to think

There are produce departments - and then there are produce departments. Yes, it is late at night, and yes I have fortified myself with a medicinal glass of single malt Scotch, but I still make perfect sense. Even if I say so myself.

What could I possibly mean with such an opening statement?

Let me put it this way.

In some produce departments every item I might look for is available, but the stock is either old, not properly ticketed, picked through and generally unappealing. There are other produce departments that are missing the basics - like no apricots in the stonefruit season or no bananas at midnight.

And then there are produce departments where every item positively stands to attention, looks fresh and inviting, inspiring me to aim for hitherto unscaled culinary heights.

What determines where your produce department fits?

It is, in my view, usually the produce manager. Yes, produce buyers and category managers play a role as well and yes, the produce manager usually does not determine the size of the department.

A skilled, committed and constructively articulate produce manager is, however, in the position of influencing those factors not directly under his or her control, such as buying and departmental foot print.

It is usually the produce manager who orders the fruit and vegetables required. It is the produce manager's job to receive and process the produce deliveries to the point where the produce is ready to be brought into the retail area. The store manager or owner/operator relies on the produce manager to ensure shoppers receive an overall positive impression of the entire store through being able to shop in a well stocked and presented produce department.

What then makes a successful produce manager?

In short - a successful produce manager understands two aspects very well.

1. Produce, by definition, is perishable and only lasts for a limited amount of time. Time is therefore of the essence.
2. Management can be defined as "directing for a purpose". All actions and reactions that occur within a successful produce department are therefore carried out for a reason.

When combining these two strands, we find that the successful produce manager usually does everything for a reason and within a tight time frame due to the perishability of the produce.

In practice this means, for example, a successful produce manager does not 'guess' the size of the daily order, he 'assesses' his needs. Assessing involves understanding average daily sales volumes, daily customer count patterns, the price/quality/attractiveness formula of an about to be ordered item, the delay factor between order issued and receipt of goods, the time of year, the short-term weather forecast, supply options and competitor reactions.

In short, a produce manager needs to be a thinker as well as a doer. Are we currently doing enough to encourage the next crop of 'thinking' produce managers? Judging by the state of some of the produce departments I get to see around the country - I think not.

Industry matters

I attended a ministerial function last week at Parliament last week, which had a dual purpose. Firstly, it introduced a new HEA report on tariffs and non-tariff barriers applicable to our horticultural export crops in other countries. Secondly, it provided the launch pad for the Fruitgrower's Federation careers in horticulture video - "Top of the Crop".

Both initiatives are very worthwhile, as well as thought provoking.

As a nation we still depend on primary exports for a large share of our revenue. Horticultural exports have grown exponentially over the last 30 years, but still can't compete with milk powder in terms of value.

Our own industry is deregulated (with the exception of Zespri) and operates very much on 'user pays' principles. No sign of any government export subsidies or incentives here. Australian apples can enter the country freely - yet ours still can't cross the Tasman. Earlier this year our stores were flooded by Californian nectarines, marketed by the Californian Tree Fruit Agreement, which similar to other US based primary marketing structures has access to both state and federal incentives.

New Zealand produces its summer fruit at the same time as Chile produces its crop. There are plenty of Chilean peaches and nectarines available in California during the US off season - but one would be engaged in a futile struggle if one wanted to find New Zealand fruit in that market.

The Fruitfed video, which also comes as a DVD, aims to position horticulture as an attractive career option for 5th and 6th formers as they make decisions about their further education.

To its credit, the Fruitfed team has cast its net fairly wide and has tried to include every horticultural discipline that exists in the wider sense in order to present a balanced picture. The video, containing a series of vignettes with successful young people already in horticultural careers, therefore also provides information about careers in plant nurseries and retail produce departments.

Two examples of how we are trying to address key issues of vital concern to our industry - market access and the future labour pool and skill set required to maintain and continue our growth.

Very worthwhile initiatives and both pointing into the same direction - industry advancing industry issues. The Horticultural Export Authority and Fruitfed are both bodies heavily reliant on industry participation, industry goodwill and industry determination to achieve their goals. Others, such as Vegfed or United Fresh, are similarly dependent.

The challenge for many industry participants is that they will not always see direct immediate returns for energy committed to industry issues. It's not like concluding a sale.

Advancing industry issues can take months or even years before measurable results are achieved. Yet, if we don't get involved, what are our chances of improving an industry problem? Especially if we are unlikely to benefit from its solution?

Let's throw them to the lions

There is nothing that focuses the mind like getting up at 5am to catch a flight to Wellington. At that hour of the morning we are able to have a real intensity of sensations, as long as we are tuned in and have cut through the mental fog that usually hangs around our brains at that hour of the morning.

For me this meant that I enjoyed driving on Auckland's motorway system - because there were hardly any other cars around.

The sunrise was spectacular, and without wind, the Waitemata Harbour was as flat as a millpond.

With a degree of clarity of mind rarely experienced in recent weeks, I started to mull about a couple of general interest items I had learned about in the last 24 hours.

The first item beamed into my living room by way of the Sky Discovery Channel. It was a documentary about the Netherlands and the way water used to be kept at bay through the use of windmills.

The second item was one that attracted my attention on the Internet, as I was perusing the e-version of a German news magazine. An article about the Roman Colosseum caught my eye.

The Windmill story discussed the conceptual and engineering feats of Dutch engineers during the last five hundred years.

The item about the Colosseum reported the findings of an architect researching ancient building techniques who had originally been fascinated by the way the organisers of Roman gladiator events had managed to have groups of lions or bears appear in the arena all at once, seemingly out of nowhere.

In the case of the Dutch, the programme concluded that the breakthrough in land/water management came when engineering minds started to look for multidimensional solutions and linked natural power elements together; i.e., wind and water.

The question that exercised the mind of the Italian architect had a very logical answer.

A detailed examination of the Colosseum ruins revealed that animals were simultaneously transported onto the main arena floor through a, for the times incredibly sophisticated, system of wooden lifts and pulleys that originated six storeys below the main arena.

The human mind sure is an amazing tool. This makes it even more difficult for me to understand why we, with more technology, automation and energy available to us than at any other time in the history of man kind, still can't manage to get consistently ripened bananas into our stores seven days a week!

This type of shonky service level delivery would have led to mass drownings in Renaissance Holland.

In Rome, failure to deliver a smooth circus act usually meant the organisers were part of the entertainment at the next performance

- more likely than not with fatal consequences. We just have it too easy today, don't we?

Summerfruit - what is that again?

Doesn't time fly when you are having fun? Its December already

- the time when retailers generally stop listing new products, homemakers groan at the thought of doing the Christmas shopping and the perversity of our Southern Hemisphere life schedules raises its head again.

Here we are, in the South Pacific, where December 25th definitely does not take place in winter - although one often can't necessarily call the time of year 'summer' either!

What do we do?

We bundle the end of the academic school year, the onset of the non-winter season, a religious date of questionable authenticity and a habit of cutting down trees that a German introduced into Victorian England with a Coca-Cola advertising symbol of the 1930s that took the shape of a jolly old fat guy and call it "Christmas".

I think we need our heads examined.

Business slows down, staff start thinking about leave, it is difficult to get any sense out of people after December 15th and convention dictates that one is to go out and spend money on Christmas presents.

Ah, yes - and it is difficult to move in the supermarkets as shoppers pretend that stores will be closed for three or four days as they used to be, which, of course, means that trolleys have to be loaded up to the gunnels, in turn quadrupling the time it takes to get the average shopper processed at the checkout.

It is into this environment fruit growers each year release their precious summerfruit - cherries, apricots, peaches, nectarines and plums.

In Europe of North America, summerfruit just has to compete with the onset of the school holidays and serves as an in-store scene setter and seasonal herald.

Here in New Zealand, it would be very easy to see the arrival of local summerfruit on our produce shelves as simply another one of those frequent range changes that happens in produce.

In fact, it is not uncommon to have seasonal off-location grocery displays mysteriously muscling their way into the produce departments, precisely at the time when the produce manager ought to open the department up and create a colourful and tempting summerfruit display to entice customers.

One of the secrets of a good summerfruit sales season - apart from giving the fruit the exposure it deserves - is having good quality sweet juicy fruit available in the first place.

This is by no means as simple or obvious as it sounds and many a customer has been turned off early on by biting into a sour or mealy piece of summerfruit.

Customers want good fruit in any event. At a time when other distractions such as the ones alluded to above influence fruit marketing, good taste experiences are vital to achieve repeat purchases. That is something growers, wholesalers and retailers will all be keen to achieve.

Come fly with me...

One of the advantages of operating a business with offices in various cities is that one gets to travel. Some might say this could be a disadvantage - and on some days it certainly looks like that.

I prefer to take the 'glass of water' approach. You know - is half a glass of water half 'full' or half 'empty'?

My glass is always half full - even if the travel element is just hopping between Auckland and Wellington or Christchurch and Auckland.

Here are some thoughts that came to mind during my last trans-Cook Strait excursion:

- Why does it take four cabin crew to serve coffee, tea or water on an Air New Zealand flight?
- Why do those flights always have a captain and a first officer? Where are the second and third officers?
- Why do I have to take my jacket off and put it through the scanner and the captain just ponces through - no questions asked?
- Why does the gate crew pretend I can't read for myself where I am meant to be sitting on the plane?
- How does one say 'you are sitting in my seat' in Japanese?
- Why does everyone insist on standing in the aisle the minute the plane has stopped, regardless of whether the door is open or not?
- Why is my luggage always last off the carousel?

Now let's apply some of those questions to the produce retail industry.

- How many staff do we need to manage a produce department efficiently and effectively?
- Do I need an assistant produce manager and a leading hand or will one of them do?
- What is the correct uniform for a produce manager? Shirt and tie? Apron? Gumboots? If yes - why? If not - why not?
- Do I need tickets for all my merchandise or just some of it?
- How large should the type font be? Large enough for customers to read for themselves or will I always be on hand to read the tickets out to them?
- How should imported produce be ticketed?
- Is my department correctly laid out so that my customers are channeled past the entire range - or am I allowing for some 'emergency exits' which

means I loosing out on sales?

- When does my order arrive? Have I planned for its arrival? Can I cope with its arrival in terms of staff on hand - or does order arrival time mean nobody works in the retail area and is available for customer queries?

Logistics issues are very similar regardless of the type of industry one is working in. Translating challenges and solutions observed in one industry into another - preferably ours- is easy and just takes a little practice. Questions are a great way of advancing knowledge and working towards achieving once objectives.

Give it a go. You can do it, too.

A basic focus for 2004

The end of the year has arrived and I have surprised myself once again by realizing that I managed to meet 50 weekly deadlines in producing this Produce Express column.

Finding a topic is not all that difficult. As long as one's eyes are wide open, suitable topics tend to crop up just when one thinks one's creative juices have finally dried up.

This week is really no exception.

I spent most of the week in Tauranga. Driving down from Auckland and driving around the area was a good exercise in reacquainting myself with the region's horticultural abundance, which manifested itself in road signs exclaiming "10 Avocados for $5" amongst others.

I did not stop to check size or quality at that particular roadside store and as a former retailer I am familiar with the costs that get added by the time crops appear on a supermarket shelf.

Nevertheless, there is often a sizable gap between prices in the production areas and the supermarkets in town.

Another example hails from Sunday's Takapuna Market, where a large Whenuapai strawberry grower was offering his wares at 5 punnets for $10 - which differs markedly from the prices the same grower's strawberries are selling for in the supermarkets.

What influences the prices supermarkets sell their produce for? There are principally two factors.

1. The cost of shipping the produce from the growing areas into the stores and the various handling stages involved in that process.
2. The place the produce takes in the supermarket's overall merchandise mix. Both steps can be optimised. Shipping produce to stores should occur as direct as possible. In some cases that literally means shipping the produce directly into store. In other cases markets or distribution centres offer the best solutions as costs can be optimised through consolidating loads. The merchandise mix position is also critical. Retail prices are influenced by expected shelf life, the degree of consumer need for the product, the advertised promotions schedule and the time of year.

No two customers are the same and what matters to one, can leave the next one curiously unaffected.

But there is one aspect that drives all customers nutty.

When one stands in front of a produce display and has decided to purchase the produce on the shelf, one needs a bag to place the produce in.

An empty bag holder is not a pretty sight and has been known to induce the supermarket version of "road rage" in frustrated shoppers.

High on my wish list for 2004 therefore is that I will not see empty bag holders in the produce departments of the country's supermarkets, regardless of the time of day I visit a store. Nothing turns customers off more.

I wish you a peaceful Christmas and a Happy New Year.

What does it take to be a competent assistant produce manager?

The local community paper ran a job ad for an Assistant Produce Manager for one of the national supermarket chains. Here is what it said:

"Joining the team your role will be to assist the [produce] manager in the smooth running of the [produce] department. You must have previous experience in the [produce] department and a working knowledge of stock ordering, assisting with managing gross profits and supervising staff. This is a "hands-on" role that calls for an enthusiastic individual with a positive attitude, good personal presentation as well as the commitment to delivering first-class customer service."

You will note that the words 'produce' are [bracketed]. That feature was not included in the original ad.

I did that.

I would like you to read the ad again, but this time, don't take any notice of the word [produce].

What you see is a pretty generic set of words, which don't really tell you much about the skills required for the job.

So, put the [produce] back into the ad - does it really enhance the ad and tell prospective applicants whether they should apply?

I think not.

Where are the criteria relating to the length of experience required? What about the issue of necessary product knowledge?

Produce managers no longer select produce these days - head office based produce buyers make those decisions.

Good stock ordering habits and consistent gross profit performance are both a function of sales.

Sales success depends on a combination of merchandise skills and attention to detail. How do I lay the department out? Does it really make sense to have Aussie tomatoes on the first bin as customers enter the department?

How wide should the lettuce display be in winter compared to summer?

Do I really need to pile bananas eight high at a time?

How often should I rotate the kumara?

When do I stop ordering stone fruit?

Successful produce management is all about answering these and other questions confidently and being able to turn the answers into actions - based on the reality of the produce department one works in.

What reality?

Well, there is the department size for a starter, then there are the neighbourhood demographics, shopper profile by trading day, range stocked to satisfy customer demand, supply and delivery logistics, the type of mirrorback, multi-deck or produce bins being used, whether the department is refrigerated - and I have barely started.

Many produce departments are not a pretty sight these days. Given the perishable nature of the fruit and vegetable range that makes up the department, it is inconceivable to be an excellent Assistant Produce Manager without having an in-depth understanding of the reality as it applies to one's department.

Ads like the one quoted above therefore will not do. Excellence requires a lot more definition than that.

The power of a brand

As consumers we take brands for granted. As produce industry managers we often get confused about what constitutes a brand and what doesn't.

The Google query "Brand definition" produced 2,170,000 hits on my web browser. One of the first definitions I came across offered this definition:

"An identifying symbol, words, or mark that distinguishes a product or company from its competitors. Usually brands are registered (trademarked) with a regulatory authority and so cannot be used freely by other parties. For many products and companies, branding is an essential part of marketing." www.advfn.com

Fair enough, but how does one know whether brands actually work? Sales result is one obvious measure, market share is another, but unbranded product can also be a strong sales performer.

Brand recall and recognition are in my view strong indicators of branded product positioning.

Companies such as Coca-Cola or Pepsi pay substantial amounts of money to get their products into Hollywood movies in order to become part of the perceived 'real' world as opposed to being a product that buys TV advertising time. And yes, both are global brands that achieve instant recall around the globe.

Here are two passages from a New Zealand short story I recently read.

"Our first stop was always at the fruit shop, first on the left through the doors of the mall. On Christmas Eve the cartons of fruit and vegetables bellied out of the doorless shop, spreading halfway across the cobbled floor. We stood in front of the cartons, mesmerised by the succulence of the piled apricots and nectarines, tiny droplets of moisture clinging on their skins; the smooth unmarked Bonita bananas, the punnets of raspberries and strawberries from Harrows' farms; the fat dark Otago cherries; Island pineapples and Riverland oranges."

Smooth unmarked Bonita bananas, eh? But wait, there is more:

"We bought bananas so we could use the Bonita stickers as false fingernails, curving them around our own nails, flourishing our hands at ourselves, palms facing, to show the tough opaque talons."

Author Kathleen De Goldi who in her story 'Old Faithful" reminisced about her 1960s Christchurch upbringing has sufficient fond memories of her fruit shopping expeditions, that she clearly recalls the bananas by brand.

One could argue that this would not be difficult, because Bonita was the only brand around in those days - but credit where credit is due! Brand recall like this is impressive.

'Smooth unmarked' sounds good too. Maybe Bonita could strike a deal with Mary-Kate & Ashley Olsen to migrate the brand from fruit into the teenage accessories market - quite lucrative apparently.

Retail is detail

I am sure I have used this heading before, in fact I am absolutely positive. I don't tire of it though, because no day is the same - particularly at retail. And details that were right today might need a heavy dose of correction tomorrow. Or vice versa.

I went shopping at my local supermarket this Sunday morning and picked up on a couple of details that could well do with adjusting.

The produce department had no loose washed potatoes for sale. I was given the choice between 4kg bags and 750g punnets. The former had a green tinge and the latter were being sold from within the refrigerated multi-deck.

The banana display was well stocked and featured Bonita promotional merchandise material about how one could win an X-box game by collecting Bonita banana stickers. Great scheme, but a minor problem arose. There were no Bonita bananas - the brand on display was Aloha.

Aloha bananas are, by the way, not from Hawaii as one might expect given the brand name but are imported from the Philippines.

Just a minor detail.

Moving right along, I tried to buy some poppy seed rolls in the bakery. "Sorry", I was told, "we aren't making these any more. We couldn't get the poppy seeds to stick."

I gave up, bought the Sunday paper and went home.

Things did not improve when I opened the paper.

The page 2 feature story reported the appearance of National Party finance spokesman Don Brash at the ACT conference. The caption under the photo read, 'Don Brash is the second National minister this month to speak at ACT conferences about forming a coalition'.

Excuse me? Have I been in some sort of time warp? When did Brash become a minister?

The job ads also offered evidence of detail not being high on the list of priorities for many people.

A Tokoroa based log processing machine manufacturer is looking for a 'Marketing Accountant'. Surely that must be a contradiction of terms. Marketing people tend to spend money and accountants tend to avoid spending it. The statement 'Ideally, applicants will have had previous experience working in a finance environment', makes me wonder what the background of less than ideal candidates is likely to be.

Creative New Zealand, the national arts development organisation that spends tax payer and lotto money like there is no tomorrow, is also looking for new staff, particularly an Assistant Arts Adviser. In case you don't know what an Assistant Arts Adviser's role is - here is what the ad had to say: 'As Assistant Arts Adviser, you will assist the specialist Arts Advisers to deliver arts advisory services.'

There, it couldn't be clearer than that.

Whether it's a supermarket, a newspaper article or a job ad, in order to be effective, a certain amount of attention to detail is required.

As for the Assistant Arts Adviser's job - the ad also mentioned that some experience in performing arts/ dance would be helpful.

Could that be an opportunity for the produce industry manager who moonlights as choreographer of the Bonita Bananas dancing girls?

The customer is king

Well, he ought to be anyway. One of the great revelations I experienced at some stage in my mid twenties was that we are all "in sales". One might not be called sales rep, but lawyer, accountant, doctor or engineer. One might not stand behind a counter or have a till in sight - but ultimately, we are all salesmen.

I would have thought that by now this would be a universally accepted home truth, but apparently this is not the case.

I recently had two examples of this. The first one relates to our bank. We bank electronically, but from time to time some manual intervention is necessary. Our office manager tried to phone the branch where our account is held. There was no listing in the phone book, other than a 0800 number. Three attempts and half an hour later she got through to a centralised call centre, only to be told that it was bank policy not to divulge branch telephone numbers to customers!

The second example relates, you have guessed it, to a supermarket.

I bought some liver sausage from the delicatessen department amongst other items. Liver sausage tastes a lot better than it sounds but I am digressing. When I got my shopping home and looked at the till tape, I found that my 250g of liver sausage had cost me $0.00 - despite the fact that the per kg and unit price were clearly printed on the tab that had been stuck on at the Deli counter. The centralised price database was obviously having a "day off". There are usually half a dozen checks and balances in place to ensure that this does not happen. Not the least of which are alert checkout operators who are meant to keep one eye on the digital display in front of their noses as they are passing one's purchases across the scanner.

I don't live that far from the supermarket and I wanted to see what the store's reaction was when I pointed the errors of their way out to them.

Upon arrival at the service counter, I presented myself to the duty manager and acquainted her with the issue by showing her liver sausage wrapper ($3.92) and till tape ($0.00).

The supervisor's first reaction was to deny all knowledge and the possibility that such an occurrence could take place in her store.

Then her mind moved on to "Hey - why are you coming here to tell me about this? What's in it for you?" Her lips never mouthed these questions but her facial expressions gave her away.

What she did actually say to me was, "Couldn't you have said something earlier? Surely, you must have noticed it when you watched your shopping being scanned?"

Well, that was one reaction I had not anticipated. Are customers now held responsible for accuracy of scan information?

It appears so, at least in this store. I should have gone and 'cornered the market' on liver sausage instead.

Needless to say that bank manager and store manager will get complimentary copies of this week's *Produce Express*.

Does it really matter which decade (or century) fresh food grocers live in?

Harold McMillan became Prime Minister of the UK. The "Sowjetunion" (remember that one?) launched Sputnik 1, the first artificial satellite to orbit the Earth. It was also the year Humphrey Bogart and the Finnish composer Sibelius departed from this Earth. Japanese car maker Honda was still producing rickshaws in 1957 and the year proved to be an excellent vintage for French Bordeaux wines.

Not surprising then that 1957 was also the year in which this writer was born - and the Harvard Business Review published an indepth article entitled, "Supermarkets Face the Future". Fresh food gets its fair share of attention in the article, enabling us to assess how much we have advanced and learned since the early days.

"Supermarkets are the pivots on which modern food marketing turns." That was Applebaum and Carson's assessment in 1957 and the statement is as relevant today as it was then. Supermarkets are obviously not the only food outlets around, but their sheer scale and size still take some beating. Back in 1935, Charles Philipps was also asking basic questions, such as "What is a supermarket?"

He answered the question, cautiously, like this: "In a general way it may be said that the supermarket is a large departmentised store in which the departmentised food sections are the only, or at least among the most important, sections operated."

Do we detect a certain weariness about the role of non-food items in the supermarket range here?

"The dangers of business on too big a scale" was uppermost on Paul Cherington's mind in 1928. "Incompetence arising from inadequate management or inefficient operation" was seen as a very high hurdle for small retailers who were aspiring to build multibranch businesses.

This would have to be seen as a statement that still rings true 77 years later. I have lost track of how often I have walked into a supermarket produce department in the early evening only to see an empty banana display whilst the sole produce assistant on duty is busy with a very meaningful task such as grading ginger or piling fresh mushrooms on top of the old ones on offer.

One of the critical issues facing supermarkets, according to the authors of the 1957 article, was "that 75% (by weight) of all food eaten by Americans requires some refrigeration between production and the time of eating. Facilities of such preservation are often inadequate.

According to one survey, spoilage of fruits and vegetables at the retail level and in the home ranged from 18% to 35%. Other losses are less evident: for instance, deterioration of flavour, attractiveness, and food values."

Well, well. Some things just do not change.

Supermarkets, according to US research and local anecdotal evidence, clock up average instore wastage figures of around 7% - just by being in business and putting produce on display. Accounted for in this percentage are naturally occurring product-specific waste and a reasonable shrinkage expectation based on the fact that the produce has to interact with staff and customers - i.e. biological deterioration and damage through human contact.

It is also understood that commodities do change price frequently and some losses - as well as gains - can be caused by stock on hand values differing from one week to the next.

Not included in this average waste percentage are bloopers of a human kind, e.g. staff tipping apples onto the display bin from an unreasonable height or stacking bananas ten levels high. Ordering more produce than is needed, not looking after fruit and vegetables properly when they arrive in the store or selling this week's stock at last week's prices are all potential shrink factors that are also not covered by the industry average figure.

Are we getting better at managing our perishable departments in 2008 than we were in 1957 or 1928? That's debatable. We certainly have more management tools available these days, such as refrigeration, information technology and modern instore fixtures.

None of these are of any help though unless we also employ staff who are committed, skilled and have a healthy dose of common sense. It's a not inconsiderable expectation. Cherington already considered this issue in 1928. "The fundamental difficulty with retailing", he said, "is the fact that the price of human brains of the type necessary for conducting a retail establishment has risen substantially during the past few years."

Here we are in 2008, with New Zealand unemployment figures pretty low and stores struggling to recruit suitable staff, judging by the state of the mirrorbacks, meat cases and deli counters in supermarket country. It looks like the price of human brains is still on the rise and supermarkets will have to dig deeper into their pockets.

So, does it matter which century or decade we live in? Well, each of us is likely to have a personal preference in this regard. In terms of problem solving, though, it does not matter, as long as we have a keen sense of history and are able to learn from those who tackled what amounts to be the same problems years, decades or centuries ago.

R2D2 is coming to an orchard near you - how long before it hits your store?

On robotic technology, consumer perceptions and retailer conundrum

The Massey University Magazine landed on my desk today. Not really the kind of publication that I would usually discuss here - but one article caught my eye. The School of Engineering and Advanced Technology at Massey has developed a robot for the fruit harvest in the apple and kiwifruit industries.

Fruit pickers of the human kind are set to get serious competition. Which is just as well, as there appears to be a perennial shortage of skilled seasonal harvest workers in this country.

And the connection with supermarket produce departments, pray tell? Well, there seems to be shortage of skilled produce assistants in your stores, ladies and gentlemen, and if it's good enough for two of our more successful perishable fruit industries to entrust their livelihood to sophisticated robotic equipment assembled by "mechanics" focused on PhD research, why don't we start thinking about automating store produce departments?

OK, it is a tongue and cheek comment, it's late at night and I just sampled a particularly pleasant drop of Central Otago Pinot Noir, but; isn't it time we started to think outside the box when it comes to giving the consumer an enjoyable produce shopping experience?

Am I sounding like a broken record? Undoubtedly, but sooner or later the message will hopefully get through.

The emergence of supermarkets in the US was a revolutionary concept in the 1930s. Ever since, change has been incremental. It is time for the next mega shift.

The Massey team putting the robotic kiwifruit picker together believe that realising effective artificial vision is the key to successful robotic development. Obviously we have a long way to go in the produce departments, as no fruit or vegetable looks the same and any apron wearing robot trying to cut cabbage or rotate a display of oranges without creating total havoc would be a sight to behold.

I don't really expect robotics to take over in the retail display area any time soon, but I would like to challenge your thinking along the lines of - "what can we do to engage more constructively with our customers?"

When did you last stand surreptitiously in the vicinity of your produce department for a few minute or two and counted the number of people heading straight through without buying any fruit and vegetables?

Running supermarket produce departments is not the easiest job around.

On one hand we are piling up loose fruit and vegetables in their natural state in stores that are getting more sophisticated by the minute with packaging solutions for the groceries in the centre aisles and the chillers. In other words, the perception gap between the merchandise divisions that make up the entire supermarket range is widening - and maybe consumers are really struggling more than we realise with the notion of buying bunches of celery and ripe tomatoes in the same place where they shop for long life milk, DVDs, eco light bulbs and toasters.

On the other hand, sophisticated fresh produce packaging solutions really only work in one category, fresh cut salads. Attempts to get clever with packing other produce categories, which go beyond offering basic consumer convenience, are usually not a roaring success. Customers appear to have a limited tolerance level related to plausibility when they consider their purchasing options.

So, how do we manage the gap between increasing sophistication of the total store offer and the consumer desire to be able to believe that the produce they buy is fresh - whatever 'fresh' means for them?

Well, that is the challenge you are faced with every day; which brings me back to robotics. R2D2 and his cobbers are actually the last thing we need to see in the produce departments or the supermarkets at large. The glue that binds a store together and provides a common denominator for grocery aisles and fresh food departments is service. Not just any service, mind you. Consistent service of a high standard is what's needed - and for that we need people! Well trained people with good product knowledge and acceptable communication skills.

Over to you.

The good old days

My recipe for getting the freshness message across to customers.

Albany on Auckland's North Shore was for many years Auckland's fruit bowl. Apple orchards were everywhere and strawberry gardens had trouble keeping up with the demand from a growing city.

The harbour bridge changed the dynamics when it was opened in 1959 and rural North Shore became an enormous building site. Our offices are now where the apple orchards use to be and the last strawberry patch in the neighbourhood is up for sale.

The pace of change has been enormous. As recently as fifteen years ago, Foodtown store managers in Glenfield and Sunnynook used to worry about the impact on their weekly produce budget from orchard gate sales and the "red shed" in Bush Road, Albany used to play severely on the minds of retail aces such as Richard Croucher, Bob Shaw, Nigel Lagdon and Mark Page.

The stores are still around and so are most of the guys, but the red shed is long gone!

With it went a lifestyle shopping option for Shore dwellers: the ability to buy produce at the orchard gate.

Orchard gates are still around as well; it's just that one has to travel further to get to them. Some people do exactly that - seek out the orchard or garden gate whenever the opportunity presents itself. And the reason these hardcorers are willing to go to the length they do, is that they have an inherent discomfort about the "freshness" of produce sold in supermarkets and greengrocers.

This brings us to a topic that keeps shoppers around the globe, as well as Sue Kedgley MP, very busy. The question they are asking themselves consciously or subconsciously as they shop is this: "how fresh is the produce I am buying today?"

As we know as produce industry professionals, there is no easy answer to that question. Lettuce, broccoli and cauliflower are probably fresher than most as these crops are harvested daily all year around.

Apples, kumara and onions on the other hand are harvested, stored and fed into the supply chain over a period of months.

Whilst this makes perfect sense to all of us who deal with produce for a living, it does not for consumers who buy produce to live!

And because they are able to buy all their produce in one place; i.e., your store, they subconsciously expect all produce purchased in your store to have similar characteristics; such as, being competitively priced, being safe to eat and being "fresh".

How do you cope with that?

Well for starters, you try to have "fresh" stock delivered to your stores on a daily basis, sometimes even more than once.

Secondly, you are committed to presenting and displaying your produce assortment in a way that communicates to your customers that you: a. care and b. know what you are doing.

Thirdly, you have a rotation and maintenance program in place that is reflective of the perishable nature of your produce.

Fourthly, you know about your produce, in fact you are passionate about your fruit and vegetables. This creates a positive energy in your department that is subconsciously communicated to customers who respond by increasing their produce shop in your store.

What is the catch phrase on those Tui beer billboards again? YEAH RIGHT!

The reality though is that you better get around to managing your departments in just that way, because the strawberry patches are not just disappearing in Albany. All over the country suburbia is stretching its muscle and the orchard and garden gates are pushed further and further out.

Consumers are looking to you for recreating the "freshness" experience for them without necessarily being able to articulate this.

So, keen to maintain market share in an economy that is headed for recession and where the price of fuel is forcing consumers to get a bit more selective about how far they stray for their food needs?

All you have to do is stick to the recipe above and get on with it because the good old days have gone.

Simple as, eh?

Working on a chain gang

One of my favourite musical pieces is “Working on a chain gang”, the ballad about former Alabama slave John Henry’s experiences during the Southern US railway construction period.

Groups of convicts from different walks of life were indiscriminately chained together for convenience sake and sent off to work, building railway tracks, construction roads, breaking rocks – the American justice system was already fairly innovative in the middle of the 19th Century!

The overseers did not really care much about how the chain members organised themselves – as long as the work got done.

John Henry’s approach to problem solving
John Henry told the captain,
"Captain, when you go to town,
Bring me back a ten-pound hammer,
I's gonna knock this mountain down."
William G. Parmenter

People having to work together to achieve a common goal? Where have we heard that before? Ah yes, supermarket chain management!

The modern equivalent of a chain gang is the supermarket catalogue! Wow, that’s a bit of a mental leap – but think about it. How does a catalogue come together?

1. The marketing department plans catalogue layout and themes.
2. The Managing Director or his nominee approves the marketing department plans.
3. Advertising designs the catalogue layout.
4. In all likelihood, the supermarket company’s advertising agency also has its finger in the pie to ensure that catalogue design and execution fits into the wider communication strategy.
5. Merchandise departments select goods to be advertised.
6. Suppliers put their spoke and discuss/select/ get told their level of involvement.
7. Operations management, i.e. the guys that run the stores, offer their opinion about what ought and ought not to be advertised.
8. Prices are set.

That is just the simple version!

Store managers love to see fish advertised. Why is the only fish advertised only farmed fish like salmon or processed fish such as crabsticks or smoked kawhai? Well, the seafood merchandise team has yet to come up with a way of predicting which type of fish is likely to jump into the fishing fleet's nets four weeks hence. Or predict whether the weather will be clement enough to allow the fleet to go out in the first place.

It's the turn of the produce department to take up a front page slot in the next catalogue. The Produce Merchandise Manager gets told in no uncertain terms buy his colleagues that only bananas, potatoes or strawberries are acceptable. Pickling onions, daffodils or shallots are definitely not on the wish list.

Catalogues have a longer lead time than newspaper ads. The Produce team therefore needs to have a pretty good crystal ball to figure out whether the banana boat will come in on time or whether it is likely to break down near the Galapagos Islands; whether the potato supplier will be able to dig his spuds the week they are needed in increased numbers; and whether there will be enough sunshine to ensure the bumper strawberry crop required to special the fruit.

What is the definition of a supermarket anyway? Is a supermarket a retail facility that sells predominantly food and products required in food production and management? Or should a supermarket also be in the business of selling park benches, trampolines, outdoor heaters and DVD players?

Once product mix has been decided, the next round of cooperation kicks in. What should the price be? Are we running we loss leaders, do we need to be in the money or can we get away with just breaking even?

What are the messages that go with the product? Who should determine what is said? Can it be left to the advertising agency to come up with the 'feel good' statements or should the department responsible for the product discussed sign off any statement made?

What am I on about? The issue of conflict and more to the point, conflict management.

Similar to a bunch of convicts working in a chain gang, the supermarket managers tasked with getting a catalogue out need to work together – whether they like it or not.

If they don't, they'll end up confusing the consumer which surely is not in their interest.

That is why I was quite disturbed by one of the recent supermarket catalogues that came through my letterbox.

On its front page the catalogue attributed a tomato handling statement to an imaginary checkout operator who claimed that ripe tomatoes should be popped into the fridge. Somehow that statement must have slipped past the guys who should no best – the produce merchandise team in this instance.

The chain gang was obviously not operating at its most efficient that day. John Henry's 10 pound hammer is not going to solve the problem, but all participants in producing a successful catalogue need to sing from the same hymn sheet to ensure credibility with customers and suppliers alike.

The Easter Bunny & Father Christmas - the annual curse of the produce department

Easter is long over by the time you read this article but some memories linger. This year in particular, I am suffering from vivid recollections of having to fight my way into the produce departments of my local supermarkets, a task very much complicated by those ever-sprouting Easter egg displays.

Fruit and vegetables are impulse purchases. The consumers' perception of what constitutes quality ensures that trolleys get 'parked' and produce is hand selected, item by item.

Produce departments are typically located at the entrance to a supermarket and not all supermarket shoppers chose to buy their produce at the supermarket.

As a consequence, produce departments need to be laid out to enable some shoppers to just cruise through on their way to other store offerings, whilst allowing produce shoppers to go about their business without having made an advance appointment with their local Accident & Emergency Clinic, as they are anticipating emerging second best from an altercation with an out of control shopping trolley or having been squashed between produce bins and off-location displays.

In order to avoid such unfortunate situations, store planners need to allow for a certain amount of empty space to ensure a smooth flow of shoppers and their trolleys.

At certain times of the year, the empty space Nazis seem to get the run of the stores and some of their worst offences seem to be reserved for the produce department.

Every bin end, every nook and every cranny are suddenly filled with chocolate, cheap seasonal merchandise imported from China, bargain wine or Christmas cookies.

A sure recipe for conflict. The marketers are busy trying to create an ambience, the produce merchandise team is keen to achieve its sales forecast whilst grocers, store operators and supplier reps conspire to fill every square inch of empty space they can lay their hands on.

As usual, it is the consumer who is missing out. Customer shopping behaviour is not a homogenous attribute that remains static as the customer moves through the store. Behaviour changes on the basis of predetermined needs established consciously or subconsciously prior to entering the store and by being exposed to a variety of instore stimuli, both positive and negative in nature.

How the store presents during the customers' visit therefore does matter and does influence spend by department and total spend.

Store managers do understand that equation very clearly in relation to store cleanliness and the ratio of open checkouts versus checkout queues but for some reason there is a blind spot in relation to enabling produce shoppers to go about their business in peace.

Where to from here then? May I suggest that cramming produce aisles full of seasonal merchandise is a manifestation of short-term and tactical rather than long-term and strategic thinking.

Stores that value the contribution their produce departments make to the overall sales and GP mix and who appreciate the long-term potential of fresh and natural versus processed goods and chocolate sales will have no problem taking my views into account when planning their Christmas layouts!

The proof of the pudding will as always be in the eating and I look forward to hanging on to "my" space as a produce shopper as the Festive Season approaches.

That's right, only seven months to Christmas and counting!

Quality - is it all that it is cracked up to be?

Where I look at the obvious - and the not so obvious!

It does not matter whether we spend 99 cents, $1.99 or $3.49 per kg of apples, or any other produce for that matter; we are looking for 'quality' when we are completing our purchase.

Quality means different things to different people though. At $3.49, I expect total symmetry in an apple's shape and perfect colour. My expectations are somewhat less at $1.99. For 99 cents per kg I will even put up with minor blemishes and puncture marks.

Regardless of the price though, I know that the experience of biting into an apple at this time of the year should be a 'crunchy' one

- and the apple will, of course, be sweet and juicy.

Somewhere in my grey matter is also the perception that the apple is 'fresh'; 'fresh' meaning in my case that I expect it to have been harvested in autumn and properly cared for all the way to my retailer so that I can have the above outlined experiences.

The various correspondents who flooded the 'letters to the editor' pages of the New Zealand Herald and other newspapers during the last few weeks on fresh produce related matters had two things in common. They all had different opinions about what constituted 'fresh' and they were all lamenting that fruit no longer tastes as good as it used to.

Summing up - there is a correlation between 'fresh' and 'quality' , but the two terms do not mean the same and are not interchangeable. 'Taste' is a key performance indicator for consumer satisfaction. If it does not taste right, all bets are off!

On an altogether different matter - I went shopping yesterday. Yes, I do venture into supermarkets and here is what happened.

I wanted to buy some sparkling mineral water. It seemed to be my lucky day, as I spotted a shelf filler in the bottled water section. Instead of picking up a couple bottles, I thought I would get smart and ask the shelf filler to get me a whole carton. That seemingly simple request started an interesting chain of events which is still going on as I write this column.

Firstly, I had problems communicating my request, as the shelf filler appeared to only speak broken English. Secondly, once he understood, he told me he was not allowed to give a customer a whole carton. Thirdly, when I insisted, the duty manager turned up and told me that my request was against company policy.

At this stage, I took my cell phone out and suggested that I would ring his area manager, the regional manager, the merchandise manager and if necessary the Managing Director until I found someone who could authorise my intended purchase of 12 bottles of sparkling mineral water in a carton.

That statement had the desired result. The shelf filler was dispatched to fetch a whole carton of sparkling mineral water for this cranky customer who appeared to know how the system worked. I proudly took my purchases home where upon "her indoors" pointed to the product description printed on the carton - STILL mineral water - and had a good laugh at my expense!

Was that a quality shopping experience? Not in my book it wasn't! I will attempt to exchange the goods tonight.

C.S.T.S.Y.B.

I re-introduce Tom Ah Chee's operating credo

Readers of our weekly Produce Express Newsletter would be acutely aware that I have had the issue of service on my mind over the last few weeks. Good old-fashioned customer service, not necessarily related to supermarkets either.

It is, however, not easy not to think about supermarkets and their service offering. Supermarkets are the 21st Century's equivalent of Mr. & Mrs. Neanderthal's happy hunting ground for berries and buffalo and as such consumers spend a lot of time thinking about their local supermarket. They might not always express their opinion when they're at their store, but boy, there is no stopping some customers when they have a forum and a willing audience.

The midnight to dawn radio talkback host on 1ZB recently provided such a forum. The discussion centered around aisle width when I went to bed at 0.30 am and when the radio sprung to action at 5.30 am to wake me up, host and guests were still at it, although the debate had shifted to meat wrapping, shopping basket cleanliness and rotten apples.

Based on the two opinion snapshots I was exposed to, there appears to be a real focus on matters relating to convenience and hygiene. The consumer wants to find the product she is looking for faster and she wants to be able to manoeuvre her trolley around the store without experiencing traffic jams. There must not be any out of stocks and all food and in-store equipment must be food safety assured and germ free.

Reasonable requests - aren't they?

When I joined Foodtown in the latter part of the last century (don't you just love the way that sounds?), prior to the eighties' sharemarket boom and subsequent crash, company founder Tom Ah Chee had already retired. The business was however still adhering to the principles he had fashioned and insisted upon, with his presence still very much in evidence.

In those days, prior to emails and computers, when letters were still being produced on a typewriter, every internal memo was concluded with the initials **C.S.T.S.Y.B.** underneath the signature of the writer.

I tried for a while without success to figure out what these letters stood for and eventually asked one of the old-timers, who was absolutely horrified that this topic had not been covered during my induction phase into the company.

Listening to his dismay, one would have been forgiven for thinking that the world had ended.

C.S.T.S.Y.B. I was told, stood for **C**onstantly **S**triving **T**o **S**erve **Y**ou **B**etter. It summed up the operating credo of the fledgling Foodtown chain as Tom Ah Chee and his collaborators expanded from their first Otahuhu store to what had become a 27 store empire by the time I joined.

C.S.T.S.Y.B. was a brilliant way of enshrining some very fundamental truths, namely: that the job is never done, there is always room for improvement, providing good service has to be part of the underlying business philosophy and acknowledgement of the fact that the customer has a choice.

Businesses today could do a lot worse than adopting Tom Ah Chee's philosophy. The customer often misses out these days. Service means different things to different people. Within a fresh produce context, I suggest that attention to detail in the following areas constitutes good service:

1. Customers do not have to go searching for advertised specials. These are readily identified in an easy to access part of the department.
2. The banana display is well stocked with bananas that are ready to eat.
3. The department is kept in a clean, tidy and hygienic state. This means no loose onions skins flying around on the floor, no rotten produce on display and no clouds of vinegar flies rising from the display tables when one claps one's hands.
4. Every item is ticketed and the ticketed price corresponds with the price loaded into the front-end scan system.
5. Before staff take their tea break, they ensure that there is no water on the floor of the retail section and any empty cartons or crates are removed from the display areas.

These are just my top five. You may well have something you might want to add. Whether you stick to my list or use your own - it pays to remember that customers do have choices and that, particularly in the case of fresh produce, there is always someone around the corner who offers an alternative.

A mango in my fruit bowl

Discussion of produce economics inspired by my breakfast ingredients.

I found a mango from Peru in my fruit bowl this morning. Right next to it were Ecuadorian bananas, a Philippine pineapple, some US oranges and local apples. They all ended up in my muesli plate, together with cereal, yoghurt and milk. As I was crunching my way through the contents of my plate, my mind started wandering back along the supply chains of my breakfast, which, of course, have at least one thing in common - they are all agricultural commodity based.

Little snippets of information popped into my grey matter as I continued to eat. Bananas arrive green and get gassed with Ethylene before we get to eat them. Pineapples have their tops chopped off lest they harbour Biosecurity risks harmful for New Zealand and because they no longer come from Australia, we can trust that they will be edible. Oranges taste either divine or foul, depending upon how well the crop has been managed as it reached maturity, was harvested, handled, stored and shipped. Local apples get to market a lot earlier these days compared to when the Apple & Pear Board tightly controlled supply.

Cereal and grain are caught up in the international biofuel debate. The yoghurt range available in my local supermarket is mind boggling compared to 1981, the year I arrived in New Zealand - and the price of milk is going off the Richter scale due to huge global demand increases.

All these products, as basic as they may look in my fruit bowl, pantry or fridge, have had value added to them before they arrived on my breakfast table.

Common sense would suggest that product that comes with added value attracts a higher price than product that comes without value add componentry.

Unfortunately, common sense does not always prevail. Supply and demand also plays a big role. Not a problem with that - but when perception gets into the way of reality, then the problem really starts.

No business can stay in business for a sustainable period unless it earns an income and gets a return on its investment.

Economic performance is cyclical - just ask any economist! So there are times when producers might struggle on the 'getting a return on the investment' front, but as long as land values continue to rise there will be some payback at the point of exiting one's land based industry.

Problems begin to occur for the entire supply chain, however, when a lack of clarity and direction leads to confusion. In the fresh produce business, confusion results in numbers of briefcase-based produce brokers appearing from nowhere at a rate of knots; each promising the world, none capable of delivering even sliver sized portions of that promise, with the net outcome being older produce sloshing around on retail shelves.

Many of you will easily recall those ridiculous debates generated by the Greens a couple of years back: What constitutes fresh produce? Every product group had its own answer for that. 'Fresh' is a lot easier to define in the case of lettuce, for example, than it is for kiwifruit or apples.

Consumers have their own interpretations of 'fresh' when they are shopping. They ask themselves five simple questions:

Does it look as if it has arrived in this store recently? Is it blemished or damaged in any way? Does it look as if it will last the distance once I have taken it home? What happened the last time I bought this item? Does the price look right relative to size, quantity and presentation?

The more questions they can answer in the affirmative, the more likely they are to buy.

So, the fruit in my fruit bowl had been subjected to some vigorous testing before it was allowed to come home and grace my kitchen.

With this in mind, the professional produce buyer ensures that the produce offered in his or her store/department arrives at the store in the most expeditious manner, in the best possible condition and in volumes that reflect trading reality.

There is no room for creating unnecessary confusion in the produce supply chain if one wants to maintain consumer confidence.

A message for store produce staff

The best wristwatch will eventually need a new strap. The most comfortable pair of shoes will eventually need a new pair of laces. The most practical vacuum cleaner will eventually need a new inner bag to contain what is being sucked up.

In each case, I am referring to an everyday product, which we either wear or have in the house. Most males these days even know how to use a vacuum cleaner, so you all know the products I am referring to!

Have you ever got frustrated, when you couldn't find the right replacement watchstrap?

Have you ever wandered between shoe shop and bootmaker and back to find the right pair of replacement shoelaces?

Have you ever felt angry because the replacement vacuum cleaner bags for your specific model are no longer available for sale anywhere other than in Eketahuna?

I bet you can at least say "Yes" to two of these scenarios - and yes you may well ask, what does this have to do with produce?

Well, if you agree with me that wristwatches are not very practical without a strap, most shoes don't work so well without laces and vacuum cleaners without bags are an environmental hazard, then my next statement is something you will be able to relate to as well.

A produce department without the right types of produce bags in the right places is next to useless!

Ostensibly, this ought to be very simple. You put the produce on the shelf and then you put the bags out. Why isn't it so simple in practice? Because staff often don't think and customers actually use the bags put out for them.

So, here is how to get it right.

1. If you only want to use one bag size, make sure the bag you offer your customers fits the largest and most awkward item on display. A 2kg cauliflower fits that bill nicely.
2. Place bags where customers need them - i.e. near loose produce, not in front of the prepacked salads.
3. If you use more than one bag size, make sure that a good balance of both types of bags is available and that the bigger bags are near the bulkier items.
4. Use a bag that can easily be detached from its roll and does not require

a science degree to open it.

5. Most importantly - never run out of bags!

Customers don't want to take up residency in the produce department. They want to select their purchases and move on. It is your job to ensure that they buy as much as possible in your department as they are passing through. They cannot possibly do this if the bags are missing, are too small or are too difficult to open.

The only skill requirement needed to get this right is common sense and produce managers usually have plenty of that. Put it to work please.

ANZAC Day reflections...

There are not many days in the year now when one can go and look at car sales yards without an overeager sales man pouncing the moment one sets foot in the yard.

Staying with the theme, but looking at it from a consumer's perspective - there are not many days in the year when supermarkets refuse to open their doors to let customers in.

I am an immigrant to the country and arrived 23 years ago. Somewhere along the line I picked up on the significance of ANZAC Day. I can't remember where and when.

The Gallipoli landings certainly featured in my German history lesson during school days - Germany was a Turkish ally in the Great War and German military advisers were working at all levels of the Turkish army.

Winston Churchill was much admired in the post WW II democratic Germany for the leadership he provided in the fight against Hitler.

I remember his involvement in the Gallipoli campaign, however, as being referred to by a description that translates more or less into "Winston's folly."

This view is also shared by a number of English, Australian and New Zealand historians, which makes the annual ANZAC Day celebration even more poignant than it is anyway.

Earlier today I, the German immigrant who somehow managed to absorb enough information about ANZAC Day to understand its significance, drove in my Japanese car to return a DVD to the video store at the local shopping centre. I then stood to watch a continuous succession of more recent immigrants of Asian descent drive up to the supermarket next door in their German cars, get out and shake their heads in disbelief when they realised the supermarket was closed.

In geological terms, 59 years is a minute time fragment. Within the historic development time frame the gulf between New Zealand of 1945, to take but one major reference point, and today is enormous.

The world has become a smaller place, modern technology has ensured that the physical distance between ourselves and other countries is less of an issue and the ethnic mix of New Zealand has undergone a major transformation.

The other thing of note, of course, is that supermarkets were unknown in New Zealand 59 years ago, coffee was an exotic drink more or less introduced by the Yanks along with milk bars when they 'invaded' New

Zealand in the forties.

Domestic refrigeration was an absolute luxury and the consumption of produce occurred along strict seasonal lines.

No such thing as strawberries from Western Australia, kiwifruit or new season potatoes all year around.

I like ANZAC Day, it might not be around forever in the way it is acknowledged now as the veterans are passing on - but as a day of reflection its worthwhile keeping. Even if the supermarkets stay closed for the morning.

Cheap pineapples - a comical tragedy in 3 scenes

Scene 1. (Sauerkraut sits bleary eyed at his breakfast table and reads the newspaper)

It appears to be anniversary time. The newspapers and TV Channels are full of the 60th anniversary commemorations of the D-Day landings in Normandy. The Herald had two photographs of French President Jacques Chirac this morning. The first one sports him trying to kiss Helen Clark's hand; the second one has him squeezing the life out of German chancellor Schröder in an embrace. Both activities are French specialities and it's a dead heat between Schröder and Clark as to who least enjoyed the attentions Chirac was attempting to bestow.

New Zealand political commentator Colin James was not going to be outdone and wrote his own anniversary story, which is also published in the Herald today. In it James takes the occasion of next Monday being the 20th anniversary of the night then Prime Minister Sir Robert Muldoon called a snap election.

James reflects on this event being an end of an era, the transition from a colonial one to an indigenous one.

As one could expect, a large part of James' article dealt with the deregulation of the economy, a process that occurred in rather a hurry when the Lange/Douglas government swept into power, following Muldoon's decision to let the voters have their say.

Scene 2. (Sauerkraut drives along the Upper Harbour Drive that connects the Waitakere area with the North Shore and is littered with fruit and veggie barns.)

Every fruit & veggie barn car park is packed and just about every item appears to be on special. Best buy of the weekend: 5 pineapples for $5 - yep, this is not a typo.

Scene 3. (Sauerkraut overhears a conversation between a Produce Department staff member and a consumer)

Consumer to produce department staff member *(whilst standing in front of miserable looking pineapple display):*

"Why is it that I cannot buy the juicy Philippine pineapples here that I can get up the road for $1.99. Who on earth wants these Australian pineapples for $6.99?"

Produce department staff member to consumer *(not really interested and busy placing equally as expensive Californian stone fruit on display):*

"Don't ask me Madam, I only work here."

Deregulation has obviously worked in the produce industry. The importation of bananas, citrus, grapes and pineapple was, when Sauerkraut arrived here, a highly regulated activity. The industry has considerably more freedom to do what it sees fit today and we can thank Rob Muldoon for calling that snap election 20 years ago.

As for that "I only work here" answer - that's the sort of answer which got a lot of Germans into trouble 1 year after the Normandy landings - in 1945.

The 25th anniversary of Sauerkraut's arrival in New Zealand will occur in January 2006. Jacques Chirac is not invited, but the odd pineapple merchant may well get an invite.

Culture - what culture?

If my version of word had Chinese characters, I would be able to make extensive use of them in this column today. Not that I know what they mean, but I sure saw plenty yesterday.

The shopping experience comes in a variety of ways these days. Strip shopping is still around, which has baker, butcher and dairy lined up more or less alongside each other. Then there are the malls and stand-alone supermarkets and big ticket item areas where The Warehouse, Noel Leeming and Bond & Bond, to name a few, congregate.

And now there are ethnic hybrids.

I found one of those on the North Shore today. A group of shops offering goods originating from India, Korea and China as well as local food commodities such as fish, meat and fresh produce selected for and presented to, people who originate from those parts of the world.

The fish shop smelled as fish shops do - but I saw types of fish in there I had not seen before.

The spice shop worked on the same principle as a 'Bin Inn' store. Spices and ethnic bulk foods were stored in clearly marked large plastic containers and one helps oneself with the aid of a scoop and a plastic bag. There were six different types of curry, cinnamon powder as well as sticks, chick peas, broad beans, lentils and at least four different types of Basmati rice.

The fact that the store in typical Indian fashion also operated as an ethnic video outlet, dry cleaning agent, local real estate office and neighbourhood meeting place, with the matriarch perched on a high chair behind the counter sipping tea and observing her customers only added to the exotic atmosphere of the place.

The last shop I ventured into was the greengrocer. Well, actually, it came out to meet me.

The shop had an awning that extended into the carpark at a right angle to the shop front itself.

It featured Okra, long thin Eggplant, Watercress, a range of Chinese veggies I failed to recognise, immaculately presented Bok Choy and spinach - as well as the standard range of produce carried by the local supermarket.

The key points that caught my eye were, apart from the wider range:

- the fruit was generally of a smaller size than is stocked in supermarkets
- all tickets were bilingual - English and Chinese

- the prices were very competitive and in some cases substantially cheaper than at the local supermarket As I was leaving the area I pondered about the wisdom of having such an ethnic culture enclave tucked away behind Kiwi shops. The folly of such thinking became obvious as I wound myself past these so-called Kiwi shops onto the main road.

I had to pass Burger King, Subway and a pub called Mad Dogs & Englishmen to reach the road. Next door was Corniche Interiors and from across the road Danske Mobler and McDonalds beckoned.

Kiwi cultural icons, the lot of them?

Yeah, right.

It's Thursday, it must be Finland

Thoughts on strawberries, bear meat, globalisation and industry co-operation

I recently had the opportunity to visit supermarkets in three European cities over a five day period - Frankfurt, London and Helsinki. Plus Brisbane a week prior.

On first glance, differences were difficult to spot. Globalisation has well and truly hit. There was bugger all difference between store layout, aisle width, checkout behaviour, etc.

When I got my fine tooth comb out though, I came up with the following variations.

The German store was the tidiest. There wasn't a speck of dust visible and grocery items were standing ramrod straight and fully faced on the shelves. Even the bananas had a certain sense of order about them.

Brisbane is still in the dark ages as far as liquor sales are concerned. You won't find beer or wine in any Woolworths or Coles stores. Plants and flowers though were sold from a separate till at the customer information desk, with the displays accessible for shoppers without having to enter the store proper.

The English are as messy as ever but their fresh food ranges continue to expand. The cheese counter at Waitrose is just awesome and when am I going to get grape tomatoes in our stores?

The real revelation was Finland.

Whilst supermarkets are the same around the world, there were some subtle differences in Finland. For starters, I could have purchased canned bear meat if I had been so inclined. Secondly, they sell a berry type called cloudberries. Cloudberries grow near the Arctic Circle and are considered a delicacy with vast quantities of the fruit being turned into Lakkalikööri - cloudberry liquor. Yum.

Beer comes in two types in Finland. Anyone wanting to drink the real stuff needs to go to the pub or an off-licence store. The beer sold in supermarkets is of the watered down variety, as the legal maximum alcohol level for beer sold at supermarkets is 4.7%.

Potatoes are eaten all year around, but a popular joke in the country is that the preferred national vegetable is sausage! This relates to the fact that no Finnish sauna session is considered complete without a BBQ and sausages after one has endured the heat, has flagellated oneself with birch switches and jumped into a lake to cool down.

The single largest fruit crop Finland produces is strawberries and when one visits Finland in mid summer as I did, one can't escape the strawberry vendors. These guys, actually good looking young women in the main, are everywhere. At the railway station, at the bus depot, at every street corner and at the entrances to supermarkets themselves!

One of the other differences is that the Finns sell strawberries by the half litre or litre. Strawberries are largely sold loose and the smiling vendor will measure the desired volume with what looks like a silver milk jug into a pottle or cardboard cup.

Finnish strawberries are red. Real red that is. None of that half ripe stuff on display that we unfortunately still find too often at the bottom of our punnets. Who picks Finnish strawberries? Funny that

- not too many Finns have fruit picking careers in mind. Where have we heard that before?

Finnish strawberry growers are therefore increasingly relying on imported picking gangs, Thailand being the most exotic labour source at present.

Whilst we are talking about strawberries - a fascinating industry project has been under way for a year now right here in Auckland. The strawberries product group of Horticulture New Zealand, HortResearch, The AgriChain Centre, Foodstuffs, Progressive, MG Marketing and Turners & Growers have all been working together quietly behind the scene and without fanfare to improve the food safety aspects of strawberries at all points in the value chain in order to ensure that all chain participants can focus on growing the business rather than getting sidetracked by health scares and consumer anxieties in that area.

This level of cooperation from one end of the value chain to the other has little precedent and needs to be encouraged. Whilst it is never easy to contemplate cooperating with one's competition, we all sit in the same boat, do we not? We rely on the consumers to vote with their wallets and in these days of rising costs, impulse purchasing decisions are increasingly difficult to trigger. All registers therefore have to be pulled to ensure that consumers have no reason to hesitate. The product needs to look good - preferably red in the case of strawberries, taste good and not lead to adverse effects after consumption. It is the latter area that the afore mentioned strawberry project concerns itself with, the invisible stuff.

Let's keep working together on that one.

Food for thought

I have been invited to present a paper on the strategic drivers in New Zealand's fresh produce industry at an agribusiness symposium in Germany in September.

As a consequence, I have done rather a lot of observing and thinking during the last few weeks.

This is by no means an isolated process, i.e. I don't tend to lock myself away in the attic for the duration.

On the contrary, a lot of my views and initial theories are formed as I go about my business or get involved in some of the household chores.

Of late, there have been quite a few banana ads in the paper, offering the fruit at $0.99/kg.

Not just for the day, not just on one or two stores on the North Shore, but right across Auckland.

Late last week I was driving along State Highway 1 between Wellington and Levin. Just about every fruit & veggie mart around Otaki was also offering bananas at $0.99/kg.

Is this part of a general price repositioning? Are Dole and Bonita battling for market share?

Is this a North island phenomenon only? Have the banana companies suddenly forgotten how to ripen bananas properly and are needing to discount heavily week after week?

To what extent are Freshmax's increased banana import activities responsible for what appears to be a retail price positioning?

Is this price sustainable? How will the consumer react when the market tightens again?

Yesterday afternoon I had to go to a garden centre. I happened to go to one that had a Fruit World next to it. Fruit World, for those non-Aucklanders amongst you, is a chain of now 10 stores that continues to grow.

Apart from the obvious that is - bananas at $0.99 /kg, there were a whole bunch of interesting things to observe. For starters, Fruit World had a decent pear display. Every variety available right now from a production perspective was available, not just DDC or Packhams.

The store carried the largest range of Asian vegetables I have ever seen assembled in one place. Both Dole golden and standard pineapples were available, as were Bonita lady finger bananas. Baby leeks were sold alongside their more mature cousins and I was able to buy Fennel - a pleasure supermarkets regularly deny me.

Everything was fresh, the prices were reasonable and the customers were buying. The produce trade is buzzing with the success of this chain and where they might be opening next and I understand that at least three more are planned to open before the year is out.

Defining the strategic drivers of our industry is an interesting exercise - lots of room for thought.

Meanwhile, there appears to be no shortage of shoppers that vote with their wallets and prefer to buy their produce at the green grocer rather than the supermarket.

I would be interested in your thoughts.

Fresh Duck &^%# !

The word 'fresh' took on a lot new meaning this morning. Saturday mornings are usually spent ferrying the teenager to his cricket games.

I enjoy cricket, although I obviously did not grow up with it. Germany does have a national cricket team of sorts, although most Germans would dispute ever having heard of it. The team consists of a group of expatriate gentlemen from the Indian sub-continent…

But I digress.

I do enjoy cricket's tranquility and the way watching schoolboy cricket slows down one's mind - I get some of my best ideas on a summer Saturday morning.

Today was slightly different though.

My son's team was playing another college in a semi-rural setting on Auckland's North Shore. The fun started with the gate to the field being locked. Chairs, chilli bins, cricket bags, umbrellas, newspaper, writing material and other essentials therefore had to be unceremoniously dumped across the fence, followed by the respective owners.

Once across, we discovered that the artificial green 'velvet' wicket served an unusual secondary purpose. The pitch was littered with duck droppings - and, of course, we did not have a broom with us.

The opposing home team appeared unperturbed. This was probably part of its psychological warfare arsenal.

We ended up scraping the droppings from the field with two sets of metal cricket stumps one of the parents luckily had in the car, part of his tool kit as youth cricket supremo for the Takapuna Cricket Club.

The game got underway on time, but not before I observed the soggy droppings breaking open and disintegrating as I was trying to remove them. Not a pretty sight. They looked fresh, but I couldn't really tell how long they had been sitting on the wicket.

This started me thinking about the adjective 'fresh', which is so often used and abused in our industry, the [fresh] produce industry.

Why have I placed [fresh] in brackets?

Well, what is fresh? Are mushrooms 'fresh'- given their liking for horse manure? Are kumara 'fresh' - after 4 months in a storage pit? Are bananas 'fresh'- after having been harvested green 3 weeks prior somewhere in South America?

They all might be 'fresh' into store - but does that make them FRESH? I don't think so.

And what about this one: 'fresh from the markets' - currently used in a supermarket advertising campaign. That is surely like saying, "here, come and have a look at this square circle of mine".

May be it is and may be it isn't. Fresh, I have decided, is all in the eyes of its beholder. The duck &^%# looked pretty fresh to me and any 'fresh' produce, regardless of how long it has been hanging around, is preferable to 'fresh' duck &^%#.

But I do believe we should also put brackets around [fresh] from now on when we use the word in connection with fruit and veggies

- just in case.

PS. We won - and whilst the home team was not 'out for a duck', they lost convincingly by 6 wickets.

Quality at a low price - challenge or utopia?

A discussion of the relationship between produce quality and produce price

Just prior to Christmas I was sitting at my desk, thinking about a theme for this month's article. I eventually settled on 'the relationship between quality and price' - which is a pressing issue in the New Zealand Produce Industry.

Right now, I have a brochure on my desk, detailing the 23rd Fresh Produce Forum, Fruit Logistica 2004, the huge produce exposition staged every year in Berlin, Germany. This year's theme is "Qualität zum kleinen Preis - Herausforderung oder Utopie?"... which, translated into English, means "Quality at a low price - challenge or utopia?"

Here we have confirmation that the quality/price equation is not just a New Zealand issue, but one that is very much on the minds of the global fresh produce trade.

So, what is the definition of quality?

In international terms, for the Japanese for instance, quality may mean sourcing an impeccably perfect apple - at a price of $12 per apple - for use during traditional religious festivals and ceremonies.

At the other extreme is the local shopper, who is looking for apricots to make jam with at Saturday morning's local Farmers Market. To her, quality means something totally different.

To a supermarket or greengrocer quality means a product has to be acceptable at the point of purchase, robust enough to get to the store and continue to look attractive and last on the shelf for a defined period- that is the general quality expectation.

Every buyer is different and therefore has different expectations and tolerance levels with regards to misshapen fruit, appearance and price.

Quality is related to who wants to buy a product, where a buyer wants to buy the product and for what purpose the product is being bought.

There are a couple of grey areas, though. Firstly, what is reasonable in terms of shelf-life? Are long shelf-life tomatoes, for example, benefiting the retailer or the consumer? How much shelf-life can a retailer reasonably expect? How long should produce last in the consumer's fridge or fruit bowl? Secondly, how much 'quality' is included in the base price? Is the shipping of nectarines or peaches in refrigerated vehicles just part of the basic quality equation or should the grower be paid a premium for that fruit? Should the retailer still expect the full retail price for prepacked oranges that had arrived in store a week prior? Does 'quality' erode over time to such an extent that the full retail price should no longer be charged - even if the produce still looks acceptable at retail?

The reality is that both wholesale buyers and consumers do shop on the basis of a price/quality equation. The way they express themselves, however, varies considerably. A banana buyer, for example, assesses fruit on the basis of the technical ripening grade it is being offered at. The consumer looks at whether the fruit presents green, yellow(ish) or spotty when making her buying decision.

So, is 'quality at a low price' something that can easily be achieved? It isn't in my view. What the produce industry, including the retail sector, needs to work on is lifting the value the consumer perceives produce to have. Only when realistic prices are obtained in a sustainable fashion will it become possible to consistently deliver the 'right' degree of quality pertinent to specific crops within a given purchasing channels.

The retail sector can play its part in achieving this goal by ensuring that consumers have as little reason as possible to question the level of produce prices. Buy the best produce available and maintain, grade and rotate your displays religiously.

Brian Gargiulo - Vegfed's answer to Robespierre?

Waking up to Radio New Zealand is one thing. Waking up to Vegfed President Brian Gargiulo's voice suggesting one way to convince government that the taxes associated with the Kyoto protocols will cripple the glasshouse industry is to instigate civil disobedience like the French farmers frequently do, that is something else altogether.

Yet there Brian was, on Rural Report this morning, offering precisely that opinion.

One of my grower friends frequently refers to himself as a peasant. He does so for two reasons. Firstly, because he is extraordinarily proud of what he has achieved in his life and likes to remind himself of the less than fortuitous circumstances he started his life on the land in. Secondly, because he knows that an enormous amount of power and responsibility are associated with being a food producer and that the achievements of our modern knowledge age society have largely been built on the backs of the peasantry across the centuries.

I can relate to that. One of my ancestors participated in the German peasant wars in 1524 - I guess that makes me a peasant from way back!

Whilst Brian was probably invoking the image of French Farmers driving their tractors to the Beehive and blocking the access roads, my mind wanders back further to the early days of the French Revolution, to Marie Antoinette's statement when she heard that the peasants could no longer afford to buy bread.

What was it she said? "Let them eat cake instead."

I can't help feeling that Helen Clark, New Zealand's modern day equivalent, would come up with an equally as inappropriate answer to the glasshouse industry's concerns about environmental taxes and the effects these will have on the profitability of glasshouse growers.

Robespierre's solution, the Guillotine, which soon became affectionately known to Parisians as the 'national razor', is not available to Brian.

But just as Dr Guillotin, the inventor of the machine that bears his name, was assisted by a drunk German carpenter called Schmidt, I am happy to assist Brian in his attempt to get his message across that enough is enough and that economic reality needs to take over from political correctness.

What would you like me to build, Monsieur Gargiulo?

The Fresh [Direct] approach

Tracing the origin of niche produce marketer Fresh Direct and discussing its new Mr. Jack's brand

I have lost count of how many produce industry companies there are which use the phrase 'Fresh' in their name. Freshmax, Fresh New Zealand Produce and Freshco are just three of them.

Fresh Direct is another. The name 'Fresh Direct' is not exactly original either. An initial Google search reveals that there are numerous businesses using that name around the world, involved in anything from fresh produce to grocery home delivery in the US, coffee roasting in Hawaii, direct-to-consumer food processing on the Eastern US seaboard as well as fruit and vegetable catering at the Ascot Races, the Henley Regatta and the British Grand Prix.

Here in New Zealand though, Fresh Direct is the name Jeffery and Peter Turner gave to their fledgling company as they departed the 'mothership', aka Turners & Growers, some ten years ago now.

As fourth generation males born into the Turners & Growers family, brothers Jeffery and Peter Turner could have reasonably expected to spend their entire working life within the family company.

When the company, however, ceased to be the 'family' company through the need to inject third party investment in a drastically changing market place, the brothers decided to leave Turners & Growers to set out on their own.

This they did - much to the industry's consternation and, from some quarters, ill concealed sniggers.

There was general agreement that the industry needed another produce wholesale and import business like a hole in the head. There was also considerable speculation about the Turners brothers' ability to succeed as a small business. The general perception was that Turners & Growers' fading fortunes at the time were to a large extent related to the company's inability or unwillingness to anticipate and react to market place changes. As both Jeffery and Peter Turner had been senior managers and directors of the family business, many industry participants drew unsubstantiated but inevitable links between leadership competence and business performance.

Well, the brothers proved the pundits wrong. Ten years on, Fresh Direct has emerged as a substantial niche focused business that pays particular attention to the floral, organics and pre-packed business segments of our industry.

Its staff size has gone from zero to 150 plus within the last ten years. From initial premises shared with a machinery importer in the Mangere Airport industrial area, Fresh Direct is now in its own custom built premises in Clemow Drive, Mount Wellington, a stones-throw from Turners & Growers.

Visitors to Fresh Direct receive immediate confirmation that Fresh Direct's owners have not forgotten their roots, as the reception area is adorned with ancestral portraits.

Now Fresh Direct has introduced another link to its owners' past

- which is the real reason this story was born in the first place.

Through either good luck, good management or a combination of both, Fresh Direct has come up with a new produce brand that intends to celebrate the past whilst assisting the business to grow further through meeting their customer needs.

The company has launched a range of pre-packed asparagus products under the 'Mr. Jack's' brand.

Remember my earlier comment about Turners & Growers originally being a family business?

The senior members of the family were referred to by their first name and the prenominal 'Mr'. Mr. Jack is actually Jeffery and Peter Turner's retired father who is being honored this way.

Mr. Jack was very partial to elegant headwear and could often be seen walking the market floors, inspecting the produce with his hat firmly planted in position.

The Mr. Jack's brand is a very smart combination of past, present and future. Mr. Jack clearly represents the link to the Turner family's long involvement in the produce industry, stretching way beyond the ten-year organisational life of Fresh Direct.

The 5 + a day logo, barcode and cooking instruction firmly anchor the brand in the present. We can no longer assume that shoppers know how to cook Asparagus, our ethnic mix has become too diverse for that. The 5 + a day logo is a neat way of creating leverage from a well publicised industry campaign whilst in turn spreading the key industry health message further. The barcode is an inevitable reality when marketing prepacked produce through supermarkets.

The FDQ logo is representative of what the future will bring. Consumers are becoming more quality conscious and increasingly concerned about food safety matters. Whilst fresh produce is generally a low risk carrier compared to other fresh food items, it is indeed possible to get very sick from consuming contaminated produce. Greater assurance and improved health standards are therefore a definite future industry focus.

Mr. Jack's Premium Selection - an excellent effort by a young produce company steeped in tradition to take produce marketing to the next professional level whilst acknowledging past achievements in a very personal way.

SARS and the energy crisis - any impact on produce?

Well, that is the $64,000 question. The initial answer has to be 'yes' and 'yes'. Here is why.

Consumer behaviour in the Asian economies has been severely affected. No New Zealand export trader appears to be game enough to quantify the impact, but some of the Australian counterparts are not quite so shy. The executive officer of the Northern Victoria Fruitgrowers Association, Stan Cornish, said in early May that exports of fresh pears and apples from Victoria to Asia could fall by up to 50 per cent as a direct result of the SARS outbreak and the decision by Singapore's health authorities to quarantine the island state's usually hectic produce markets. Victorian fruit growers had budgeted to export about 17,000 tonnes of pears and 3500 tonnes of apples to Singapore, Hong Kong, Malaysia and Taiwan this year and reap about $40 million of export income. Asian markets account for 85 per cent of all northern Victoria's fruit exports, or about a quarter of its total harvest.

Here in New Zealand, SARS has meant that air cargo space for export produce is getting even rarer, as Air New Zealand has cancelled a number of its regular flights to Asia. No bums on seats usually translates into fewer planes. It is called economic reality.

This part of the equation adds up to more New Zealand produce staying at home and entering the local market and probably more Australian produce ending up on this side of Tasman. The net result should be attractive wholesale prices for key export product.

Then there is the energy crisis. Produce growers are no different from any other producer. They require energy - a lot of which comes in the form of electricity. Not every glasshouse complex comes with its own nuclear power station - although some of them are now reaching a size where they probably could justify entering into negotiations with the 'Dear Leader' to obtain North Korean energy know-how of the 'glowing' kind.

Seriously though, glasshouse crops do require more heat in winter, heat equals energy and energy supply will either be disrupted, more expensive or both.

My money is on 'both'.

Will that mean higher produce prices? Well, not necessarily. There is always SARS, remember?

It is probably best to look at things from this point of view. Produce prices are determined by a wide range of factors that interact with each other. This winter there just will be a couple more. And there are bound to be some bargains to be had.

How will one hear about those?

That is where the supermarket with the ability to buy locally is definitely advantaged compared to those stores that are tied into a more disciplined centralised buying regime.

Many export growers are gloriously unfamiliar with the way the domestic market structure works. Often, the first response to needing to shift a serious volume of export grade produce onto the domestic market is a phone call to the nearest supermarket. If the store is able to react and take up the offer, a very attractive deal can often be struck. Those stores, which cannot react themselves and have to pass an offer up the line to a buyer sitting 500 km away, tend to miss out. Growers are only human and it is human nature to pursue the path of least resistance.

Yes, I know, I am walking on quicksand here. Isn't it heresy for someone from a corporate produce buying background to suggest a degree of local buying might be in order? One would have thought so. On the other hand, there is always the customer to consider. What is our job as produce retailers, whether we are greengrocers or supermarket produce buyers & managers?

Isn't it to satisfy the customer?

'Local' customers have this habit of expecting to have the ability to buy 'local' produce - particularly in the provincial parts of the country and can get quite shirty if they find that 'their' local store does not sufficiently support the local growing community.

Contrary to popular wisdom and the fervent belief of the centre aisle jockeys, aka the groovy grocers, produce management is very challenging and demanding as the category is still very much commodity driven and full of raw emotion.

SARS and the energy crisis will just add a little bit of extra spice to an already very volatile industry.

Opinions 285

Summerfruit, boatbuilders and the need for action

Somewhere in Christchurch, Steve is building himself a boat.

As all good boat builders do before they start building boats, Steve first built himself a shed. Once the shed was built, boat construction could start in earnest. Boat building materials were shifted onto the site, helpers appeared and, accompanied by all the necessary side effects, i.e. noise, dust and air-suspended fibreglass particles, boat building commenced. At some stage during the process Steve the boat builder discovered that the boat he wanted to build required a larger shed, so the boat building shed was extended.

The Minister of Economic Development, Jim Anderton, would undoubtedly be pleased with Steve the enterprising boat builder, as the boat building industry is potentially a major income contributor to the New Zealand economy.

All is not well though. Whilst Minister Jim might want to encourage Steve the boat builder, there are a number of people in the garden city of Christchurch who are increasingly getting exasperated - not only with Steve the boat builder, but also with the various authorities which, at least in theory, are responsible for enforcing the by-laws and rules Steve the boat builder needs to operate by.

These people are Steve's neighbours.

You see, Steve the boat builder is located in the middle of a residential area in inner city Christchurch, Living Zone 4 to be precise, and it seems that Environment Canterbury, the Christchurch City Council, OSH, the noise control people, police and the fire department are all able to pretend that this problem does not exist and therefore does not have to be dealt with. At the very best it is "someone else's" problem - which is a bit strange given that Steve the boat builder did not have resource consent to put up his boat shed in the first instance and is, in theory, prevented by zoning restraints from operating a boat building business and storing hazardous chemicals on the premises.

After exhausting all other avenues and having being told by various officials from the Christchurch Mayor down, "there is nothing we can do about this", fed up residents now see "Fair Go" as their last option to get what they consider natural justice.

At certain times of the year the produce industry is quite capable of being equally as ineffectual in solving a problem. The way summerfruit is presented to consumers can be a classic example.

Growers harvest the fruit - and want to get paid. Packhouse operators pack the fruit - and want to get paid. Transport operators truck the fruit up and down the country - and want to get paid. Wholesalers sell summerfruit by the pallet-load - and want to get paid. Retailers would like the consumer to buy plenty of summerfruit

- and they want to get paid as well.

But when a consumer brings a peach or nectarine back into the store because of brown rot, chill injuries or mealy taste - it is often "the other fellow's problem" and no one link in the supply chain is prepared to accept responsibility.

Customer satisfaction is dependent upon the supply mechanism being efficient and effective. Summerfruit needs to be harvested at the correct time, packed and stored the correct way, transported at the correct temperature and handled correctly at the retail rear store and at the point of sale. If just one of the parties involved does not do its part of the job correctly, the entire customer experience is jeopardised - which, in the case of summerfruit, usually means consumer dollars are transferred from summerfruit to bananas, Californian oranges or early season apples.

The New Zealand Summerfruit Council is this year keen to improve customer satisfaction and has commenced an industry education programme aimed at all parties in the supply chain with the goal of improving the consumer satisfaction strike rate when purchasing summerfruit. This initiative is not only very timely, but also absolutely vital in ensuring that consumers will not loose confidence in the New Zealand summerfruit category. I would therefore urge all retailers to support the Summerfruit Council in its endeavours. Waiting for consumers to shout "Fair Go" is not the preferred solution - growers, intermediaries and retailers all need happy shoppers who make repeat purchases.

Some of the good citizens of Christchurch, meanwhile, do not have much confidence left in the various service providers and regulatory bodies responsible for their health and well being - which just goes to show that relying "on the other fellow" simply does not work and that taking action is the only way to progress any issue in need of a solution.

Cause & consequence

One of the challenges with writing this column is that there is a four-week gap between my fingers flying across the keyboard and your eyes and minds absorbing the information presented.

This means that in order to maintain your interest, I have to restrict myself to matters that not only maintain relevancy but are also very topical at the time the magazine lands on your desk.

And, of course, this being an FMCG based publication with a distinct fresh edge (pardon the pun), there is a limit to the topics one can really write about.

It doesn't take a crystal ball, though, to figure out that October heralds the beginning of the local strawberry season and that, this year, some extra spice will be added by the discussion time table about the lifting of the moratorium on genetically modified organisms.

Incidentally, the first European trial of genetically modified strawberries was harvested in Scotland way back in 1996. Scientists successfully introduced a gene from African cowpea to strawberry varieties Symphony and Melody. The gene, known as CpTi, disrupts the digestion of chewing insects such as vine weevil, preventing them from developing normally.

Whilst this undoubtedly is an important topic, as retailers, we should also be concerned about some of the more mundane issues, such as where we get those strawberries from in the first instance, our strawberry ordering patterns and of course, our strawberry merchandising strategies.

Last week I had occasion to visit one of Auckland's 24 hour supermarkets, just before midnight. As I walked into the produce department, I was greeted by a stack of Persil automatic and a stand-alone bin display of over-mature Californian cherries. Not a pretty sight. Further in the department, the high tech mirrorback's automatic misting system sprung into action, providing H2O sustenance to everything in sight - which included loose potatoes, pre-packed tomatoes and bean sprouts!

When the produce manager inspects his department the next morning, he or she will hopefully pick up the 'consequence' - soggy produce. But what about the 'cause'? How well will that be understood?

Too often, unfortunately, people get highly excited about the consequences of a particular action, without fully understanding the cause. Yes, the consequence matters and needs to be dealt with. You can't leave soggy washed potatoes on display. They will rot and they will stink. Don't stop there, though. Figure out how the situation arose in the first place. Determine a solution and implement it.

I went back to that store yesterday and the loose washed potatoes were still in the same position, and sure enough, they were moist when I picked them up.

That store appears content with dealing with the consequences - or not as the case may be - and cannot be bothered about dealing with the cause.

The store's pain threshold is obviously at a level where excessive wastage on loose washed potatoes does not register, which suggests that the real money is in pre-pack spud sales.

But just imagine that the strawberries were sitting in one of those "ve vill gif you vater vhether you like it or not' locations. What would the pain threshold be then? Which brings me back to October, strawberries and summer merchandising.

Here are some suggestions. Order your strawberries daily. Don't leave them sitting around the rear store. Put them into the cooler.

In terms of retail merchandising, I suggest you start by observing the customer flow through the department. It might even be an idea to plot this on a piece of paper. A produce department with the reputation for quality strawberries can enhance total store sales. The opposite is true as well.

Your strawberry display should therefore be eye catching, easy to access, well stocked at all times and irresistible. The price ticket should be easy to spot from a distance and the display should be checked, rotated and restocked every hour.

Shortcuts will get you nowhere with this highly perishable product. And if something goes wrong with your strawberry display

- don't just deal with the consequences. Please try to understand the causes and create a more permanent solution.

Do tomatoes fart?

It generally pays to stay away from politics, but on occasions I find myself compelled to comment on matters that have some connection or other with the Beehive.

During the Produce Plus Conference Week in late July, Brian Gargiulo, the President of the New Zealand Potato & Vegetable Growers Association, delivered his key note address to delegates.

The main theme of Gargiulo's address was the Government's proposed "flatulence tax".

This tax is a direct consequence of our Government's decision to sign the Kyoto Protocols in which member nations commit themselves to reducing global CO2 emissions into the atmosphere, which are deemed to be responsible for increasing world temperatures and raising sea levels.

I don't want to start a debate here about the validity of the scientific arguments surrounding this highly controversial issue. Government, for one, is clearly convinced of the arguments' authenticity and intends to act upon them.

In practice, that means a levy will be introduced next year that would ostensibly raise funds from agricultural and horticultural businesses to research ways by which CO2 could be reduced.

Prior to conference, I had not processed what that would mean in practical terms for the produce industry, although I had seen some figures that would apply in the meat sector. Rural publication "Straight Furrow" had estimated that the levy would be applied at the rate of 9c a sheep, 54c for each beef animal and 72c per dairy cow.

Brian Gargiulo, in his speech, talked about costs of $150,000 per year for a reasonably sized coal burning tomato glasshouse property.

The debate on this levy is heating up.

Government is indignant and feels that primary producers do not want to accept their responsibilities. Minister of Agriculture Jim Sutton asks publicly, 'how else could the Government meet its Kyoto commitments?'

Farmers are being accused of having their heads in the sand and not wishing to deal with reality. The Convenor of the Ministerial Group on Climate Change, Energy Minister Pete Hodgson, says that agriculture is the source of more than half New Zealand's greenhouse gas emissions.

National claims it will repeal the tax if it gets into power and accuses the

Government of duplicity on the way it deals with the Kyoto issues. According to National's estimates, New Zealand is will have to give up one-third of its energy use to meet its 2012 reduction targets - a wholly unrealistic undertaking in anyone's book.

The mechanisms agreed to by the signatory Governments to the Kyoto Protocols for the reduction of CO2 emissions are fairly complex and not only involve reduction targets but also a regime of 'carbon credits' which can be traded.

Without the space to delve into the fine print, I merely question what has happened to common sense in this debate.

The net consequence of being politically correct and signing the Kyoto Protocols means that the cost of New Zealand food production will be going up. No one argues with the need to protect our environment and safeguard it for future generations.

There is also general agreement that we can't be an isolationist Amish style society at the bottom of the world, pretending that the world has not changed and that global problems do not exist.

But let's get real for a moment. How large a contributor can tiny New Zealand actually be to the world production of CO2 emissions? Do we really need to lead the world in bovine and tomato flatulence research?

Is the rest of the world moving forward on this issue? It does not look that way. Most European countries that have signed up have very little chance of meeting emission reduction targets, with the exception of France, which is stubbornly introducing more nuclear power plants.

And what about Uncle Sam, currently impersonated by the one-man brains trust from deep down in Texas? How is he getting on with cutting emissions?

The short answer is - he isn't.

One of George W's first acts, when he eventually got his feet under the desk in the Oval Office, was to withdraw from the Kyoto Protocols. He deemed them unrealistic and not in the USA's national interest.

Common sense from an uncommon source - at least in that instance.

We should be so lucky - political correctness appears to be one of the fundamental platforms of our current Government, which means the 'Fart Tax' is on its way. Costs will increase, primary produce will be more expensive in the domestic market and less competitive offshore, but, hey, we will be able to sleep at night because we are doing the right thing.

Brian Gargiulo and I have been known to spectacularly disagree on certain issues, but in this instance he is right. This tax is a nonsense.

Local or imported, 'for sale' or merchandised?

A discussion on fruit seasonality and the value of merchandising

The world has become a global village. Anyone who disputes this should just stroll through a busy supermarket produce department and pay attention to the origin of the fruit on sale. Bananas from Ecuador and the Philippines, grapes, stone fruit and citrus from California, strawberries from Western Australia, pears from Victoria, kiwifruit from Italy and the list could go on.

Seasonality has gone out of the window. If a decent crop of a desirable product can be found somewhere, our importers will have a crack at bringing it into the country.

Inevitably, there are consequences to shipping fruit between countries or even hemispheres.

Firstly, there is a difference at wholesale level between marketing a local crop and importing a quantity of fruit for sale. A local crop of oranges, for example, will reach maturity at a certain time of the year, with the time of harvest being more or less predictable within a two to three week time frame.

The state of the crop, its quantity, as well as eating and keeping quality, will be determined by the prevailing growing and climatic conditions. Growers, packhouses and wholesalers then set about marketing the whole crop.

Importing oranges is more precise. An acceptable specification is set, fruit is ordered to meet that specification and the retailer sets about selling the fruit he has ordered. Prudent importers will not order fruit on the basis that they might be able to sell it, but aim to agree to an import programme with their retail customers that enables them to import fruit with the knowledge of the agreed volume having been pre-sold, subject to meeting the retailers' quality expectations.

Secondly, local fruit tends to be packed into reusable crates for its journey from packhouse to store, whilst imported fruit usually travels in cardboard cartons or Styrofoam boxes. This means that storage and handling requirements can differ. Stacking cardboard boxes full of oranges on the rearstore cooler floor is not such a smart idea - cardboard and water don't mix well together and I have yet to see a cooler that remains dry for any period of time.

Thirdly, local fruit is most likely fresher, as it will have spent less time traveling than its overseas cousins. This usually extends into a longer shelf life for local fruit, something produce managers often misinterpret as: "I can put this stuff into the fruit bins and not worry about it." Wrong attitude - but I am digressing.

Fourthly, imported fruit has often been exposed to a number of temperature variations between leaving its orchard to arriving at the New Zealand retail store. This means the fruit's tolerance level for further temperature changes within the local supply chain is often different to that of local product. Storing, handling and rotation regimes for imported oranges, for example, can therefore differ from the way local fruit is treated.

Consumer expectations can differ too. The shopper who thinks nothing of buying four punnets of strawberries at a time during the height of the season, might only buy one punnet a fortnight during the New Zealand winter. A crop that serves as the main dessert in summer suddenly becomes a treat for a special occasion in the colder months.

Yes, price has something to with the equation, but even more important is consumer mindset.

What are the meals that are being prepared? What is 'right' for this season? Am I buying this fruit for snacking or as a gift?

Mindset can be influenced. Exercising influence over consumers at point of sale is called merchandising.

Different strategies are required for merchandising produce with steady demand all year around, produce on promotion, produce during its seasonal peak and produce available, at a price, out of season.

The well-trained produce manager understands the differences between the four merchandising strategies and is capable of using all of them.

The produce department that wants to optimise its turnover potential needs to have a well-trained produce manager and staff.

The supermarket that wants to sell more produce to its existing customers needs a produce department that delivers.

Leverage & standards

I endured what is commonly referred to as "Auckland Malaise" recently. You know, getting stuck in traffic on the Harbour Bridge and not being able to move either backwards or forwards.

There is a limited amount of stuff one can do in this situation, such as checking cell phone messages, using a Dictaphone or fiddling with the radio.

Ideally, of course, one should not do any of that, as it is less than safe.

Once I had exhausted the 'unsafe' activities, I decided to play it safe and started to look out of the window.

In the lane next to me stood what I considered to be one of the best 'marketing campaigns on wheels' I had seen for a long time.

It was a sewage tanker! One of these trucks that gets called when one's septic tank needs emptying.

The driver's door was adorned with a simple statement - J. McDonald Contractor. The number plate read 'Big Mac' and the tank itself sported the following message:

'McDonald's Takeaways'.

Basic, to the point and effective.

Great leverage in terms of offering a variation on a global theme and as far as the 'other' McDonald's is concerned - what can they do when one is using one's own name to create an effective marketing tool or advertising message for one's business?

There are obviously limits to how many instantly recognisable brands we can create in the produce industry, but I am sure we can do a better job than we are currently doing.

Mention advertising to anyone in the FMCG industry and people immediately start thinking about money - which in this industry often comes in the form of rebates.

Rebates have also been on the mind of MG Marketing lately. A letter sent by the company to growers and suppliers recently suggested that commission rates would effectively have to go up in order to afford paying the rebates retailers were expecting. MG Marketing suggested that this burden should in future be a shared one, with growers shouldering their share to the tune of 1% of invoice value.

The industry being what it is, letters like these soon make the round and this letter caused quite a bit of speculation amongst competitors.

I, for one, cannot understand why that letter was written in the first place. Surely, it not only had the potential to disturb supply relationships, but also provides a focus points for those retailers who until that letter was delivered had not enjoyed a rebate?

The underlying issue is, however, more complex. What is really going on is that the produce industry does not have an effective trade marketing strategy. There are no norms and no models to follow.

Produce is a commodity with changing fortunes and therefore fluctuating prices. The traditional grocery based FMCG trade marketing models are too rigid and cannot be effectively deployed.

The supply base is not operating on a common structure. Market companies, such as Turners & Growers and MG Marketing, are trying to stretch the traditional 10% commission across an ever increasing number of tasks expected of them - and the blanket no longer fits!

Other merchants create flexibility by trading in whatever produce they sell, with margins being based on what they can get on the day. As this varies, there is little room for a coordinated trade marketing strategy in the 'co-driver's seat'.

Growers supplying directly to retailers in essence negotiate marketing contributions on a per crop or per relationship basis. That can hardly be called trade marketing though, as it occurs behind closed doors and is very much driven by the retailer's direct requirements.

However, times are changing. I believe that we are at a very crucial point of our industry's journey towards consummate professionalism.

The Progressive/Woolworths merger has reduced supply channel options, but speculations that The Warehouse will enter the produce industry in Wal Mart fashion simply will not go away.

The exposure our fledgling private enterprise apple exporters are getting in conducting business in mature well structured overseas produce markets right now, will in time create increased opportunities to introduce trade marketing strategies into the New Zealand market.

The Turners & Growers/ Enza merger, the appointment of a Marketing Manager at Freshmax and the Foodstuffs' companies seriously investigating centralised produce distribution are but three examples that illustrate the industry understands the need to become more professional.

Increasing produce sales and staying profitable

Taking a look at the weekly juggling act between dollars in the till and dollars in the bank

Well, isn't this just the goal of every produce retailer? It is easier said that done though. Retail price reductions do not automatically lead to increased sales, as not all produce is purchased on impulse. Getting the volume increase/ price reduction equation right can be compared to playing Russian roulette. It is entirely feasible, after having had a fantastic week of catalogue sales and a real sense of achievement, to discover that the only tangible financial outcome of the exercise was a drastic reduction in gross profit - which can take a couple of weeks to recover.

What happens when a store runs a special on, for example, 10kg brushed potatoes? Sales of that line will increase, whilst sales of 3kg and 5kg brushed potatoes will drop, with the severity of the decrease being dependent upon the attractiveness of the 10kg special.

Sales of pre-packed washed potatoes will also slow down, but probably not to the same extent, as the potato market has over the years been segmented sufficiently for washed potato users to develop a certain degree of immunity against bulk pack specials of brushed spuds.

On the surface, our hypothetical store has had a good result. Potato sales volumes are up significantly in direct response to the attractively priced special. Gross profit is likely to be down by at least 3% - unless, of course, the store had compensated for the anticipated loss of earnings on 10kg potatoes by taking an increased margin on another line.

Hopefully, the produce manager had anticipated not only the need to order more 10kg bags during the week, but also to adjust the orders for the other potato packs downwards to match the reduced sales in that area. A produce manager who is really onto things, would also understand in advance how the entire potato category would react in financial terms during the 'special' week. Potatoes represent approximately 10% of produce department turnover. The category can therefore impact significantly on overall produce department results.

A produce manager wishing to compensate for the gross profit reduction in the potato category would have to either 'buy better' (a favourite term in produce retail circles) or lift his prices in another category.

This price lift would have to occur within another substantial category in order to achieve the desired result. Doubling the price of pickling onions isn't enough. It would have to be apples, bananas, tomatoes or mushrooms that bear the consequence of an attractive potato special.

This, of course, does nothing to endear the produce manager to the apple and tomato growers who will grumble about our produce manager taking too high a margin and consider themselves to be 'ripped off'.

Whilst there is a certain validity to their argument, it also has to be said that the produce manager has a range of produce to manage, a range of produce to sell and a range of produce to balance.

The nature of commercial activity dictates that at some point in the supply chain the consumer is presented with choice. In our 'first world' economic model that choice is managed within the four walls of the retail store or supermarket.

Choice attracts risk and risk requires astute management. As a consequence, retailers have to balance the needs of a product against the greater needs of a range of products, which is usually referred to as the 'department' and in our case the 'produce department'.

Good produce managers have good tools. Having a sharp knife to slice a cauliflower in half is an essential rear-store tool.

Good financial tools are also essential. Unfortunately, these are not all that prevalent in rear-store produce departments.

One of the key issues that needs to be understood is the difference between mark-up and margin.

Establishing Sell Price excl. GST	**%**	**Values**
Cost Price		$100
Mark-up %	40%	
Mark-up $		$40
Sell Price		$140
Sell Price = Cost + (Cost * Markup)		

Calculate Margin excl. GST	**%**	**Values**
Cost Price		$100
Sell Price		$140

Margin	28.6%
Margin = (Sell Price- Cost Price)/ Sell Price	

The thing to remember is that mark-up calculations are expressed as a percentage of cost, whereas margin is the mark-up expressed as a percentage of price.

Unless our produce manager can clearly differentiate between these two financial factors, he or she is gambling every time an advertised produce special is being run. And we run those every week, don't we?

Fresh produce marketing -the 'not so' basics

Where I raise three key issues of interest to all produce retailers

On one level, fresh produce marketing is deceptively simple. Get the produce to the store, get the produce onto the shelf and your customer will buy it...

Sounds good in theory, but as readers of GR will know the practice is often substantially different.

Each of the three steps involved comes regularly under scrutiny - and so they should. After all, efficiently managing the distribution, merchandising and sales of produce on a consistent basis is what being a successful produce retailer is all about.

How to get even better at it is not just exercising the minds of the local trade, but appears to be a worldwide phenomenon.

Getting the produce to the store

In the UK, one of the political parties represented in the House of Commons, the Liberal Democrat Party, published a report on supermarket environmental practices in 2004.

Among the suggestions made by report author Norman Baker MP, are calls for supermarkets to buy a certain amount of local produce and to source a certain amount from wholesale markets, to use returnable crates as standard for fresh produce and that targets for organic produce should be written into supermarket corporate policy. It also criticises the amount of lorry mileage used by supermarkets as unnecessary.

Geoff Wells, president of Liverpool Markets Tenants' Association was skeptical on the issue of local sourcing and the achievement of recommendations to procure five per cent of produce locally and through wholesale markets in 2005, rising to 10 per cent in 2010. "It would be nice as it would make wholesale markets stronger," said Wells. "But it is not workable in practice. How can you force the supermarkets to buy from the markets?"

The Freight Transport Association has condemned the report. "These claims are nonsense," said a spokesman. "UK supermarkets have led the world in the efficiency of their logistics and distribution and the very high level of vehicle utilisation they have achieved, removing empty running as far as possible and making every journey count...The whole population relies on the supermarkets and others to deliver goods to stores all over the country with the maximum of efficiency and the minimum of cost, to the mutual benefit of retailers and their customers alike. The comments are naïve and misguided."

Getting the produce onto the shelf

The US Armed Forces have their own supermarket chain - the commissaries. One of the perks US soldiers enjoy, in addition to visiting exotic locations such as Iraq and Afghanistan, is the ability to shop at their local commissary, where all goods, including fruits and vegetables, are priced at cost plus 5%!

In a recent worldwide competition named "Produce - A World of Variety" 250 commissaries from around the world focused on regularly stocking, showcasing and demonstrating how to select and prepare the less popular fruits and vegetables in their range. One of the winning commissaries reported sales of mangoes increasing by 50%, pistachio nut sales growing by 75% and blueberries skyrocketing by 120%. When you get your produce onto your shelf and "build exciting displays and offer more variety and let your customers sample some new fruits and vegetables, you build sales and ensure repeat business," said Caroll Allred, the US Defence Commissary Agency produce category manager.

Your customer will buy it

Do customers buy produce? They sure do. Do customers have expectation and standards? Indeed, they have. Especially when it comes to quality, food safety, range/variety and price. As produce retailers know these factors are all related when it comes to fresh produce and not one single factor can be treated in isolation.

The range/variety expectation has probably been the least developed until now. It has only been in recent years through the availability of modern technology that consumers have witnessed the evolution that transformed strictly climate governed local seasons for fruit such as strawberries, apples and nectarines to name a small example, into products available at any time of year, as long as one tolerates exotic origin and higher prices.

Now innovative produce marketers are taking produce marketing a step further. A grape-tasting apple from the United States has proved a big hit with shoppers in the UK. The fruit, called a Grapple, gets its distinctive flavour through using a secret process. Mature Washington apples are immersed for several days in a marinade, which apparently creates the taste of Concord grapes.

The Grapple's sweet flavour and juicy texture has enabled growers in the US to market them as a way of encouraging children to eat more fruit and so help combat obesity. "Kids love them because they are very juicy and sweet. They also smell a bit like bubble gum," said one US marketer who was initially very dubious about the idea.

In a nutshell then: -elsewhere in the world politicians are thinking about the environmental and social impacts supermarket produce operations are generating;

- unlikely retailers are growing sales by succeeding with basic merchandising techniques;
- new technology will create new products. We no longer need to rely on evolution. Any guesses then what new produce marketing and merchandise developments we will see in New Zealand this year?

How to...

I recently met an eleven year old girl who had some interesting eating habits. She eats lettuce but no tomatoes, potatoes but no kumara, carrots but no mushrooms and certainly no leek, pumpkin or garlic. She likes strawberries but will not touch bananas, eats pears but barely tolerates apples, loves cherries but will not go anywhere near oranges.

Getting 5+ A Day into a fussy eater like that is therefore a daily struggle. Where does her menu selection originate from? Not sure, but that's the way things are right now. The 5+ A Day message is neat - but totally wasted on those who don't want to change their eating habits.

A "*How* to get the little darling eating more fruit and vegetables" message with practical tips on how to get consumption up without starting a food fight would probably be welcomed by many an exasperated parent.

"*How* to..." seems to be one of the big issues in our modern society with regards to the consumption of fruit and vegetables in any case.

How to introduce new Asian immigrants to potatoes?

How to teach the next generation of homemakers to prepare vegetables?

How to satisfy consumer food safety requirements?

How to ensure the produce has sufficient shelf life left by the time the consumer actions the purchase?

I could probably come up with a few more "How to ...?" questions, but why should I be having all the fun? I am sure you can think of a few yourself.

"*How* to...? questions are pretty cool because they often lead to new knowledge being acquired or a new skill being learned.

How to get a display set up that looks attractive and does not use up a truck full of fruit?

Dummy the display up.

How to dummy the display up?

Well, there are a number of ways - you don't need me to list them for you.

I am sure you get the picture.

Ask "*how* to...? and your horizon potentially expands exponentially.

On the other hand, you might not be able to cope with all the new knowledge. In this case, just carry on the way you are. Let others ask "*How* to...? instead. But step aside, because they will soon overtake you in the quest of more knowledge, greater job satisfaction and an improved income.

What has all this got to do with the eleven year old drama queen I referred to in the first paragraph?

Nothing at all, other than that the question of how to get her to eat her veggies probably remains unsolved at this stage.

Unless one introduces ice cream into the equation - or rather the withdrawal of said item from the regular menu!

All that Timmy wants

Where I conduct an impromptu English supermarket shopper focus group

In early December I ended up in the UK unexpectedly, and specifically, in the small market town of Buckingham, near Oxford.

Having been collected at Heathrow Airport by one of my more eccentric colleagues, a seventy years young Scottish feudal baron with a penchant for hurtling his Maserati Quattroporte down the M1 on a miserable and wet December Sunday morning whilst casually mentioning to me that he was having a "wee problem" with his right leg, I was more than ready to have a cup of tea and become reacclimatised with quaint English customs by the time we reached home base - the Baron's 16th century manor house in the charming village of Milton Malsor.

After a refreshment stop, we headed into Buckingham to attend what was meant to be a surprise birthday luncheon for the said Baron at the home of his business manager (known in "Baronese" as Baron Sergeand).

There, the 'Sergeand' had laid on a scrumptious spread and invited just about anyone she could think of, who had at some stage or other worked with my host. The gathered group of around thirty included, amongst others, about half a dozen of very strong minded and outspoken women in the prime of their years, many of whom I had met several times over the last 10 years.

I had difficulties believing my luck. My very own focus group of six English supermarket shoppers with at least 250 years of experience as supermarket shoppers between them. How lucky could I get!

I did not have to wait long. The food, the liquid refreshments, the convivial atmosphere and the time of year all contributed to experiences being shared and robust views and opinions being exchanged.

The discussion started with the shabby High Street Tesco stores of thirty years ago, which had the only redeeming feature of issuing Green Shield stamps with grocery purchases. The ladies reached general agreement that Tesco really took off when it abandoned the stamps programme and replaced it with a 15% price drop across the board. Today's elaborate loyalty schemes appear to be wasted on these battle hardened English consumers. This seemed to be particularly the case with Timmy, a people magnet who had not lost her ability to attract attention, despite no longer being a member of the spring chicken department.

Timmy has a minimalist approach to food, having spent the last few extended summers cruising the Mediterranean with her husband on their yacht. Not being a boatie, I got the impression that the vessel was definitely larger than a trailer-sailer, but somewhat smaller the than Royal Yacht!

All trimmings and trappings are wasted on Timmy - she sees through it all. Timmy has signed up to every supermarket loyalty scheme she has come across, but is terribly frustrated by all of them. All that Timmy wants is instant recognition at the checkout of her loyalty status, all communication to be handled there and then, rather than having her letterbox clogged up by offer after offer she has no intention of taking up.

If supermarkets would only understand all that Timmy wants is the food that she likes, when she likes it, preferably on special, no more overflowing letterboxes and all loyalty points converted into cases of her favourite wine, thank you very much. And without asking any questions, as the stores should know the type of wine Timmy buys throughout the year!

Around me, all of a sudden, everyone started sharing similar views and experiences and none of them differed substantially from Timmy's tale.

The connection with produce? Well, produce did not get a mention. The focus of my informal focus group was very much on organisational behaviour and values - what the supermarket companies were standing for and how they were satisfying their, the customers, need in a holistic fashion. The debate no longer revolved around categories, products, meals or meal components, but attempted to measure the overall satisfaction level.

Having the fruit and vegetable department ranged correctly, being able to buy organic, tender meat or being able to choose from a extensive selection of fresh ready meals are no longer differentiating factors - in order to get the customers' repeat business, the overall shopping experience has to be greater than the sum of all the departmental 'successes' enjoyed by a customer on her way through the store.

Be afraid. Be very afraid.

Shoppers are developing immunity to supermarket marketing tactics, just as bacteria have begun to ignore penicillin.

I will visit England again in 2008. Maybe I should ask the Baron to get Timmy & Co together again for a more organised session?

Opportunity lost

2004 has certainly started on a high note. The weather has been fantastic, summer has arrived with a decided level of assertiveness, the politicians are too busy taking holidays at our expense and most of us would have had some time to reflect on our personal highlights for 2003 and the lessons we can learn from the things we did not too well.

I spent today at Ruakaka beach, just south of Whangarei. My younger son is a junior surf life saver - which means one gets to visit some very nice beaches during the season as one transports one's son from one surf carnival to another.

All the Northern Region carnivals are sponsored by X-Box, which means that the brand is heavily represented by way of caps, beach flags and banners.

Each participating club erects its own marquee on the beach on carnival day to provide shelter and a meeting point on carnival day. These shelters are often also sponsored - more often than not by a parent who happens to operate a suitable local business.

I was sitting under the Mairangi Bay shelter today, next to a woman who had managed to manhandle the entire content of her fridge into her chillibin - at least that is what she informed anyone who was within hearing distance in her rather distinct voice. I paid close attention when she rattled off the chillibin content on an item-by-item basis. When she had finished I asked her this question: "why did you not bring any fruit or vegetables in that portable fridge of yours".

She thought about that for a minute and responded. "They are just not convenient." Obviously the woman was an extremist of sorts. I can't think of anything more convenient than a lettuce leaf to put in a sandwich or a banana.

The response is fascinating though. Here is a consumer who literally dragged most of her chilled food, as well as bread board and knife down to the beach but fruit and vegetables are perceived as "just not convenient."

A sample of one is obviously statistically not very sound, but where there is smoke there is fire.

Deep in thought, I set off to the clubhouse to see man about a dog. On my way I came across a local radio station crew that had erected a burger kitchen on the beach. The queue was quite long and I felt pleased for the organisation that would eventually benefit from this fundraising effort. At least that is what I thought this was.

Upon my return I noticed something odd in the behaviour of the Burger recipients as they reached the head of the queue. They appeared to just take a Burger and move on. I did not detect the motions usually associated with handing over money in return for goods or services.

I joined the queue and when it was my turn I got the answer to the puzzle. The Burger Cook's assistant handed me my Burger, smiled sweetly and said, "Here is your free Burger with the complements of Watties."

Sure enough, most of what Watties manages to stick in a can was imprisoned between my two Burger bun halves.

Another wonderful marketing opportunity and not a fresh produce marketer in sight.

Supermarkets - do they still work?

Where I take a slightly provocative look at supermarket food offerings

Supermarkets have their fans and their detractors. Both parties agree that supermarkets sure offer a lot of food under one roof. The differences of opinions arise about whether it is necessary to have as many brands of toothpaste as there are, whether the organic produce is truly organic or just marginally so and to what extent supermarkets are responsible for dead dolphins caught in tuna nets.

There is no doubt that supermarkets fulfil an important function in our society. With the time pressures on modern households, the demographic make-up of said households and the increasing consumer demand for meal solutions instead of just componentry, supermarkets and their incredible ranges are like manna from heaven.

Until one gets stuck at the check-out that is. :

Jokes aside - it is difficult to imagine our society without supermarkets.

And yet…

Why is there one bakery chain after the other opening up? Why is the Mad Butcher continuing to expand like there is no tomorrow? Why do we suddenly have another fresh fish market at the Auckland waterfront? Why are greengrocers and farmers markets enjoying a sudden renaissance?

There is something afoot in our society and to fully understand it we need to look beyond the 12 months horizon so many food businesses have now adopted as their strategic planning boundary.

In fact, we also have to go back in time and appreciate what happened a generation or so ago.

Tom Ah Chee, the founder of Foodtown started off a as a greengrocer in the 1950s. By the time I started working for the company in 1987, the business had grown into 27 stores. Here is what we did not stock: milk, wine, beer, greeting cards, garden benches, more than three or four types of cheese, Swiss Deli sausages, farmed salmon - to mention a few.

Every Thursday night Foodtown head office executives stayed late in the office at Favona Road and had dinner in the cafeteria together. The reason? To show their support for store staff who had to work the Thursday late night. Stores were still closed on Saturdays.

We have moved on light years from where we were 18 years ago, in terms of what supermarkets are offering in their range now.

If we then add the influx of new immigrants, the repopulation of the inner city areas and the increase in single parent household into the equation, we can safely say that the country has changed almost beyond recognition.

What has changed in supermarkets?

Yes, they now sell milk, wine, beer, greeting cards, garden benches, lots of cheese and continental sausages and farmed salmon. Some stores have even added ethnic or international food sections, instore coffee grinders and sushi bars.

Supermarkets, however, have also spent considerable amount of time, energy and money to improve their supply chains. Category management, centralised distribution, cool chain improvement being some of the buzz words that got supermarket operators in general and fresh food managers in particular, excited during the 1990s.

The mere thought of being able to teach unruly categories like fresh fish, summerfruit and beef cuts some rules and behaviours akin to the very compliant cans of baked bean had fresh food experts positively frothing at their mouths.

The prospects for improvement seemed endless and most of the potential benefits highlighted when that particular business phase commenced made perfect sense at the time.

Lettuces can be shipped from Gisborne all around the country. One central meat breakdown plant strategically located means stores no longer need to be supplied with skinned and bled beef carcasses. Refrigerated cabinets save in-store labour because the displays no longer have to be stripped at night and reassembled in the morning. But then there are the customers.

Supply chain optimisation is not something they necessarily understand. Timaru shoppers want to buy Waimate strawberries when they are in season and not the Auckland ones their supermarkets are offering them.

Levin customers do not like Auckland tomatoes and Auckland shoppers do not just want camembert. They want hand formed organic goat's milk camembert, thank you very much.

All our Asian immigrants know that there is more to Chinese vegetables than just Bok Choy and lettuce growers up and down the country who suddenly cannot get their crops into their local supermarkets are trying to get their product directly to the customer via farmers markets.

Supermarkets are incrementally yet increasingly failing to satisfy a growing part of their fresh food clientele. Dissatisfied shoppers are turning to speciality outlets to deliver the food experiences that matter to them. The problem is that every customer is different and category management has its limitations when it comes to corralling the human mind.

Don't get me wrong. Supermarkets will be with us for years to come. In order to prosper though, rather than just survive, supermarkets must refocus on their local customers and the specific needs of that group - and the centralised fresh food buying, distribution and merchandising model may need to undergo some radical surgery if supermarkets want to remain a serious fresh food choice for the discerning consumer.

Some simple maths on groceries and grapes

I went shopping at Pak N'Save on Sunday in a different part of Auckland. I don't usually shop on Sundays and Auckland's North Shore is not exactly well endowed with Pak N' Save stores - I can therefore class my visit as an experience.

At 3pm in the afternoon every checkout was open and customer queues at each checkout were 4-5 deep. My trolley was pretty full and so were all the other trolleys within sight. It took the checkout operator 5 minutes to process my order from the time I put my first items onto the counter to the time I had handed over my cashflow card and thus completed the financial transaction which cost me $150.

If we extrapolate from my experience and assume that for the hour between 3pm and 4 pm the number of people shopping and the volume in their trolleys remained relatively static we end up with this formula for the store's turnover for that hour:

23 checkouts * (60 minutes/5 minutes = the number of customers processed, i.e. 12) * $150 = $41,400.

The answer, $41,400, probably has a 5% margin of error, but is nevertheless quite respectable.

One of the items that did not end up in my trolley were grapes. Not because I don't like grapes or because there weren't any grapes

- but I did not like the grapes that were there! I had seen grapes advertised in the store's flyer for either $2.89 or $2.99 per kg - I can't quite remember.

When I worked my way through the produce department, I could initially not see any grapes. I eventually found the display. Not only was it fairly insignificant in size, but it also featured two types of grape packaging. One lot of grapes was being sold in their little shatter bags straight out of the import tray. The other lot were punnets filled with fruit that looked as if it was celebrating the first anniversary of its instore arrival a week prior.

Not a pretty sight.

How many of the 276 paying customers I estimated (23 checkouts *12 customers) in my first calculation who were passing through the store that hour would have taken advantage of the 'grape in punnets' bargain?

Not too many, I would suggest. People who like a bargain still expect quality of sorts.

May be only 30% of those customers would buy their produce at the store anyway. If those 30% got offended by what they saw, then the equation about the amount of produce business one could loose might look like this

Business lost = (276*30%)*$20*52= $86,112, with $20 being the assumed average weekly produce expenditure.

Again, there might be room for error - but the principle stacks up. Scary stuff - it does not pay to put produce of below quality up for sale - regardless of the price.

And why were those grapes in such a state? Any grape importer who might wish to comment should drop me a line.

Competence, capacity & consistency

Where I ponder 2008 uncertainties from a retail produce perspective

GR editor John Winter made reference to the new year starting with "a degree of uncertainty" in his February editorial. John came to that conclusion having analysed the 'big item' topics of New Zealand food retailing which revolve around the future of The Warehouse, the Commerce Commission approach to the big red sheds attracting suitors and the strategic direction of Australian supermarketing which, like it or not, impacts on the local scene.

There are probably a few produce growers out there in rural New Zealand who are also experiencing a degree of uncertainty - in their case, though, the issue is more immediate. In particular, they are probably asking themselves three questions at this point in time.

1. What impact will the sudden disappearance of Progressive's Divisional Manager Produce the week before Christmas have on my business relationship with that company this year?
2. How can I turn the opening of Foodstuff's new Auckland Fresh Produce Distribution Centre into a new business opportunity for me?
3. What's this I am hearing about more produce being sold through the markets again in the future?

Are consumers interested in these questions or the answers to them? Not really; consumers just care about getting the right produce, at the right price and in the right quality - every time they enter the store. At least those consumers who are still buying their produce at supermarkets and have not yet switched to greengrocers or farmers markets. Don't get me wrong. Supermarkets will as long as they continue to exist have a significant fresh produce market share but at the very least, this share is no longer growing at the rapid rate that it did in the eighties and nineties and I am going to stick my neck out and say: growth has stopped. This means that when one or other of the supermarket chains proclaims that their fresh produce market share has risen in a particular period, it is likely to be at the expense of the respective supermarket competitor rather than the independent sector.

There are three key components in every working business relationship. These are competence, capacity and consistency. Poor growers do not (and should not) stand a chance to be picked as a supermarket supplier. Supermarkets do not deal in a crate of this or a crate of that but in truck and trailer units, thank you very much. And surprises on a daily basis are not appreciated.

Growers and suppliers who can deliver against these components will assist supermarket retailers to satisfy their produce customers.

Get it wrong and customers will move through your produce department without giving your fruit and veggies the consideration you think they deserve. The customer is king and unfortunately New Zealand's chosen form of government, a parliamentary democracy with all the bouquets and brickbats associated with that status, prevents retailers from introducing compulsory automated cash extraction mechanisms that are triggered when customers get within two feet of a produce display cabinet.

Customer trust needs to be earned the hard way and it is just as well that New Zealand produce growers, packers and suppliers have been through many a change over the last twenty years and know exactly how to satisfy the retailer need for competence, capacity and consistency when it comes to getting the produce to the grocers on a daily basis. In fact, let me stick my neck out again. There are a number of New Zealand produce growers who are operating at a competence level that is right up there with the European and US standard setters and these guys do not need to hide their light under a bushel.

I, for one, would like to see a lot more certainty this year in relation to the retailers' skills in keeping the produce in top notch condition *after* it has been delivered by the supplier and before the consumer places it into her trolley. Looking after produce at retail is a skilled job and it requires skilled people who take pride in their work. They also need to have competence, capacity and consistency or the produce department they are working in is on the slippery slope.

Give this some thought please because it matters.

In praise of maturity

Reunite supermarket fruit & vegetables departments and mature sales assistants, I say.

Mother England still has a lot to answer for in certain areas and the fruit and vegetable industry is no exception. At one end of the spectrum British Universities keep on generating research papers with grandiose titles such as "Understanding the nature of collaboration within fresh produce value chains" (Cardiff University), which discusses, amongst other things, how growers, wholesalers and retailers should in an ideal world work together to consistently deliver optimum value to consumers when those shop in supermarket fresh produce departments.

At the opposite end of the spectrum, populist author and disgraced Tory politician Jeffrey Archer has immortalised fictional Cockney fruit barrow boy Charley Trumper, The Honest Trader, in As the Crow Flies. Sales patter such as " 'alf a pound of your King Edward's, a juicy grapefruit from South Africa and why don't I throw in a nice Cox's orange pippin, all for a bob, my luv?", and "I have some lovely bananas just flown in from the West Indies. Ought to be selling 'em at ninety pence a bunch, but to you, my old duck, fifty pence, but be sure you don't tell your neighbours.", conjures up beautiful word pictures about the fruiterer / customer relationship of old.

Unfortunately, this is not the kind of dialogue heard in local supermarket produce departments today.

With academia producing reams of paper on the topic and supermarkets relying on continuous technical improvements such as quality assurance schemes for growers, dedicated produce distribution centres, refrigerated transport, and chilled sales cabinets with temperature zone options, the rational observer could be forgiven when assuming that *All is Well on the Western Front* (Ernst Maria Remarque) and that consumers are gloriously happy with the quality of produce on display in supermarkets, both in Old Blighty as well as in God's Own.

Unfortunately, this is not quite the case!

Letters to the Editor, web blogs and chit chat in suburbia hone in on fruit and vegetable price and quality at the slightest provocation - and there is plenty in these times of high interest rates, commodity values and petrol prices. So why do consumers perceive there to have been a drop in fruit and vegetable quality in their supermarket produce departments?

How about this for an answer?

When supermarkets discontinued the use of manned weigh stations in the produce departments in the early nineties and integrated produce weighing into the check-outs, the mature women, who until then were a prominent feature of all suburban supermarket produce departments, faced extinction. Weigh station staff were no longer required in the produce department. Supermarket bean counters rubbed their hands together in glee, congratulated themselves on a job well done and focused on alternative investment options for monies saved. Shoppers were told that this innovation had been introduced with them in mind. Shopping would become a lot easier, now that one no longer needed to queue in the produce department to get one's fruit and vegetable purchases priced.

A slight problem soon emerged.

What had been overlooked was the fact that the mature weigh station assistants did not just stand next to their scales all day waiting for customers to approach them with to be weighed and priced fruit and vegetables.

In between weighing spurts, these women also restocked the banana tables, graded the tomato display, gathered up the loose onion skins accumulating in the root crop section and removed the soft fruit from the peach display.

In other words, the weigh station activity was a component of an integrated continuous improvement process of critical importance to maintaining the daily presentation and quality standards of the entire fresh produce department.

Think about it for a moment.

> The produce department of your local supermarket does not just contain the obvious, i.e. fruit and vegetables, but potentially also the odd vinegar fly buzzing near some overripe nectarines, ethylene gas generated naturally by maturing fruit, bacteria gathering on a potato that was damaged by the automated harvester and microbial growth on soft fruit not handled properly at some point or other in the supply chain.

Without the weigh station attendants problems soon materialised. The solution? Labour hours were put back into those stores but in their wisdom, supermarkets went for school leavers instead.

Even the most intelligent teenager cannot multi task like a mother of three school age kids. Nor does the average youngster have the social skills to have a chat with customers as they peruse the produce on offer; and are teenagers really capable of answering product related questions posed by discerning shoppers in search of information not found on the price ticket?

In conclusion - even if the produce is of exceptional quality as it enters the store, what one finds on the shelf will be affected if it is not maintained correctly.

It is time the mature women came back.

Of cabbages and kings...

There are those items in the produce department that provide all year colour or consistency, such as bananas or potatoes. Then there are the seasonal highlights, luscious strawberries or tender asparagus

- and then there are the staple greens. The items one does not necessarily pay any attention to when shopping in a produce department, but expects to be there anyway. Cabbages, cauliflower and broccoli fit into that category.

These vegetables can be found on the mirrorbacks or in the multidecks of every produce department or greengrocer's store in the country without fail.

Produce ranges have undergone substantial changes in the last thirty years and Brassica, the botanical name for this group of vegetable, have been a significant part of it. Yet, this is not something that is immediately obvious when standing in front of them.

In many cases, 'development' in the produce department has meant the introduction of prepackaged items, an increase in variety, seasons stretching out through imports and brand development on either product or at point of sale.

This 'development' seems to have bypassed cauliflower, broccoli and cabbages.

Or has it?

On first glance it has. A quick walk along a mirrorback reveals no major brand introduction, there are no PLU stickers in evidence, there is no sign of new varieties and a consumer convenience focus appears to be lacking.

Three or four stores later and a similar overall picture emerges. But there are some exceptions. Leaderbrand Broccolini is being sold in one store. Another retailer is featuring wrapped cauliflower and a third one has a big sign up stating "we cut your cabbages in half if you ask us."

None of these initiatives were happening across the board though, which suggests that the Brassica corner seems to be escaping the attention of the retail teams.

What has happened to prepacked cauliflower and broccoli fleurettes? Do stores really still cut all their cabbages on the dirty bench in the rear store? Where are the mini cauliflower that are all the rage in Europe?

Traditionally, there has been very little value attached to Brassica. They are a commodity, a product the retailer perceives where he can turn the tap 'on' and 'off' as it suites. To a degree that is correct.

But if we want products to earn us a consistent margin, we need to evaluate them in the context of how the consumer uses them and what that means for the way we need to present the product in order to grow our business.

Cauliflower does need some protection in transport, but we are still carting more green leaves from the paddock into the stores than it makes economic sense. What happens to those green leaves when the cauliflower gets into store? We cut them off and dispose of them. Couldn't we leave them in the paddock in the first place and pack cauliflower like the Dutch? Pre-trimmed, head up, six in a crate. Yes, we would probably fit fewer in the truck, but that cost could be offset against the cost it takes to trim the cauliflower at retail and dispose of the leaves.

This highlights the next problem in developing an under performing category such as Brassica. Costs are being incurred at different ends of the supply chain (grower versus retailer) and until the parties sit down and understand that they are in the same business and should jointly reduce costs to grow the business, growth will not occur.

How did we start this article? "Of cabbages and kings…"

Produce marketers need to become more aware that the consumer is king and that the fortunes of cabbages, the other Brassica crops and everything else offered in the produce departments hinges upon our ability to listen to and interpret consumer needs and deliver accordingly.

Convergence

Convergence will occur as a result of achieving operational excellence in the areas defined by the preceding six CON-Factors. It is an outcome, rather than a process. By achieving operational excellence in CON-Factors 1-6, organisations will either be ready to become effective demand chain leaders/ builders or be more flexible in how they fit into a chain put together by others.

I have been looking forward to starting this chapter ever since I decided to use the CON-Factor structure as the underlying architecture of this book. The previous CON-Factor chapters, Thought Pieces and Opinions are all about experiences - and experiences by definition are in the past. Whilst we need to have an appreciation of our experiences in order to understand what the future might hold, the future will just happen to us if we do not take an active interest in anticipating and managing it. Convergence brings the various strands of our lives, be these professional, personal or a combination thereof together, allows us to evaluate what has been before, understand where we are at now and, most importantly, puts us in the position to attempt to appreciate what the future has in store for us.

Convergence is the Action part of life!

Convergence happens at every level. On the personal level, I am sitting here on a sunny January morning in 2010 starting to write this chapter and enjoying every minute of it. There are a few other things I have deliberately 'parked' for today. There is the Australian research project into fresh food packaging that needs to be scoped, I need to have a serious conversation with the Bursar of IMCA, our Action Learning Business School, who is based in Buckingham England, a Dutch colleague is wanting to discuss marketing strategies at Fruit Logistica in Berlin, the accountant wants me to herd the prospective trustees of our Action Learning trust together so that the Trust Deed can be signed - and I am going trout fishing tomorrow.

The AgriChain Centre has a publishing division and I have just hired my first professional editor and will stop filling that role myself. Our fruit survey team has work coming out of its ears in the area of imported fruit inspection. Biosecurity training relentlessly grinds on week after week and Food Safety concerns are taking on greater importance in consumers' minds rather than becoming yesterday's fad. As a business we are involved in all of these areas on a daily basis. We also take on complex industry research projects and offer strategic advice to producers, trading businesses, retailers, grower organisations and government departments. I have a real difficulty with answering the typical question, "and what do you do for a living?" in under five minutes.

Am I the only one with this problem? Certainly not. Retailers have started importing fruit instead of leaving it to the importers. Strawberry growers are turning themselves into retailers, competing head on during the season from temporary or mobile premises, preferably within a couple of hundred meters of a retailer's premises. Many apple growers are bypassing the established fruit export firms and are taking on the job themselves.

My mobile phone has undergone a real metamorphosis in the last 20 years. My first model was the size and weight of a building block and needed to be moved via wheel barrow. Today's version has morphed into a communication device that delivers phone calls, messages, texts, emails, the web, twitter, plays music, acts as a GPS unit and weighs so little that when I sit on it accidentally, I don't even notice it.

In addition to being the Managing Director of The AgriChain Centre, I am the publisher of HortSource, a Member of the United Fresh NZ Executive, the Chief Executive Officer of the International Management Centres Association, a Trustee of the 5+ A Day Trust and Chairman of the International Federation for Produce Standards. Yet I can still sleep at night. So what is going on?

The AgriChain Centre

The reason that this business is doing so many things with a relatively small number of staff members (17 at the time of writing) is that's what's needed for survival. New Zealand is a small country with just on 4 million inhabitants. Whatever one's business activities in New Zealand, the market is small and highly specialised businesses operating in small market are very vulnerable. The degree of our diversification acts as an insurance policy against changes in market place behaviour, economic downturn and unwarranted customer perceptions, all of which have the potential to seriously impact upon a business' bottom line.

A business needs to be a dynamic, responsive and responsible organism in order to survive, grow and prosper. Dynamic in terms of change driven by the market place and its customers; responsive in terms of messages received from the market, shareholders and staff; and, responsible in the way it goes about implementing change.

Survival, growth and prosperity are key objectives for any business.

Survival, in particular, was quite topical in 2009 - but no business has a long term future if survival is the only objective. Growth can be a double edged sword - and growth for growth's sake is not a tenable long term position. Opportunities for growth need to be assessed and selected or discarded, not allowed to pass by or hopefully happen on their own accord. Prosperity is the ultimate goal for any 'for profit' business. In a balanced world, this means prosperity for shareholders as well as prosperity for the team that makes it all possible - employees.

Profit is not a dirty word but a fundamental premise in order to generate and maintain private sector employment. This is achieved through reinvestment of profits into the business, maintaining relevancy in the market place as well as responding to and generating new business opportunities.

Being able to multi-task, deploying one's skills across a range of different business opportunities and being comfortable about entering unchartered waters as long as the vessel is seaworthy will continue to be the norm for The AgriChain Centre and many other companies which are following suit.

Growers / Importers / Exporters / Retailers

What all these players have in common is that they are part of the value chain. What they also share is the belief that they know best, have the skills to perform the functions of other value chain participants and are therefore able to improve the value they extract by squeezing the margins of the other players. On one level all of them are right - on another level though, what is being played out has the potential to become an unmitigated disaster.

Philosophically, there is of course nothing to stop any business from expanding its horizons and to learn how up- or downstream functions support its own role. From there, it is only a small step to 'we might like to try having a go ourselves.' This is all very well when one understands the functions of the other players completely, has the resources to do the job properly and understands all the risks associated with getting involved in the first place.

An apple grower taking charge of his own export operation is suddenly no longer solely focused on the production, harvest and packing of quality fruit. Could this have a consequence? Marketing fruit offshore is not a cheap exercise and with the odd exception retail produce buyers have the attention span of five year olds. If one is not constantly in their face, they soon forget about one. It would therefore be advisable to have more than just one or two varieties to market but enough scope to maintain a presence through the entire apple marketing season - or even better, the whole calendar year. But doesn't that mean the grower who is now an exporter would have to market other people's apples? Precisely, our grower is now a marketer - and most likely a market agent or broker for other apples. Apart from this aspect of the operations needing to be financed, who in the meantime is worrying about what happens on one's own orchard, which by the way also has a healthy appetite for devouring cash in terms of maintenance, crop husbandry, expansion and development?

One's fellow apple growers are naturally delighted with one's foray into fruit marketing. "It needs a grower to deal with these retailers," they say. "Only a grower can make this work in the long term". Great, plenty of support then. No sooner has this support been expressed, than our growers demand their progress payments - "just like the exporters make them. If you can't cope with that, then may be you should have stuck to growing." Brilliant, absolutely brilliant that is. And just as one is coming to grips with the fact that one's brethrens have a very short memory, the bill from the shipping company comes in. "What do you mean, that is the cost? Over the last three years my average shipping rate per carton was a lot less than that . What is going on here, day light robbery?"

"Not at all my good man - it's just that you were benefitting from consolidated bulk rates over the previous three years which your exporter had negotiated with us on the basis of the total volume he was contracted to sell. Your volume does unfortunately not come close to it. And then there's exchange rate variation, increased port charges, a lack of suitable vessels, the extra handling because you are really just shipping a minute amount and, and, and ..."

Meanwhile in the retail corner, someone has decided that they should import their own bananas. Yes, there is the potential to improve the margin, because one can cut out the dreaded middleman, the importer. So the bananas are coming into the country and are ready to be sold, with the importer just clipping the ticket? Actually, no. There is the small matter of getting green bananas, because that is the state in which they arrive, to turn into yellow bananas. This procedure requires ripening rooms, personnel skilled at ripening bananas, a plentiful supply of ethylene gas - and of course storage space needed to hold the green bananas that are still waiting to be ripened and the yellow bananas after they have come out of the ripening rooms and before a retailer buys them. The latter better take no time at all, otherwise one's yellow bananas will become black fairly promptly.

It is clearly possible to save costs in terms of the importers' margin, but it appears that there are fixed costs related to getting bananas ready that will be incurred regardless of who actually is the importer of record. Another consideration is the assumption of risk. A retailer who buys his ripened bananas from his local banana importer does not assume responsibility for the fruit until it has been delivered to his distribution centre or store and he has formally accepted the shipment. A retailer who imports his own bananas takes responsibility for the fruit as it is loaded onto the vessel in faraway Ecuador or the Philippines. The effort it takes to get the fruit into a saleable state after it arrives in the country where it's be sold are considerable. How far should a retailer's focus extend? Yesterday they were selling produce they bought at auction. Today most corporate retailers around the globe purchase a significant amount, if not all, of their produce needs directly from producers and retailers importing their own exotic fruit are becoming increasingly common. What will tomorrow hold? Retailers who buy the farms where their bananas are grown to control the volumes released onto the market? Why not?

I'll tell you why not. At the end of the day, in a consumer driven market economy, consumers notice when retailers begin to loose their focus. Consumers operate on the assumption that the primary focus of retailers should be on their customers, the shoppers and consumers who frequent supermarket stores. When stores loose that focus it shows through what happens on the shelves - or more to the point what does not happen on the shelves! We have turned from a society of hunters and gatherers into ... a *modern* society of hunters and gatherers. The difference being that today we *hunt* by way of working in return for money and then *gather* what we need at one or more food outlets.

In the same way our ancestors moved on from berry thickets which were no longer yielding good or sufficient numbers of berries, our modern equivalent selves abandon tired stores and tired displays in favour of new hunting grounds, such as better managed stores, farmers' markets and the like.

Store owners, a generic term which encompasses anything from the corner dairy to a multinational corporate food retailer, have taken over from Mother Nature. Once upon a time, Mother Nature caused us to change behaviours -

when one food source dried up, we moved on to the next one. Today, supermarkets consider themselves to be the ultimate consumer advocate, albeit self-appointed, and drive our behaviour in relation to food sourcing through their catalogues, store layouts, pricing policies and range determinations.

To top it all off, food is no longer a supermarket's main consideration. The wider offer may differ from country to country. Walking into a typical English Tesco or Sainsbury store enables one to deal with all household insurance requirements including pet related ones, pay utility bills, book holidays, check the bank balance, see the optician and purchase new glasses, get dietary advice, order one's wedding bouquet, buy a new computer, organise broadband access and, of course, get one's groceries.

If that is not convergence, I do not know what is.

Convergence can at one level therefore be described as the ability of individuals or business entities to combine multiple functionalities in terms of identities adopted, activities conducted and services offered.

How is this possible though? Why does the person or organisation practicing convergence get away with this without suffering a nervous breakdown of sorts? What makes this possible in the first place?

This last question - "what makes this possible?" - is the one we ought to tackle in the first place in order to gain a better understanding of the wider phenomenon.

What makes convergence possible?

There are several drivers that contribute to convergence becoming a common format in individual and organisational behaviour; namely, communication technology, distance management, resource considerations, time constraints and value attitudes. These drivers have existed across time and for many generations. They have not always been called by these names but they have always been there.

This book is related to the fresh produce industry. My focus in discussing the drivers related to convergence is therefore firmly based on how they impact upon that particular industry sector. The underlying principles however apply to all industries and all cultures.

Communication Technology

Mobile telephones, fax machines, personal computers, the Internet in general and social networking tools, such as Facebook and Twitter in particular, were not known in 1981. Neither were acronyms such as LAN and WAN, the former standing for Local Area Network, whilst the latter describes a Wide Area Network.

Computer systems were big brutes, housed in air conditioned rooms and certainly had next to zero ability to talk to each other - apart from the embryonic work that was in progress already in the US Department of Defence and selected US universities and which ultimately became the forerunner to the Internet as we know it today.

In the absence of these technologies existing, the processes that delivered 'messages' were separate from each other and mechanised. The delivery of a letter, for example.

Today, I can use my laptop to create a financial feasibility study, write a proposal to go with it, attach both documents to an email, fire it off and ring the recipient via Skype to warn him or her of the message's pending arrival. And approximately one hour after I have sent it all off I start fidgeting because I have not yet received a reply.

Not only am I able to use one and the same device to create my message and communicate it, but the fact that the device; i.e. my laptop, is capable of doing so and this has therefore become the new norm, my expectation has changed in terms of when I expect a response. Hearing from my prospective client three days later is no longer good enough, I expect the answer to come back a lot sooner.

The time we are saving by using converging technology and the nanoseconds required to dispatch our messages to all points of the globe has altered our expectation in relation to the time that conducting business itself should take.

Distance management

Fruit and vegetables have always defied distance. The old Romans used to ship fruit around the Mediterranean and the importation of "zuid vruchten" (literally translated as southern fruit, and originally a term for oranges travelling north) was a common event on the Spanish/Dutch trade routes of the 16th century.

New Zealand pioneered frozen meat shipments all the way from Timaru to London in the 19th century, so the concept of distributing perishable produce from producer and consumer is well established across all primary produce categories. And yet....

There are always risks involved with sending perishables from A to B. Fruit and vegetables need to be handled correctly, they must be transported and held at the correct temperature and if fruit and vegetables had not been packed correctly in the first place, one needs to expect trouble in any event.

Then there is the matter of the correct picking time. When is fruit ripe - as opposed to mature? What do you mean, there is a difference? Go on!

Managing the quality of fruit and vegetables in such a way that the distance between production area and market does not become an insurmountable barrier is a major convergence exercise in its own right.

There are so many factors that contribute to success or failure that fresh produce logistics management is not a job for the faint hearted or those lacking industry skill and knowledge.

Resource consideration

Everything is called a resource these days - labour units, i.e., orchard workers and shop assistants, money, time, energy, you name it.

Typically, just being able to access one type of resource is insufficient to survive in business. In order to stand half a chance of harvesting a decent crop, a grower needs to ensure his lettuce plants have sufficient water. If he is lucky, rain will suffice. If that is not the case, the grower needs access to water for irrigation. No water, no lettuces, no money, no grower, no lettuce.

A supermarket with full shelves and in full swing will come to a grinding halt if someone suddenly cuts the electricity supply. The store is still there and so is the produce but without light to see what one is being offered, without refrigeration to keep the crop fresh and without the checkout operators being able to transact the sale at the front of the store, customers will relatively fast become scarce.

Time constraints

The clock starts ticking even before the crop is harvested. Once the crop is out of the ground or off the trees, the urgency only increases. Crop deterioration begins the minute the harvest process has been completed. Postharvest structures and behaviours aim to optimise the period between harvest and when the consumer is being presented with the opportunity to purchase the produce. Mucking around at that point is not an option.

If you think about it, mucking around isn't an option at any stage, right from the point in time when the paddock is being prepared for planting. And right through the production process the time constraint concept raises its head across the spectrum.

When it is too dry, plants can wilt on the spot. When it is too wet, one cannot dig or maintain the plantings. When it is too hot, crops can experience exponential growth. When it is too cold, crops are likely to be stunted. There is a right time for everything and every aspect of crop management has to be performed within a certain time frame.

The same goes for the retail aspects of the industry. How far ahead should produce be ordered? When is the best time for delivery? How long does it take to unload a truck, break down the load, stack it away and still have the shop looking good for the first customers?

Value attitudes

What is an apple worth? More than a banana? Less than a cabbage? How should the price be established in the first place? Cost of production and a bit of a profit for the producer? Or do we work backwards from what the consumer is prepared to pay?

There is continuous debate in this area. On one level, growing vegetables, for example, is a far less complex process in the eyes of the consumer than processing the vegetables in a cannery - which is why most consumers happily pay whatever price is on canned tomatoes, but argue about the price of fresh ones.

How value gets established, what the contributing factors are that assist consumers coming to grips, or not as the case may be, with the value equation for everything they need to obtain in order to survive, is one of the most contentious issues across the fresh produce industry globally.

Arbitrarily setting a price is easy. "$1.99 it shall be", says the manager. "Right you are," responds the assistant and slaps a price sticker on the product. Oh, if it were so easy.

Convergence, in short, is achieving harmony between these drivers. It is not something that gets taught at school, be that kindergarten or graduate school. Convergence is a state that we subconsciously try to attain every time we tackle a process.

Convergence - something new?

We are actually familiar with this concept. The word itself is relatively common in the English language. A Google search brings up more than twenty-five million hits. We live in a converging world. Not only are technical solutions, concepts and processes converging right around us, but the convergence process itself is speeding up exponentially as a result of our collective learnings as a thinking species being synthesised faster with the aid of technology and communication faster through the web, social media, viral marketing and the like.

And while we are on that theme - are we a *thinking* or a *sinking* species? A new generation of young thinkers emerging around the world is suggesting that part of our problem as a race is our unwillingness to acknowledge that we are part of nature, albeit a highly developed part, and act accordingly. I do not want to dive too deeply into fundamentalism etc, but ask yourself these questions:

What is the function of the fresh produce industry?

Why does the fresh produce industry exist?

What condition/situation had to occur or evolve in order to 'legitimise' the concept of shifting fruit and vegetables from the growing areas into the places where people who need to eat congregate?

We don't think about the meaning of life every day. We get caught up in the operational issues of growing produce, harvesting it, getting it to market and seeing it purchased by eaters.

In medieval times the eaters were called peasants and burghers

- today we know them as consumers. And instead of sickle and ladder we use combine harvesters and the like to start the process of getting our daily needs to the table.

So, on one level nothing has changed. On the other hand, our life expectancy is around eighty years instead of the forty-odd which was the average three hundred years ago and eating food produced in distant parts of the world has become the norm rather than the exception.

The plate

Another very important type of convergence happens every day right in front of our eyes, every time we sit at the dinner table and fill our plate with food. It doesn't matter whether you are eating Spaghetti Bolognese, a Hangi, Chicken Kiev, Beef Wellington, Sushi, Pork Fried Rice, meat and three veg or a vegetarian meal. Each of the meals consists of several food ingredients, each being the end product of its own unique supply chain - and these supply chains are converging in front of us on the plate. That is every food supplier's dream - to be on my plate one night - every night actually!

That raises another interesting question. At what point of the supply or value chain do we switch our thinking from a food or ingredient focus to a meal focus? Is it when we sit down and write the shopping list? Is it when we enter the store? Is it as we pick up the individual food items and place them into our trolley? Or is it on the night - when we start thinking about combining some of these individual items into a common product - our dinner?

Wherever the precise point is where we change from a separatist to a wholistic view - can that point be transformed? And should consumers be the only ones thinking about this or not? In other words, is it OK for a food marketer to come up with the meal solutions? If so, at what point? Through advertising material in the store? By having little fridges at the supermarket aisle ends that promotes whole chicken, frozen mixed vegetables, a sauce mix and a bag of potatoes as a mixed deal? By offering complete microwave meal solutions in both fresh and frozen formats?

My older son went through a few interesting phases during his four years at Otago University. One year he came back in the semester holidays, convinced that he needed to be on a cave man diet. You know, only eat meat and the equivalent in terms of greens and pulses that the women would have gathered in the cave man days, before agriculture was en vogue. For reasons that still elude me, travelling complete with an electric juicer and juicing all vegetable and fruit in sight was part of the scheme, to the extent that we were wondering why the fresh fruit salad my partner made every evening for breakfast the next morning was disappearing at a rapid rate of knots - University had obviously taught him the odd shortcut and 'hunting' for fruit salad to feed his juicer was a lot easier than having to peel the apples and oranges himself!

On the bright side, I was really pleased that he was abandoning fast food solutions in favour of wholesome options. Unfortunately, cave men are not too keen on cleaning their juicing equipment... but that is another story.

My point is this: Our stomach is the ultimate convergence location. Fruit and vegetables must play an important part of the mix that meets in our stomachs several times a day because our digestive system is a whole lot more conversant with digesting fruit and vegetable fibres than it is with turning meat into usable energy. So how can the produce industry become more professional with its marketing efforts? What else can we do apart from producing commodities and dispatching these around the globe?

We need a strategy.

Strategy

Over the last eighteen months I have been involved with the development of an industry strategy for Horticulture New Zealand. This involved working as part of an industry advisory group with the appointed contractor responsible for delivering the strategy. The advisory group was made up of two directors of Horticulture New Zealand, the organisation's chief executive, two representatives from the Government's trade agency, NZ Trade & Enterprise, a representative each from the kiwifruit and pipfruit industries, an exporter, a retired process company executive and I. What we had in common was that we were all white middle aged males who understood the fresh produce industry in one form or the other. Growers' knowledge of the processing part or the pipfruit industry's representative's appreciation for the finer points of retailing or the exporter's understanding of what really happens in the orchard was likely to be a bit hazy - but collectively we covered the entire produce supply chain.

The contractors worked for an international professional consultancy firm. The closest they came to a direct association with horticulture was that the team leader had at some stage in his checkered career (his words rather than mine) worked as an agricultural drainage contractor - before he changed career paths obviously. One of the outcomes of contractors and advisory group working together was the determination that the contractors needed to get out and about and talk to as many growers as possible in order to ensure that the industry at large was consulted adequately. Out of that emerged an intense debate as to the definition of the term “industry”, a topic I was not unfamiliar with and have covered in the opening pages of this book.

The outcome of this debate mattered operationally during the strategy development process in so far as NZ Trade & Enterprise were of the view that it was funding a 'whole of industry' strategy, with the term “industry” including packers, merchants and exporters. On one hand, organisations which exclusively engage in packing, selling and exporting do not necessarily consider themselves to be part of the *horticultural* industry, whilst on the other hand, many growers are now vertically integrated to the extent that they are running their own export operations.

The strategy clearly needed to focus on adding value to the production sector as it is the point of origin of any supply chain whilst offering options to the industry at large, given the existence of both separatist and convergence models.

Value drivers

The process of developing an industry strategy invariably involves an avalanche of information that needs to be assessed, sorted, organised, analysed and put to use in a way that achieves results.

The term value driver designates all factors and characteristics, which impact on the worth of a business or in this case an industry. I spent many years forming my views of what constitutes a value driver - and what doesn't - and fed the outcome of my deliberations into the strategy forming process. From there, the strategy development team ultimately settled on the following as being the industry value drivers:

Consumer Consciousness	Customer Responsiveness
Market Access	Intellectual Property Realisation
Product Differentiation	Economy of Scale
Resource Availability	Value Chain Reach
Commercial Awareness	New Zealand's Unique Advantage

Value driver analysis then led to a robust strategy being developed. More information about the strategy itself is available from Horticulture New Zealand *(www.hortnz.co.nz).*

The bugger index - or organisational health check!

Strategic documents and the strategies contained within are utterly useless, unless they can capture the imagination of the intended audience, otherwise they become door stoppers and dust gatherers.

Imagination is best captured through a degree of involvement and with that in mind I developed the "bugger index". That phrase is of course politically not correct, which is why it emerged as "organisational health check" in the final strategy version. Growers and other interested parties are essentially guided through a self-evaluation process which has them addressing several questions about their own business related to the industry value drivers. They are asked to answer the questions with the aid of a six point Lichter scale.

0	1	2	3	4	5
Bugger!	Barely coping	Basics in place	Some work to do	Nearly there	You beauty!

At the end of the process, participants have a biased appreciation of the state their business is in. How solid the information is and what the next steps should be is entirely based on the degree of honesty used in answering the questions in the first place. This puts the accountability fairly and squarely exactly where it belongs - on the shoulders of the business owner.

Orchardists turn into exporters. Growers of all walks of life critically assess their business against a common set of criteria - the sort of stuff accountants and other professional activities often used to get involved in. If that is not convergence of functionality, I do not know what is.

Convergence at retail price level

Growers produce horticultural products and either market the product themselves or are represented by an agent or broker in their endeavour to get the produce into a distribution channel so it can reach the consumer. At some point on the journey, all the discrete horticultural products turn into produce, the stuff sold in produce departments. Whilst consumers might go into a store to buy bananas and are certainly able to find bananas at a specific price, the supermarket views bananas as part of the product mix that needs to deliver a certain weekly return - and every product has to play its part in it.

Bottom up and top down planning meet like the Tasman Sea and the Pacific Ocean meet at Cape Reinga, the northern tip of New Zealand and sea conditions can at times get rough!

The produce buyers and category managers respectively responsible for sourcing bananas, apples, oranges, potatoes, lettuces, tomatoes and the like will purchase these products to forecasted and predicted volumes and at specified quality levels, negotiating for the "best" price they can achieve. Meanwhile, the overall business has an expectation that the overall produce department generates sales and gross profit of certain levels determined by departmental, store and company budgets. The question which is therefore constantly on the examination table is - "how does one structure the overall pricing mix across the department in order to achieve overall objectives?"

There are several constraints which come into play at this point. These include the need to remain competitive to ensure shoppers do not perceive the offer as being overpriced; the fact that some products are more perishable than others, i.e., onions will last longer on the shelf than strawberries; some produce items get bought more frequently than others. A "half price" offer on pickling onions would have a negligible impact on departmental profitability where as a steep price reduction on bananas would be very successful but blow the profit for the month.

Successful produce retailers understand that the mix needs to be managed like an organ concerto. The melody might be played on the keyboard for all to see. The feet need to be quite active on the pedals below though and at times considerable stretch is required to make sure the music does not get out of tune.

This approach would not be possible if every item on sale was to be dealt with in isolation. The various fruit and vegetable products purchased from a number of different sources therefore need to converge both in a physical sense, i.e., in the produce department, and in a virtual sense when it comes to the decision making processes that determine the financial success of the offer.

Finally, the critical bit

Old conventions are changing. Wine bottles no longer come with a cork.

Have you ever watched a young waitress who has only been trained to remove a screw top, having to tackle a 2002 Riesling i.e., a wine which is still secured with a cork? Not a pretty sight. First, she needs to go back to the kitchen and rummage for a cork screw when she realises she needs to do some actual work for collecting a corkage fee for opening my BYO bottle. Then she is blissfully unaware that the corkscrew should be driven straight down the centre of the cork and not at an angle of 45 degrees! And to add insult to injury she had absolutely no appreciation for the need to apply leverage in order to get the cork out of the bottle in one piece. Yet not so long ago, the fact that wine bottles came with corks was just about a law of nature and cork extraction was one of the first things table waiting staff had to learn before they were let loose upon the unsuspecting public.

Phenomena like these are an ongoing issue in a converging economy and particularly in discrete converging business entities. The AgriChain Centre, as mentioned earlier, provides services such fruit surveys and food safety assessments, it is a Biosecurity trainer, a magazine and directory publisher as well as a strategic consultancy. A totally bizarre mix by any man's standard. How do we train our team members? What are the skills we are looking for in new recruits? Where does cross-training fit into all of that and who is in charge? In fact, can there actually be someone in charge or has the tail started to wag the dog?

We need to eat and so do people in other parts of the world. Should we grow our food here or should we import it and focus on doing other stuff in a macroeconomic sense that has the potential for higher returns to the overall economy? The answer to this question is YES. YES, we need to grow at least SOME of our food here, because it makes perfect sense. YES, we should import those food components which we do not want to, cannot or ought not grow ourselves. YES, we need to start doing some other stuff as well in order to optimise our earnings as a nation. And - all of this is already in play and under way.

The overriding objective of the Horticulture New Zealand strategy is, in the absence of scale, to achieve proxies for scale. This means a greater focus on cooperative efforts, more energy being spent on establishing business beachheads on foreign shores rather than just exporting product and an absolute determination to develop, capture and market intellectual property in a way that we collectively earn money whilst we are asleep, through our expertise and services in the agribusiness domain working for us 24/7 around the globe!

Convergence is a frightening concept for the uninitiated. It can also be very rewarding when the need for paradigm change has been accepted by the organisational decision makers. In today's world, convergence and all it entails are no longer an optional extra. It is happening all around us. We therefore need to embrace the need for convergence and get on with it or we accept that we will be left behind.

End.

www.ingramcontent.com/pod-product-compliance
Lightning Source LLC
LaVergne TN
LVHW091146150826
845672LV00005B/1052

* 9 7 9 8 5 0 9 7 8 4 4 2 2 *